D.C. 230 Fashionable Hotels along Collins Ave.,
Miami Beach, Fla.

Also in the series

MIAMI

A Cultural History

Anthony P. Maingot

Interlink Books

An imprint of Interlink Publishing Group, Inc.
Northampton, Massachusetts

First published in 2015 by
INTERLINK BOOKS
An imprint of Interlink Publishing Group, Inc.
46 Crosby Street, Northampton, Massachusetts 01060
www.interlinkbooks.com

Library of Congress Cataloging-in-Publication Data available
ISBN 978-1-56656-983-5

Printed and bound in the United States of America

To request our 48-page, full-color catalog, please call us toll free at 1-800-238-LINK, visit our
website: www.interlinkbooks.com, or send us an email: info@interlinkbooks.com

Contents

Foreword

Many of the historical and social changes that Tony Maingot describes in this book may be visible to an observant visitor to Miami. But that visitor will also have other, more general, questions: how did Miami become what it is today? What are the city's outstanding characteristics, good and bad? What is its future likely to bring? Will it be yet another Hispanic city of the US, or will Miami-Dade be a unique sub-region? Maingot answers these questions, and that is why this book is so relevant.

A bit of autobiography. I have been both a witness to and a participant in the evolution of this city. I was a University of Miami graduate in the late 1950s, a Florida State Legislator in the mid-1960s, City of Miami Commissioner in the late 1960s, and Mayor of the City of Miami from 1973 to 1985. In the mid-1990s I was a Miami-Dade County (MDC) Commissioner. I have served on the Miami-Dade Expressway Authority for seven years and currently serve on the Florida Transportation Commission, which oversees all surface, sea, and air transportation issues in our state. In the 26 years I have given to public service in Florida, I have focused on two urban areas: the internationalization of Miami and its infrastructure. It is my strong belief that Miami's future is not only as a gateway to Latin America and the Caribbean, but also as a trading center. A trading center exists not only to buy and sell goods and services, but for a much wider interchange of knowledge, technology, and education. None of the above can happen unless Miami and Florida have the airports, seaports, downtown commercial infrastructure, roads and highways, public transportation, and transit systems—both urban, intra, and interstate—needed for the future. Infrastructure compliance also requires the build-up of educational institutions, cultural centers, and entertainment amenities that will make Miami unique.

In many ways the existence of Miami is circumstantial. Its founding was a fluke that would not have occurred had Henry Flagler not extended his Florida East Coast Railroad south from its original terminus at Palm Beach in 1896. Nor would Miami exist but for the advent of electricity to work the pumps, to make it mosquito free, to drain and keep dry the reclaimed marsh areas of the Eastern Everglades, and to work our air conditioners and elevators. Modern Miami could not survive without its airports and seaports. There is no community in the world of almost six million people (South Florida), with over 25 million visitors annually, whose economy is so dependent on its airports and seaports.

There was a time when Miami had the illusion of competing with Atlanta as the capital of the US South. That dream is long gone. Now Atlanta, Orlando, Houston, and others want to compete with Miami as the gateway to Latin America. These aspirations are possible but highly improbable because of geography, demography, and the historical circumstances of Miami.

As Mayor of Miami I dealt with such traumatic events as the race riots and civil disturbances of the early 1980s, the drama of Mariel, the arrival of many Haitian boatpeople, and the cocaine cowboy shoot-outs in local parking lots. I have lived through the modern metamorphosis of Miami. This has led me to pay special attention to what both Miamians think of their city and what serious outsiders say about it.

Among the first things to note are the demographic changes and political ramifications that the ongoing Latinization of Miami has caused in Florida. Arguably, most important in 2012 is that the Cuban-American vote statewide continues to decrease proportionately. Ten years ago Cuban-Americans made up almost two-thirds of the Hispanic vote in Florida. In 2008 they accounted for 40 percent, and today Cuban-Americans represent only 36 percent of the 1,473,920 Latino voters registered in Florida, 13.1 percent of all Florida registered voters. One of the fastest growing groups is comprised of neither refugees nor immigrants, but US citizens moving to Florida. *Caribbean Business*, a respected weekly periodical based in Puerto Rico, reports that the Puerto Rican population of Florida has surged by 75 percent in the last decade to 850,000 of whom 350,000 moved from the island during that period. Interestingly, most of the adults moving north are college graduates with a profession or trade, and they are moving mostly to the Orlando area. For those coming to Miami, what kind of city will they find?

Florida is at the bottom of the table of most national social, health, and education indicators. We are told that it is cheaper to live in Florida than elsewhere because taxes are lower, and this, in conjunction with the subtropical climate, engenders a higher quality of life than in many other places in the US. The latter may still be the case, but low costs are a thing of the past. In fact, while wages are lower in Florida and job opportunities are fewer, the cost of living is creeping up. Since Florida's population has, for the first time since World War II, fallen for two years running and our economy has been mostly based on growth, the fact that we have no state income tax puts an unbearable burden on the less-well-off through regressive real estate and sales taxes.

Nationally, African-American unemployment in September 2011 was a staggering 15.9 percent, almost twice the 8.1 percent unemployment for whites. But here in Miami black unemployment stood at 29 percent in Liberty City and 26 percent in Little Haiti. Currently, 40 percent of African-American males who work in the construction industry are unemployed in Miami. This is the underprivileged side of Miami-Dade that Maingot deals with. But he also describes a more fortunate side, citing the example of master developer, Jorge Pérez. The apartments in Pérez's Icon Brickell project, a high-luxury three-tower complex, sold out quickly after the condominium was completed. Luxury condo prices in downtown Miami have crept up from $298 a square foot in 2009 to $304 in 2010 and higher in 2012. In 2009 the new condos built in Downtown and Brickell were at 62 percent occupancy, 74 percent in 2010, and currently are pushing 90 percent occupancy. The Brickell Avenue high-end financial district now has up to 70,000 mostly occupied residential units. Downtown, Midtown, and Brickell is where the new Miami is taking shape.

It was no surprise, therefore, when Hong Kong-based Swire Properties announced in April 2011 that they planned to build Brickell City Center, a five million-square-foot luxury project. In addition, in late May 2011 the Malaysia-based Genting Group announced the purchase of fourteen acres of downtown waterfront prime property for $236 million. Genting has since purchased additional adjoining acres, and more is to come. By the time Genting reaches forty acres in downtown Miami, they will pass $800 million land cost for a proposed $4 billion casino project. As of the time of writing, the pros and cons of this proposal are being heatedly debated in the community, in local government, and at the highest levels of state government. The 2012 Florida State Legislative session that concluded its yearly ninety-day deliberations on March 9th did not pass any Destination Gaming (mega-casino) laws. Expert opinion is that casino interests will continue trying and eventually will succeed in getting new destination casino gambling legislation for Florida passed.

The Genting Group casino project is a classic Miami nice/Miami vice counterpoint so often seen in the city's past and present. But who can deny that this potential "game changing" casino project is very much in the mold of the inflated visions of Miami pioneers? Henry Flagler, George Merrick, Carl Fisher, Glenn Curtiss, Cuba's Education Minister José Alemán, and so many other visionaries saw in Miami an opportunity to make millions by leapfrogging from the existing small town to a grand metropolis.

Of course Miami has evolved. All urban centers develop in different directions. But Miami is, in 2012, a quintessentially American city, and if it is still changing architecturally and ethnically, what has not changed is its underlying essence as an American frontier town, constantly living under the threat of disaster by hurricanes, overgrowth, lack of potable water, and weakened by poverty, income inequality, and lower educational attainment levels—significantly so among its black citizens. Yet none of this signifies that Miami will not continue to have a fascinating and dynamic future: Miami, the "Magic City," perhaps even the "City of the Future."

The most interesting aspect of Miami's ongoing metamorphosis is that the Caribbean and Latin world of the New Miami is Americanizing quicker than Miami is Latinizing. The end result is already apparent: while Miami has assumed the patina of a Hispanic, Brazilian, and Caribbean cosmopolitan metropolis, it is also developing into a prototypical twenty-first century American city. The reason, as I see on a daily basis, is that American culture is so strong that it absorbs others in the well-established pattern of immigrant assimilation. Now, it seems, such assimilation includes its fifty-years-in-residence "historic" Cuban exile community. This should lead us to reconsider some widely held views on Miami.

First, one cannot listen to any Cuban radio talk show today without hearing that Miami "was a small, sleepy, Southern town till the Cubans arrived in 1961." In fact, by the early 1960s Miami-Dade County had passed one million full-time residents—hardly a "sleepy, Southern town." That said, there can be no doubt that Cuban entrepreneurial talents and cultural exuberance have contributed mightily to Miami's special Latin flavor. Cuban-Americans are still the Hispanic backbone of Miami-Dade County, although they are only 35 percent of its total population.

Second, the perception of non-assimilation into the United States is mistaken. This perception is based on studies limited to recent arrivals to our country, i.e., those who have not had sufficient time to assimilate. The longer the US residency, the deeper the integration into our society, the sooner migrants become US citizens, own their home, get better paying work, and speak better English.

Third, it is a fact that the immigrants who arrived between 1990 and 2010 are better off than those who arrived between 1970 and 1990. In 1990 only 35 percent of male Latino immigrant workers in the US had incomes higher than the poverty level. In 2008 that number was up to 66 percent. In 1990 only 9.3 percent of Hispanic immigrants in the US were home owners; now it is up to 58 percent.

What will, unquestionably, further integrate Miami, its citizens, and residents with the Western Hemisphere is trade. *World City*, an international trade and commerce journal based in Miami, announced that in 2010, although trade between Mexico and the US was third after Canada and China, Miami was number one among the top ten cities that traded with Mexico. And Miami is number one in trade with Brazil. Although that giant, now the seventh economy in the world, only buys 10 percent of its imports from the US, it buys more from the US than does Russia.

It is global geography that makes Miami viable as a transportation hub. Most people would think that traveling from the West Coast of the US to the West Coast of South America, say from Los Angeles to Lima, Peru, would be a direct flight along the Pacific Ocean. But the shortest distance, on the great circle, between LA and Lima overflies Miami. That is because almost all of South America is east of Miami. Miami International Airport has over the past thirty years consolidated its hub position. The Port of Miami, with the deepening of the main channel to fifty feet and the advent of the Post Panamax expansion of the Panama Canal by 2014, will also become one of three global hub seaports on the US Atlantic seaboard.

The importance of these contacts, interests, and expansions goes a long way towards explaining why the Miami-based Spanish-language Univision Network announced a major expansion of studios and filming in Miami. It fully intends to overtake NBC, ABC, CBS, FOX, and CNN in all TV program fields by the end of this decade.

There are also encouraging developments in an area Miami has emphasized a great deal: architecture, design, and preservation. In discussing the development of culture in Miami, master developer Craig Robbins, whose company Dacra owns 60 percent of Miami's Design District's

700,000 square feet of mixed-use commercial property, told the *Miami Herald* columnist Lydia Martin, "There may have been a hedonistic element to the Beach's rebirth, but there was also a lot of cultural substance to it. We are very seriously restoring historic Art Deco and Mediterranean Revival structures (in Miami Beach). It was also born out of a tremendous influence by the fashion industry and the music industry. And there were a lot of artists living and working on the Beach then, and they continue to have a significant influence on the art world." Robbins later said, in reference to the new Miami Art Museum (MAM) currently in construction on the Bay (diagonally across from the Port of Miami and across the street from the Miami Arsht Center for the Performing Arts), "it could be [Swiss architects] Herzog and De Meuron's most beautiful structure. But if we end up with a top museum, it will also be because our private collectors will get together and give [donate] some important work. There is much art here in the hands of the collecting community. I am not saying everybody has to donate their entire collection. But it's possible for all of us to make the MAM into a great public collection by all of us contributing. I'd like to give the community some of my work." This, in brief, is the Miami Spirit.

Despite the spectacular rate of change in Miami-Dade over the last half century, surprisingly few major books have been written about the contemporary city by historians, social scientists, economists, or journalists/essayists—and these are mostly by non-Floridians. Most Florida-based historians prefer to keep writing about Julia Tuttle, Mary Brickell, Henry Flagler, James Merrick, Pan American Airways, and all the people and events of the first 25 years after Miami's incorporation as a city in 1896. Further, if you are a historian writing about modern Miami and are not fully versed on Cuban, Haitian, Puerto Rican, and Central American history as well as the historic US fascination with the Caribbean Basin, it is difficult to understand what has happened to Miami in the past half century, or where it is headed today. Thus the value of Tony Maingot's book.

In conclusion, this book does not claim to address, much less unravel, all the complexities of this unique city. But, it does shed much light and raises many issues that deserve further study. Most of the negative hype generated about Miami as a vain, cultural wasteland and the half truths that perpetuate its image as the reverse of Disney World do not withstand intelligent analysis. Can Miami develop into something more substantial than its past? From grandiose to grand? From hype to metaphor?

I am pleased that contrary to the popular cliché that "Miami is the closest foreign city to the United States," Maingot and I agree that the city's welcome Latinization is counterbalanced by the forces of an America which has always encouraged renovation and change. Acting together, they will ensure that the city will become a dynamic new version of "Miami, USA."

Maurice A. Ferré

Introduction

GRAND AND GRANDIOSE

Few visitors will arrive in Miami free of very strong ideas about the place. There have been too many television shows, films, and a whole genre of pulp novels to allow anyone to have ignored it. Yet whatever preconceptions exist—and there will be many—they will not be all of one cast. Neither mainstream Americans nor foreign visitors have ever known quite what to make of Miami. To arrive at Miami International Airport is to receive the impression that you have entered a Spanish-speaking country—not a totally mistaken impression since Spanish is the first language of 67 percent of Miami's population. It is the uncommon nature of this phenomenon which leads a keen observer like Joan Didion to conclude that "Miami is not exactly an American city as American cities have until recently been understood." It is rather, she says, "a tropical capital."

Leaving aside any attempt to decipher here the multiple meanings and connotations of that word "tropical" and the fact that Miami, geographically speaking, lies in the subtropics, it is evident that Didion's perception is but one of many of this city. There have been plenty of others. To *Esquire,* Miami was "The City of the Future," to *Newsweek* it was "America's Casablanca," and *Time* dismissed it as "Paradise Lost." Television viewers, in the United States and abroad, became addicted to *Miami Vice* and Hollywood enjoyed a blockbuster in *Scarface.*

Finally, and inevitably perhaps, came a show about Miami that is not merely about drug barons and elegant gangsters: Bravo TV's *The Real Housewives of Miami.* It attempts to probe a modern, national reality: the world of "desperate" wives and spoilt beauties. Yet once again the city's "Latin" culture is presented in predictable stereotypes which led the *New York Times* in February 2011 to describe the show as "set in South Florida, where hedonism reigns and the imbibing is professional grade." Even the *Miami Herald,* while welcoming the fact that the show presents Miami as something other than "a corrupt hellhole of narco-traffickers, serial killers, and transvestite porpoises," was anything but charitable in assessing both the presentation—and the reality—of its own city. The paper conceded with more than a tinge of self-loathing that the show does strike a realistic note by acknowledging Miami's "indisputable achievements: Our indolent trashiness. Our incandescent superficiality."

There appears to be no end to the popular fascination with Miami and death by foul play, a phenomenon we highlight in Chapter Six. *Miami CSI* is the enduringly popular TV series on how new forensic science helps solve the multiple and bizarre murders that occur in the city.

Mercifully, more established literati have had a go at describing this complex city. In 1987 T. D. Allman presented his *Miami: City of the Future*, a full-length version of his earlier essay in *Esquire* magazine. David Rieff decided to probe deeper with his *Going to Miami: Exiles, Tourists, and Refugees in the New America*. A later edition of his book left unchanged his interpretation that Miami "was and is an invented vision, a fantasy of ideal living... a city which dealt in illusion." By late 1987 Joan Didion felt no need to give her work an elaborate title and settled simply for *Miami*, resting comfortably on the assurance that the name was enough to conjure up a city she portrays as "long on rumor, short on memory, overbuilt on the chimera of runaway money..." (There is nothing new here since one is immediately reminded of the historian who described the film *Money, Money, Money* as being enormously popular in 1920s Miami.)

Unfortunately, many of the more sensational descriptions of this city rest on superficial analyses of the mix of immigrants and the ethnic enclaves they have created. Invariably travelogues dealing with "immigrants," "refugees," and the allegedly peculiar and exotic "illusions" they brought with them—or came looking for—assume that all was, and is, in flux. The reality, however, is a much more settled "American" city, which means that it is more complex than the invented and transient community so often evoked. Indeed, Cubans and Haitians are examples in a long tradition of iconic "hyphenated" ethnic groups, i.e. "Cuban-Americans" and "Haitian-Americans." Cuban-Americans now wield near hegemonic economic, cultural, and political power in the city. Their influence on national foreign policy shows clearly that they are punching above their weight. Their role in developments in Cuba—through travel, remittances, and arguably ideas—is growing, providing us with ample reasons to speculate on what the future might hold. We deal with that uncertain future in the final chapter.

Haitians are now similarly "Haitian-Americans," controlling the politics of North Miami and attracting the attention of all serious candidates for office in Haiti itself. They are hardly the only ones settling in. The Colombian community has elected its first state representative and the relatively new Venezuelan and Brazilian communities have already shown great economic prowess and entrepreneurship. Given that all these groups are naturalizing in large numbers, and that the US has a new tolerance for dual nationalities, political participation and influence cannot be far behind.

Interestingly, much of the ever-growing because ever-popular travelogue-style writing about Miami runs parallel to but is hardly congruent with recent scholarly thinking on cities such as Miami. Stand-alone cities, it is argued, are entities of the past. The future belongs to what Kenichi Omae calls "city regions": metropolises with sufficient economic power to draw whole regions into their sphere of influence. Miami, it is claimed, is well on its way to becoming such a metropolis. In this vision, the "Gateway to the Americas" is close to becoming the financial and entrepreneurial epicenter of the Greater Caribbean. A powerful reason for its regional importance, says Scott Page, is that Miami has the kind of demographic ethnic diversity and fluid (even "messy") organizational structures that lead to entrepreneurship and creativity. This certainly is a theme to which we will often return in this book.

Miami's doers and shakers (promoters like to call them "visionaries and dreamers") have not only accepted this interpretation of reality but added a less admirable dimension: grandiose self-congratulation. The propensity to hyperbole in all things, from being cosmopolitan to being grand in sports, is neither new nor exclusive to Miami. It appears to characterize the boosterism of the whole state, indeed, of the whole nation. It was Alexis de Tocqueville who said famously that Americans lived in "the perpetual utterance of self-applause." In Florida that applause has always seemed particularly loud. The "Sunshine State," noted a promotional brochure from Central Florida in the 1920s, "is now entering upon the most extraordinary era of substantial growth and business activity ever known in the history of the world." In Chapter Two we will see how this bombast coexisted comfortably with a Jim Crow regime replete with sundry racists and hateful nativists such as the Ku Klux Klan.

Miami, even as it was tightly controlled by a segregationist elite, represented a penchant for braggadocio writ large. Miami, the boosters repeat like a mantra, is a "world class" city, a city "on the cutting edge," a "cross-roads" not just of America but of all the Americas. "The world," says the editor of Miami's *Business Enterprise* magazine (21 January 2008), "has taken notice." Even those who would not speak in terms of "the world" merely lower the rhetoric a notch when they claim that Miami is the new dynamic center of the Caribbean and even Latin America.

Accompanying such rhetorical flourishes is a feverish drive to make the city physically ready for its projected new role as the export hub of southeastern America, including the rebuilding of its erstwhile links with Cuba. All this suggests why the preferred mechanism is to build on a grand (or is it grandiose) scale: newly expanded airport and cruise port, new stadiums, new universities with the name "international" in them, new tunnels, new civic centers, and—if the law eventually permits—new mega-casinos. Such is the boom in real estate that short of expansion into the Everglades National Park there are lamentably few green spaces left but much concrete—or, as they are prone to say, much "cutting edge design." As we will note in Chapter Seven, the latter claim does carry considerable merit since it is undeniable that in many cases the city's new architecture is rightfully considered grand. Known as "MiMo" for Miami Modern, "Miami architecture," says Mimi Whitefield with established authority "has become as hot as the blazing sun..."

Alas, one does not have to dig too deeply below all this full-throated promotion to discover—as Maurice Ferré points out in his foreword—that the city has experienced some knotty and persistent problems. Not unlike other cities which undergo explosive growth, Miami often finds it difficult to contain that growth and to plan with due diligence. What is intended to be, and could very well actually be, "grand" can end up being merely "grandiose." No amount of rhetorical flourishes can make these problems disappear. One past and one recent example will suffice at this point. In the 1950s what one architect called "the steroid-driven egos and ambitions of Miami's civic leaders" led to the planning of a monumental "city within a city" called the Interama Theme Park. For years, a team of the world's most renowned architects and urban planners worked on the design for this multi-purpose exposition which, it was argued, would "influence culture and ideology in the whole Hemisphere." By the late 1960s the helium had gone out of the balloon with the result that today the site holds a satellite campus of the state university system and a dump.

A more recent case of the blending of the grand and the grandiose is the architectural and cultural crown jewel, the erstwhile Carnival Performing Arts Center, so-called after the first private donor Miami-based Carnival Cruise Line. Its planning and gestation, the critics maintain, mirror the collective psyche of the city's elite. "Miami," said Mary Luft, director of a prominent performing arts company, "is a land of speculation. They want it big, they want it fast, they want it now." And they got it in the Performing Arts Center. While many question her judgment that Miami received a "gorgeous piece of architecture," few disagreed with Luft's opinion that Miami is not yet the beneficiary of a truly grand performing arts center. The fact that after nearly three years and hundreds of millions of dollars, the complex has not been able to fill its seats, spurs on the criticisms. A high profile activist aptly operating under the *nom de plume* Alan Farago, punningly called it the "Carnivorous Center of the Performing Arts." "It reflects," he said, "this patina that the city fathers hope will catapult the city into some kind of glorious future."

Even as all such carping turned out to be somewhat premature, the critics did have a point: the elite, beguiled by their enchantment with architecture, left out rudimentary elements of proper city planning. Missing, the critics rightly complained, were parking space, public transportation, street level security, and a top-notch resident philharmonic orchestra. Even worse, the costly building bordered on a decaying and impoverished neighborhood which had yet to reap any benefit from city planning and renovation or, indeed, from this architectural leap forward.

Yet the history of the Carnival Center did not end there; it is evolving. In fact, this changing history exemplifies how Miami has somehow managed, once again, to overcome potentially disastrous undertakings through the actions of modern-day fairy godmothers or godfathers, native and foreign. Typically, only one year after it opened as the Carnival Center of the Performing Arts, unpaid bills were threatening its closure. Fortunately, and once again typically, a loyal citizen, a savior with deep pockets, came to the rescue. With a biography which mirrors the self-proclaimed ambition and style of the city itself, banker Adrienne Arsht anted-up the needed cash. The complex is now called the Adrienne Arsht Center for the Performing Arts of Miami-Dade County, revealing a degree of personal, commercial self-interest very much in keeping with American philanthropy, except this time with a touch of New World self-promoting panache. This gesture and so many others which are further developed throughout this book are not to be underestimated.

Be that as it may, there is reason to believe that the next great "cultural" leap forward, composed of the development of Brickell Avenue, a rejuvenated Downtown, and the planning of a $3 billion casino and mixed-use building where the *Miami Herald* building now sits might well create a whole new urban complex. This will also include the American Airlines Arena and give new life to the Arsht Center. Additionally, the Hong Kong-based Swire Group, which already owns the Mandarin Oriental Hotel (and one of the few five-star restaurants in the city), is planning a major Brickell CitiCenter complex. The hiring of Miami's own glitzy Arquitectónica architecture group promises a splendid aesthetic outcome. Predictably, the inflated boasting had to take place. Perhaps tongue in cheek, Jane Wooldridge of the *Miami Herald* (19 June 2011) said, "Maybe South Florida has finally become the center of the universe—and not just for South Floridians."

CITY IN FLUX

None of this, of course, will alleviate the stark social and racial contrasts which bedevil the city. Critics warn darkly that the juxtaposition of Miami's haves and have-nots is so evident and the political implications so ominous, that anyone who knows the history of race riots in this city must sit up and take notice. That said, there is no stopping the propelling of present-day Miami from city to future metropolis. Beyond geography and demography, there is an inherently self-fulfilling quality to such thinking.

This book will highlight periods when the actions of the city's elected officials and business elite took place with little accountability and even less transparency as well as periods when they acted with sobriety, honesty, and admirable administrative skills. In other words, we will forthrightly address the issue of modern Miami's less than grand past in order to answer the question: will Miami anytime soon stop being a "city on the edge," as an important study of ethnic tensions in Miami phrased it? The issue cannot be avoided since concern with race and ethnic relations has certainly been a frequent theme in much of the scholarly work on the city. Even as Miami has become America's "great immigrant city," there are those who question the absorption of these immigrants into the mainstream. Unlike Los Angeles or Houston, says historian Melanie Shell-Weiss, where critical black-brown alliances were formed among African-Americans and Latinos, "the particular demographics of Miami's immigrants and the southern norms they encountered caused distinct black-white divides to remain in place even as the city became more international and ethnically diverse."

Shell-Weiss' portrayal of Miami is in a general way accurate except for her claim that Miami was a "southern" city. As we shall demonstrate in greater detail later, Miami, while containing distinctly "southern" patterns of race relations and neighborhood segregation, was never part of the south as defined in terms of slave-sustained plantation societies. Miami was, and largely is, an American city with all its bad (viz., residential segregation) and good characteristics (viz., opportunities offered to newcomers and re-formist leaders). It certainly is more akin to New York than to the state's capital city, Tallahassee, 600 miles to the north. This may explain why, for instance, both black and white Bahamians migrated to the city and estab-lished a distinct presence. "Miami," a black Bahamian recalls with a char-itably selective memory, "was a young Magic City where money could be shaken from trees." Indeed, according to immigration experts Raymond A. Mohl and George Pozzetta, between 1900 and 1920, one-fifth of the entire population of the Bahamas and substantial numbers of other West Indians had migrated to South Florida. The relations between these black immi-grants and the native blacks were anything but cordial. The testy relations between these groups of the same race continue to this day, evident in the tensions between native blacks and Haitian immigrants and refugees. Of course, as we explain in Chapter Five, the peculiarities of the initial Haitian migration mitigated the tension to a degree.

The point is that the fluidity and adaptability of the city's social pat-terns have their limits but, as distinct from the northern part of the state, have never been like those of the "Deep South." Rather than the settled patterns of ex-plantation societies, Miami tended to see rapid changes in leadership—a virtual circulation of elites often brought about by new money from the northeast, mid-west, or south of the border. A genera-tional change in the present dominant Cuban-American elite cannot be long in coming.

At the Greater Miami Chamber of Commerce June 2009 Goals Annual Conference, Dade Community Foundation's president Ruth Shack said, "I don't know what Miami will be next. I can't wait to find out what that will be." She is right. Differences of opinion among serious observers such as Joan Didion, David Rieff, and T. D. Allman as to whether Miami is "Paradise Lost" or "The City of the Future" can in part be ascribed to the fact that in a little over a century Miami has had four completely different configurations. With just a few years separating each, Miami has gone from a true frontier village to a boom-and-bust town through post-World War II expansion until finally, and critically, the arrival of the Cuban exile community in 1960. Miami is now in the midst of yet another metamorphosis, but it is still in chrysalis form, which might produce a homely moth or, finally, a lovely butterfly. What exactly is Miami going to be? Can the many grandiose plans and actions of Miami's public and private leaders eventually mature as something truly grand? Might it be true that, like some proverbial self-fulfilling prophesy, the dreamy superlatives metamorphose into down-to-earth community transforming actions? Can such maturing and grounded sophistication take place in a city with the present—and ever-growing—ethnic pluralism fed by what appears to be an endless influx of immigrants from countries with their own ideas of urbanity? Might the eventual opening up of Cuba propel Miami into a truly global and cosmopolitan phase?

This book makes no claim to elucidate all the complex questions that equally complex cities engender. What it strives for, rather, is to avoid flippant critiques, odious comparisons, and exuberant boosterism. It aims to help the reader discriminate between what is grand and memorable about Miami—in the material, cultural, aesthetic, and intellectual sense—and what is merely grandiose, that is, pretentious, bombastic, and self-congratulatory.

One crucial historical fact should be borne in mind: Miami is barely more than a century old. When Havana and less so San Juan and even Ponce, Puerto Rico were seigniorial cities, Key West the most populated city in Florida, and New Orleans and Charleston refined communities, Miami was still a swamp. Not until 1896 did its pioneer citizens manage to gather 368 "registered voters" to incorporate the city. Many of these "voters," moreover, were Seminole Indians and fully 162 were blacks emancipated from slavery only decades earlier. These marginalized groups were voters only for this one occasion. This was the humble—and frankly opportunistic—origin of the city we consider in this book.

If nothing else, it compels us to say, "You've come a long way Miami!"

DOWNTOWN

Miami was originally laid out as a grid composed of northern section, southern section, western section, and, on the eastern side, Downtown. It presently comprises an area of 55 square miles (92.4 km²) with a population of 410,000.

Downtown's first business location was on Miami Avenue (originally called Avenue D), with Flagler Street to the north, the Florida East Coast Railway to the west (now NW 1st Avenue), the Miami river to the south, and Biscayne Bay on the eastern side (see 1 on map).

North and south Miami are connected by I-95 which, like the railroad before, divides the City of Miami into east-west sections. The Miami river is a working, navigable river from its mouth on Biscayne Bay up to SW 12th Avenue.

GREATER MIAMI

The initial expansion to the south (across the river) was residential. By the 1960s it had become Miami's major banking area (see 2). The expansion to the north included Overtown and to the west, SW 8th Street (Little Havana today). The expansion northward also included the suburbs of Wynwood, Design District, Liberty City, Lemon City (Little Haiti), 3 on map. Expansion southward included the suburbs of The Roads, Shenandoah, and Coconut Grove (see 4).

MIAMI BEACH

Miami is connected to South Beach by the MacArthur Causeway (past Watson Island, the Port of Miami, and Dodge Island), and by the Venetian Causeway (passing over the Venetian Islands). It is connected to North Miami Beach by the 79th Street Causeway (through North Bay Village).

KEY BISCAYNE

The connection to Key Biscayne is on the Rickenbacker Causeway, passing through Virginia Key.

The City is connected to Miami International Airport (MIA) by the East-West Expressway (State Road 836).

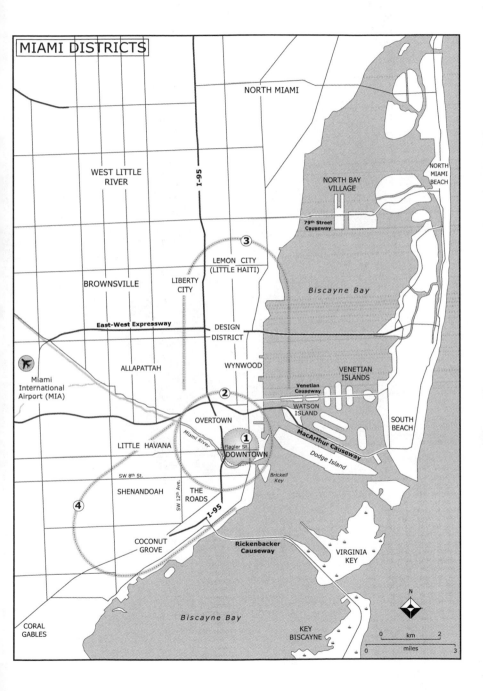

MIAMI DISTRICTS

NORTH MIAMI

WEST LITTLE
RIVER

I-95

NORTH BAY
VILLAGE

NORTH
MIAMI
BEACH

79th Street
Causeway

③

LEMON CITY
(LITTLE HAITI)

Biscayne Bay

BROWNSVILLE

LIBERTY
CITY

East-West Expressway

DESIGN
DISTRICT

WYNWOOD

VENETIAN
ISLANDS

Miami
International
Airport (MIA)

ALLAPATTAH

Venetian
Causeway

②

WATSON
ISLAND

SOUTH
BEACH

OVERTOWN

MacArthur Causeway

LITTLE HAVANA

Miami River

Flagler St.
①
DOWNTOWN

Dodge Island

Brickell
Key

SW 8th St.

SW 12th Ave.

SHENANDOAH

THE
ROADS

④

I-95

COCONUT
GROVE

Rickenbacker
Causeway

VIRGINIA
KEY

Biscayne Bay

N

CORAL
GABLES

KEY
BISCAYNE

0   km   2

0   miles   3

Chapter One

CONQUERING THE NORTHERN
FRONTIER

SETTLING SOUTH FLORIDA

Daniel Boorstin described the nature of "frontier" towns such as Miami by noting that since they lacked monuments from the past or walls to defend, they were prone to be overwhelmed by their imaginary present greatness and their debt to the future. "They measured themselves," he argued, "not by their ability to keep out invaders, but by their power to attract immigrants." But Boorstin's interpretation has wider philosophical implications for a city such as Miami since he argues that the American belief in progress and the identification of life with continued progress was rooted in such open cities. "Open" cities have a different type of frontier because it is a more peaceful one than cities which experience considerable combat and changes of masters.

It is an interesting historical characteristic of Miami that until quite recently it neither had to repel invaders or accommodate many immigrants. None of the naval powers so prone to conquer and settle foreign lands ever fought over Miami and South Florida. Despite the fact that as English, French, and Spanish fought over St. Augustine in the northeast or Pensacola in the Panhandle—cities which today proudly fly all the flags of their colorful pasts—Miami was ignored. The only part of South Florida which was settled was Key West. There was quite evidently no reason, economic or geopolitical, for any of these powers to wish to control the Miami area. Even the Indians who settled there off-and-on were simple hunters and gatherers. This was not so in the northern part of Florida.

THE EARLIEST SETTLERS

It is believed that the original pre-Columbian Indians were part of that great Trans-Siberian migration into present-day Alaska some 12,000 years ago. Known as Paleo-Indians, it is not known when they trekked down to northern Florida. It is a fact that by the time the Spaniard Juan Ponce de León arrived in 1513 looking for the "Fountain of Youth" and Pedro

Menéndez de Ávila established the city of St. Augustine in 1565 (fifty years before the English landed in Jamestown), various of these Paleo-Indian tribes were settled. Nothing of the grandness of the Aztecs, Mayas, or Incas here, but rather, rudimentary villages of people who cultivated the land, fished the rivers and coastal waters, and hunted the forests. They left just enough physical evidence for modest efforts at archaeological reconstruction later on.

In the panhandle of northwest Florida they were called Panzacola (hence present-day Pensacola), Apalachicola (hence present-day Appalachicola), and Calusa (a confederation of tribes largely in southern and western Florida, hence Calusa County). In southernmost Florida there were the Matecumbe in the Keys (from there Matecumbe Key), and the Tequesta at the mouth of the Miami river. We shall deal with the latter in due course as we come across the only archaeological site presently attributed to the Tequestas, the "Miami Circle."

Looking for treasure was only one, albeit the most important, of Spain's goals in settling the "land of flowers" later called Florida. There was also supposedly the search for the so-called Fountain of Youth by Ponce de León. Both St. Augustine and the state of Florida have made much of this search but, in fact, as J. Michael Francis has pointed out, Ponce de León was never in search of any such fountain. It was well after he died in 1521 that Spanish chronicler Gonzalo Fernández de Oviedo y Valdéz attacked Ponce de León's vanity and stupidity, citing the search for the illusive regenerative waters as evidence. And it was thus that the mythical fountain came into history to become one of Florida's most persistent legends, arguably its first grandiose claim to fame. As the saying goes, when "facts" become legend, promote the legend. True to form, future Florida boosters simply adopted the myth, integrating it into the promise of rejuvenation offered by a trip to Florida. Gary R. Mormino put it nicely: "A refuge and a dream, a time-warp and brave new world, Florida provided a new home to millions of Americans wishing to reinvent themselves." Seldom has a story with so little historical veracity endured so long and served public relations so well.

Conversion to the "one true religion" was another of Spain's goals in the New World, and in Florida that was best done by the Franciscans. Thirty-one missions have been documented. It is calculated that they contained 26,000 Christianized natives. There was much to commend the

Spanish Franciscans in their treatment of the Indians. In general, however, the Spanish settler was, as described by Father Juan Rogel in 1568: "…wherever we Spanish are, [we are] so proud and unrestrained that we try to trample everything under foot…"

It would not take long for things to turn nasty between the natives and the *conquistadores* or *adelantados*, and the missionaries who accompanied them. Evidence of the natives' hostility from the very beginning was the fact that Ponce de León himself died from an infected wound caused by a poisoned Indian arrow.

Two processes brought the Franciscan missions to an end, and with that an end to any humane consideration and treatment of the Indian. First of these was the lagging of the original Franciscan missionary ardor. It was, as historian Michael Gannon put it, "as though a kind of Florida weariness had overcome them." Then there followed the wars between the European powers and their constant battles to expand their overseas territories. Soon these geopolitical skirmishes took on a religious dimension. The Franciscan and Jesuit missions were savaged by an invasion led by the English Governor of South Carolina. Interestingly, it was largely English, Scottish, and Welsh settlers from Barbados who populated South Carolina and formed its expansionary hordes. By the time of the Treaty of Utrecht in 1713, Spain had to cede Florida to England in exchange for the English ceding back to Spain Havana, which they had occupied during the so-called French-Indian War. As we shall see, by then the original Paleo-Indian tribes of Florida in the southern part (including the Tequestas) were, for all practical purposes, gone—either migrating to Cuba with the Spaniards or devastated by the white man's diseases.

The same did not hold true for the northern part of the state, i.e. that section north of the line running from present-day Pensacola, through Tallahassee, and east to St. Augustine. That was Florida's first frontier, a frontier with many military fronts. Not only did the combative white men fight each other, they also had to deal with the Indians who were already settled and once these were decimated by epidemics, with the tribe which began to enter Florida from Georgia around 1717. Having migrated south after conflict with the white man in Alabama and Georgia, these new Indian settlers were of a considerably more belligerent nature. They were the ones we now know as Seminoles. The name comes from the Spanish word for escaped and wild Indians *cimarrones*. There is nothing mystical or contrived about the Seminoles; it was their fierce resistance to the white man which shaped much of Florida's early history and eventually led to the existence of quasi-independent Indian "nations" within the state. These white-Indian conflicts were but one of several wars which took place in northern Florida: wars mostly related to imperial expansions. These wars produced some key historical watersheds generated by imperial successions, to wit:

1763: the French and Indian Wars led Spain to cede Florida to England. The English divided the peninsula into two colonies: West and East Florida, both fundamentally plantation slave societies. The distances were daunting. Pensacola, the capital of West Florida, and St. Augustine, the capital of East Florida, were a 28-day wagon ride apart and there were no navigable rivers connecting the settlements. Instead of flowing south, the navigable rivers emptied west into the Gulf of Mexico. Not surprisingly, during Florida's Spanish phase, with the territory governed from Havana, their settlements had better communication with Cuba than with each other. During the British period, a vast fleet of ships capable of circumnavigating the peninsula kept the settlements in constant contact.

1783: because Spain sided with and aided the American revolutionaries, Spain regained Florida and the English settlers left.

1819: due to continued pressure from American settlers moving south, Spain ceded Florida to the new American nation in 1819 in exchange for the United States assuming $5 million in Spanish debts to the American settlers. This was nothing to sneer at given that the Louisiana Territory was bought for $15 million and much later the US paid Denmark $17 million for what are today the US Virgin Islands. A major factor in Spain's decision to be rid of the colony as best it could was the presence in Florida of Andrew Jackson, the hero of the War of 1812 against Britain, and a man whose reputation for military aggressiveness—not to say cruelty—was already legion on the frontier. Jackson had led an expedition into Spanish Florida in 1817 to punish a rebellious group of Seminole Indians who were harboring escaped slaves. Ironically, these Indians were survivors of the so-called Creek War of 1813–14, which Jackson brought to a bloody conclusion. So began the American phase of Florida's northern frontier, which also brought to an end a period of relative prosperity for the Seminoles. In fact, historians John K. Mahon and Brent R. Weisman speak of an American "invasion" which had "cataclysmic" and "traumatic" consequences for the Seminoles. Also ended was any hope of a Spanish reconquest. When Spain, which had given the American rebels critical support during the Revolution, invited Americans to settle as a bulwark against British incursions, US Secretary of State Thomas Jefferson saw a clear opportunity. As he told President George Washington: "I wish 10,000 of our inhabitants would accept the invitation. It would be the means of delivering to us peacefully what must otherwise cost us a war."

No sooner said than done! In 1821 Florida became an American Territory and in 1845 a state of the Union. The concept of "Manifest Destiny" had just witnessed its geopolitical unfolding in inexorable phases: get an invitation to settle, settle in considerable numbers, secede and establish an independent "republic," petition to join the American Union, become a full-fledged state. It occurred in Florida and then in Texas.

The occupation of the rest of Florida was considerably bloodier since it involved three wars with those other "new" settlers, the Seminole Indians. These Seminoles were an independent-minded people with a tradition diametrically opposite to British and American interests and ideologies: they rejected all forms of slavery and as such gave safe haven—in a form of feudal vassalage to be sure—to all escaped slaves. By the second decade of the nineteenth century there were 31 Indian Seminole settlements and three Black Seminole villages in northern Florida. It is worth noting that when the white settlers of northern Florida voted in 1838 to petition the federal government for admission to the Union, the territory had 48,222 inhabitants of whom 21,132 were slaves and 985 free blacks. Indians were not counted. When Florida was admitted as the twenty-seventh State of the Union in 1845, it became an integral part of the slave-holding south. Because Britain had abolished the slave trade in 1808 and abolished slavery in 1834, securing new slaves from Africa was difficult. This made the existing slaves already in America all the more valuable to plantation owners. Seminole resistance to handing over the blacks among them as well as other rebellious attitudes became increasingly threatening to whites moving into new lands to establish slave-worked holdings. The white settlers fully intended to do something drastic about it. The results were three separate "Seminole Wars" which can be summarized as follows:

The First Seminole War was from 1817 to 1818, in which Andrew Jackson defeated the Seminole rebels. Jackson wrote that it was necessary to close the escape route used by Georgia slaves, and to "chastise a savage foe combined with a lawless band of negro brigands." But Jackson also made one of the earliest public announcements of the desire to annex Spanish Cuba as another slave state. "Give me some shipping and more troops," he wrote to President James Monroe in 1818, and "I will assure you that Cuba will be ours in a few days." This was an early indication that in one form or another, Cuba has always figured in Florida's history.

With the Seminoles defeated, in 1823 the US government officially recognized the Seminoles as an Indian Nation and moved them to a reservation in Central Florida. Unable to grow enough food to feed themselves, the Seminoles began another struggle for more land which predictably resulted in clashes with the increasing number of white settlers from Georgia and Alabama. The result: the Second Seminole War (1835-42), the bloodiest by far. Unable to field large numbers of warriors, the Seminoles carried out a punishing guerrilla war, inflicting 1,500 casualties on the US Army. By then the Seminoles were under the leadership of skilled fighters including a half-Scottish warrior named Osceola. Osceola's military skills against overwhelming odds were the object of world-wide marvel. He became, in the words of his most credible biographer, Thom Hatch, "the most famous Native American in the world." Hatch's 2012 book, *Osceola and the Great Seminole War*, carries the appropriate subtitle, "A Struggle for Justice and Freedom." The struggle was for freedom for his fellow Seminoles and for the escaped slaves already known as Black Seminoles.

Osceola was eventually betrayed by the Americans while under a white flag truce, and he subsequently died in a jail in St. Augustine. But the tactics of what would now be called "irregular warfare" are today part of the Seminole history of heroics and are best described by one of the few eye-witnesses of the events, John T. Sprague, in *The Origin, Progress, and Conclusion of the Florida War* (1848). It might very well be, as historian Michael Gannon says, that none of the American officers, with the exception of General Zachary Taylor, acquitted themselves with distinction. "The more durable heroes that emerged from the protracted agony," says Gannon, "were the chiefs and war leaders of the tribes..." These included Osceola, the mixed-blood John Horse (Juan Cavallo to the Spaniards), the full-blooded Seminole Coachooche ("Wild Cat"), and a large number of Black Seminoles who carried out one of the largest slave revolts in US history. None of these rebels knew the meaning of the word surrender. By the end of the Second Seminole War it was generally agreed that the Semi-

Osceola, Chief of the Seminoles

noles fully deserved to call themselves the "Unconquered People," a designation paid for in blood many times over. In 1835 the US Congress passed the Indian Removal Act and 3,824 Seminoles were forced to move to Indian reservations in Oklahoma. Black rebels received no such consideration, so that those who survived were either executed or returned to slavery.

A Third Seminole War broke out in 1850 from which perhaps 300 braves survived by escaping into the Everglades, a watery "river of grass" fed by Lake Okeechobee. These were the forefathers of today's Seminoles. The white man did not develop an interest in this swamp area until South Florida became populated and it became clear that it was the sole aquifer of the area. With their flight into this wilderness, the Third Seminole War came to an end—and so ended, in Gannon's words, "one of the darkest chapters of Florida's history."

We should keep in mind, however, that it was part of the history of the northern frontier, not the south, which was yet to be settled. The southernmost battle during these wars was fought north of Lake Okeechobee—and that was fifty years before Miami was even chartered as a city. Beyond that, it should also be understood that what had ended was the warfare episode of white-Indian relations. The hardy Indian survivors of the three wars, now settled deep in the Everglades and removed from white control, began to rebuild their lives and culture to the extent that in the 1880s the Bureau of Ethnology of the Smithsonian Institution in Washington sponsored a major study of their economy, architecture, colorful clothing, diet, and relations with the ever-increasing numbers of whites settling in Central Florida. The resulting study, *The Seminole Indians of Florida* (1887), bears witness to their inherent cultural strengths and predicted with great prescience steady progress for the tribe.

The way to understand the history of the Seminoles is to see it as a metaphor for the history of the state of Florida. Like so much of that history it exemplified the rise of a grand and heroic people, their fall (often through betrayal), and their later ascent. We will again encounter the Seminoles when their descendants living in southern Florida made their presence felt. Historian Jerry Wilkinson quite correctly calls our attention to the fact that when Florida became American property the Seminoles had already been resident there some 120 years. He then makes the peculiar assertion that "They were Native Americans, but not native

Floridians." This, of course, begs the question as to who, after the Paleo-Indians disappeared during the Spanish period, were "native" Floridians. It is a question which resonates to our day but which in the final analysis is academic, at least for the Florida south of the northern frontier, given that that history of settlement is so recent and so replete with "invasions" of people. It has been one of the enduring and arguably endearing features of South Florida and Miami in particular that such newcomers tend to become instant natives.

Quite clearly, when Florida decided to join the Confederacy of slave-owning states by seceding from the Union, it was an act which involved people and land nearly exclusively in the northern and western sections of the state. All that existed some 600 miles south of these populated plantation areas—beyond swamp and lands inhabited mostly by Seminole Indians—were two isolated forts which remained in Union hands: Fort Taylor in Key West and Fort Jefferson in the Dry Tortugas, an American archipelago south of Key West. The only part of southern Florida that was populated was 140 miles south of Miami, the city of Key West, settled by American Royalists who fled to the Bahamas and from there began moving to this southernmost part of the US. We will return to these "Conchs," a term dear to their independent hearts, later.

None of the Civil War and then the so-called Reconstruction activity involved what would later be Miami and its south-eastern environment. In other words, Miami was not at that time part of the post-Civil War "southern ways" which evolved into what is generally known as the "Jim Crow" south. To be sure, Jim Crow traditions would be brought by the many southerners who later migrated to Miami. Significantly, it was not until 1868 and the Fourteenth Amendment to the US Constitution that blacks were granted citizenship. Additionally, it took another constitutional amendment in 1870, the Fifteenth Amendment, to grant blacks the right to vote. Whatever the legal rights accorded by the amendments to the Constitution, Jim Crow practices made certain that blacks did not benefit from them. In northern Florida, the practice of white supremacy became the law of the land. Since this included stopping blacks from voting, it was a travesty of history and more than ironic that in 1896 the Miami founders would need blacks, who were legally citizens, to become voters (albeit voters-for-a-day) to finally incorporate Miami as a city.

BIRTH OF MIAMI

Who were the few white settlers who in 1896 rounded up Indians and blacks and persuaded them to vote on a one-off basis, and why did they push for the incorporation of this city? According to Miami historians Arva Moore Parks and Gregory W. Bush, who have done the major collecting of the writings of some early settlers, they were a hardy bunch of pioneers. They had to challenge established opinions and prejudices about ideal places to settle. Florida was certainly not perceived as such a place. Representative John Randolph of Virginia opposed the US's acquisition of Florida in 1821, vehemently stating: "Florida, Sir, is not worth buying. It is a land of swamps, of quagmires, of frogs, and alligators and mosquitoes... No man would immigrate to Florida—no, not from hell itself!"

Representative Randolph did not mention Seminole Indian attacks, which although infrequent were always of concern. But the greatest bother by far were the ever-present swarms of mosquitoes, which made life a misery as well as bringing "the fevers." The result was that many a grant of land went unoccupied. Another obstacle to settlement was securing title to the land. Some did manage to secure title and sell. Others just settled in the first acceptable plot they could find, regardless of title. Historian James M. Denham quotes a French naturalist who visited Florida in 1838 to the effect that if any proper title holder ever attempted to assert his authority, he would receive "no more response than a bullet from a rifle." In 1890 Mrs. Emma Gilpin described how the whole stretch from west of the Miami river down to Coconut Grove was owned by a Mr. Brickell. According to Mrs. Gilpin, this was not the case on the east side entrance from the Bay on the Miami river: "This is the favorite point for beauty on the whole bay, but it is owned with such uncertain title that no man is willing to buy it, though all want it."

What existed on this side, which is where Miami was born and grew, was a small fort ("Dallas") on the northeast bank of the Miami river. It was built in 1845 by the US government during the Indian Wars and was where the few settlers went in case of Indian attack. In one very rare assault in 1836 a small Seminole group traveled as far south as Cape Florida where they burned the Light (lighthouse) and killed one of the first white settlers of Miami, Henry E. Perrine (after whom the city of Perrine is called). As Edward Clifford Anderson from Georgia noted after visiting the single settlement on the Miami river in 1844: "I have no idea... that Miami will ever be much more than it is. I have never in all my travels met with such an immense numbers of horseflies and other insects..." Another visitor, Rose Wagner Richards, recalled that in 1858 there were only two family-run starch processing factories on the river. The starch came from the coontie or West Indian arrowroot plant and was used in the making of puddings. There were no systematic plantation-type crops, and the wild-growing arrowroot was harvested from the surrounding area. The isolation of the settlers was only broken once a month when the mail boat from Key West brought what news there was from what Richards called "the outside world—never much but eagerly looked for." Later settlers who grew produce, such as pineapples and avocado pears, or those who made starch had to transport their products by boat to Key West, and from there these were shipped on to New York.

Frances Leonard Sturtevant, mother of grand pioneer Julia Tuttle, believed that it was the isolation and small population which constituted "the charm of this mode of life." She was full of praise for the courage and tenacity of her fellow settlers, and in 1876 she wrote the following about the small colony on the Miami river:

> Our people tend to gravitate independently, which is not surprising...
> A few of the descendents of the fearless class who remained through the
> Indian troubles are still here... When inclined to seek a new location the
> majority of them can readily transfer their worldly possessions to the
> boat and have ample room for the family during the transit...

She fully realized that that isolation and way of life would eventually change. "As civilization advances," she said, "it will become a thing of the past." Today, curious people can see what that past looked like by a visit to "The Barnacle" house, a State of Florida Historic Site in Coconut Grove, built by another pioneer of that time, Ralph Middleton Munroe. In his 1930 memoir, *The Commodore's Story*, Munroe waxes poetic about the "sailor's paradise" that was Biscayne Bay. He was nostalgic about the "simple and genuine life" they led in "isolation and mutual dependence." A later example of this early type of housing is the home built from hand-carved rock at 2521 South Bayshore Drive, Coconut Grove. Whether it was "The Barnacle" or the house built from local rock, simplicity of design was the style, ventilation and sturdiness the ultimate architectural goal.

11

Ralph Munroe's "The Barnacle," Coconut Grove

Life did have its attractions and comforts, mostly in the variety of food available. This certainly compared favorably with the meager diet of the American and European urban working-class neighborhoods of the time. Mary Barr Munroe always referred to herself as a "pioneer woman" and despite the great loneliness was not willing to take many backward glances at "the comforts of a civilized home" or "the great outside world." This was possibly because of the table she could set: "Johnny cake, sweet and plenty of it, stewed venison, ash baked sweet potatoes, boiled Seminole squash, corn pones, roast wild hog, and wild turkey, coontie pudding… Reef bean soup, turtle fry, and fried chicken."

Far from the luxurious plantation houses in the north of the state, these Miami homesteads were simple households with many children and "no one to assist in the daily and hourly work"—in other words, no slaves. They certainly did believe that things would improve, and the idea of progress was seemingly built into their DNA. Consider Julia Tuttle who in 1891 in Miami saw herself as part pioneer and part missionary of the

Baptist Church. Living in the middle of the wilderness, she wrote to her fellow Baptist friend, John D. Rockefeller, praised him for having "the most charming country home" and invited him to visit them in Miami because "I too am going to have a beautiful home." She demonstrated the same spirit in persuading Rockefeller to contribute to the building of Miami's first Baptist church, and on another occasion when she persuaded Rockefeller's partner, the great railroad-man and hotelier Henry Flagler, to extend his railroad from Palm Beach to Miami. Julia Tuttle can truly be considered Miami's first and foremost promoter. She was grand because her efforts were geared to benefitting the commonweal, not in grandiosely promoting herself.

PIONEERS AND RAILROADS

Aside from Tuttle's persistence, there were other simultaneous circumstances which together helped propel the growth of Miami. First was inclement weather up north; two deep freezes in a row convinced the citrus growers in the northern and middle parts of the state that they had to plant further south. It certainly helped convince Flagler to look further south than Palm Beach, where his railroad ended. He brought his railroad down to Miami in 1896. Second was the competition between Flagler and another railroad and hotel entrepreneur, also named Henry. As Flagler developed on the East Coast, Henry B. Plant developed on the West Coast. Both were as visionary as they were wealthy, and both moved in different directions to develop the state but had additional grand schemes which went beyond Florida. Specifically, each saw the opportunity of one day incorporating Cuba. Both had Key West as a key port on the route to Cuba. Plant's railroad shipments went south to Tampa, Punta Gorda, and then connected by steamer to Key West and Cuba. Flagler's East Coast Railroad and steamships served Havana, Nassau, Key West, and Palm Beach. The story of both Henrys explains Tampa's and Miami's early interest in Cuba.

Of special relevance to Miami was the fact that the whole East Coast was Flagler's to develop. He started with three luxurious hotels in the 1880s in Florida's oldest city, St. Augustine—the Ponce de Leon, the Alcazar, and the Cordova—before he even considered moving further south, first to Daytona and Ormond Beach and then on to Palm Beach. It was in Palm Beach that he built the grand Hotel Royal Poinciana. With beds for 1,200

Ponce de Leon Hotel, St. Augustine, 1902

guests, it was at the time the largest in the world. He also built the Break-ers, which having succumbed to fire several times over the years rose like a phoenix again and again, standing today as arguably Florida's grandest hotel. Compared to Plant's Tampa Bay Hotel with its Moorish design (today the University of Tampa), Flagler's Royal Palm Hotel in Miami was built in colonial revival style with an open colonnaded portico, a columned rotunda, and verandas around the whole. Although the Royal Palm Hotel has long since been demolished, it set the standard for what Miamians since then have called "casual tropical splendor." It remained the city's dominant structure until the 1920s but, sadly, it hardly influenced the ar-chitecture that would follow.

No sooner had these two railroad and hotel projects been accom-plished than events in Cuba—where Spain ruled but America invested—pushed both Tampa and Miami into the front lines. In 1898 the American naval ship USS *Maine* exploded in Havana's harbor, causing an American intervention in that island's War of Independence. With the American in-vasion the conflict became known as the 1898 Spanish-American War. In the ensuing mobilization it was evident that Tampa was a more developed city and port than Miami. This explains why Tampa, not Miami, became the main gathering and launching port and base for the US intervention in the war, with Plant's Tampa Bay Hotel the US Army's center of operation. Predictably, the other Henry would not sit still: it was not in Flagler's nature to be a mere observer in the face of evident economic opportunities. He soon convinced the federal government to deploy thousands of troops in the Miami area. Unfortunately, as Les Standiford put it, the area did not have much to offer: "What they discovered was a town consisting of a hotel shuttered for the season and a clutch of raw buildings that might have dropped down from the sky." A soldier stationed in Miami described the desolation in even starker fashion: one had to walk but a quarter of a mile out of town, he said, "to come upon such a vast wilderness as can be conceived of only in rare nightmares." Another soldier billeted in Miami was hardly alone therefore when he complained saying, "If I owned both Miami and Hell, I'd rather rent out Miami and live in Hell."

Miami was indeed in the "boondocks" and yet it kept growing. By 1896 it boasted a newspaper, the *Miami Metropolis*, the forerunner of the *Miami News*. Miami journalist and historian Howard Kleinberg reprinted Vol. 1, No. 1 (15 May 1896) of that newspaper showing the entire merchant class in the front page of the six-page paper. Miami had a mere

Watermelons for sale, Downtown, 1896

"thousand souls" but this did not stop the editor, Walter S. Graham, from referring to the city as "the Metropolis of South Florida." Boosterism, which had had an early start with the fable of the Fountain of Youth, had now taken on its modern form.

By 1907, only eleven years after Miami's incorporation as a city in 1896, there were three banks operating. One, the Bank of Bay Biscayne, was opened the same year the city was chartered. Six years later, the First National Bank opened its doors and a year later the Fort Dallas National Bank was in business. Soon all this banking activity would provide an example of another early pattern in Miami: grand ideas and grandiose openings followed by spectacular failures... with the city left holding the bag. The Bank of Bay Biscayne rapidly ran into trouble, unable to collect on two major loans intended to make the city more liveable by building a streetcar service and building a new hotel, the Halcyon. That said, another more positive feature of what would later be a Miami characteristic became apparent: community spirit coming to the rescue. The fact is that this first financial crisis of the city could have been much worse had it not been for what the *Miami Metropolis* described as large deposits made into the remaining two banks by "Patriotic Citizens" and a loan of $110,000 in cash from a bank in Jacksonville. There clearly was great faith and incipient community spirit in the young Miami. On 5 July 1907 the *Miami Metropolis* described the local rescue of the Bank of Bay Biscayne, remarking:

> No more beautiful tribute than this can go out to the world. In the face
> of possible loss, financial ruin, and even poverty, if the bank went under,
> they took their chance fearlessly and willingly, and helped save the day...
> [Miami's] people have demonstrated their worth as citizens.

This was but one example of the early "spirit" of the Miami pioneers, always willing to put their money where their pride in the city was. Julia Tuttle showed such a spirit when she offered Henry Flagler 140 acres of her own land to bring the railroad down from Palm Beach. Joseph Smoot, owner of a cattle ranch in what is today Hialeah, donated 160 acres for the building of the Miami Jockey Club, later to be the Hialeah Race Course. George Merrick donated 160 acres for the building of the University of Miami. None of these philanthropies, however, was done anonymously or in silence. At all times there was the need to proclaim their beneficence to the four winds. One who did not need to broadcast his accomplishment was Henry Flagler, the man who connected the whole East Coast of Florida with railroads and magnificent hotels. This truly grand figure deserves special mention, for his deeds and for the vision behind these.

Henry Morrison Flagler made his millions as co-equal partner with John D. Rockefeller in developing Standard Oil. As distinct from Rockefeller, who secured his place in American history by sticking to the oil business, Flagler was a restless spirit who did things not just for the money but to see the presumably impossible become the possible. John D. Rockefeller put it quite nicely when he said, "Think of all that money out on a whim! But Henry was always bold." The boldness was best appreciated when you consider that "civilization" in East Coast Florida ended in Palm Beach and south of Palm Beach little existed except bush with a bad reputation. Michael Grunwald in his comprehensive book *The Swamp* described the Catch-22 which kept South Florida so underdeveloped for so long: "Who would extend a railroad to a settlement without settlers? And who would settle in a settlement without railroads?" The "who" in this case was Henry Flagler.

Gregg M. Turner's *A Journey into Florida Railroad History* notes that "If any one American state eventually smiled upon railroads, gave them a free course over the expanse, and greatly relied upon them to open up the land… it was assuredly Florida." True, but perhaps too much "free course." Between 1836 and 1939 there were 251 railroad companies operating, each with its own rail gauges and rights of way. Flagler's grand feat was to unite the rail system running from Jacksonville to his two favorite stops, St. Augustine and Palm Beach, and then be so bold as to continue south.

It is critical to understand that even as we call Flagler without a bit of exaggeration the "man who built Miami," the fact is that his interest in Miami was minimal. When in Florida he stayed either in St. Augustine or Palm Beach; preferably in the latter. Miami was a launching base for overseas expansion. When the federal government rejected his idea of dredging the port of Miami he turned his attention to Key West. A thriving port and commercial center since the 1820s, it was only in 1822 that Key West was chartered as a city and a federal court was established as part of the US Navy's suppression of piracy. Wrecking then became the main business, followed by Cuban cigar-makers. When Flagler decided to undertake the Key West Extension, the 140-mile "Bridge across the Sea," Key

West had a population five times bigger than Miami's. There were perhaps 200 cigar factories with workers hand-rolling close to one million cigars with tobacco imported from Cuba.

Key West was to be the "American Gibraltar," the port which could only benefit from all other events taking place around the world. As Les Standiford explains in his splendid small book *Last Train to Paradise*, Flagler's public relations bulletin made his goal very clear: "As has been intimated, the assurance of the Panamá Canal made the world look at the Keys of Florida and Key West from a new point of view. The canal opens in a moment tremendous vistas and pushes our commercial horizon across the seven seas."

In the midst of a wider milieu composed of the new Manifest Destiny advocated by what Mark Twain called the promoters of the Gilded Age, by the American defeat of Spain, and by the building of the Panama Canal, Miami was small-change to men like Flagler. Their vision was global and they were not deterred by calamities, either man-made or acts of God. They had to be special people and certainly Flagler was the grandest. In the building of his railroad across the sea he had to import everything. Labor came from wherever, but ultimately his favorites became the Cuban and

KEY WEST EXTENSION, FLORIDA EAST COAST RAILWAY

Cayman Island workers. In terms of materials, special underwater hardening cement from Germany, steel rods, timbers, sand, and even water were all put together in the middle of the ocean. One after the other, the 180 arches went up and stayed up despite some horrific weather. Between the start of the project in 1905 and its termination in 1912 the Keys were hit by three hurricanes which did not stop the work for too long. When the 15,000 citizens of Key West went out to welcome the first train carrying a by-then very feeble Flagler, they were joined by the Governor of Florida, Albert Gilchrist, and the President of Cuba, José Miguel Gómez. Entertainment was provided by a Cuban circus. Flagler died soon thereafter but his great dream had been achieved.

Nothing, however, prepared Miami and Key West for the devastation caused by the hurricane of Labor Day, 1935. That great storm, which preceded the naming of hurricanes by almost twenty years, roared in with winds of 200 miles per hour. It is still the strongest hurricane ever to make landfall on US soil. It brought the whole railroad structure to an end. Perhaps 500 people died in the Middle Keys. Even though the reinforced concrete bridges survived the devastation, there was no rebuilding the East Coast Railroad. Two events led it to receivership. First, much of the import-export commerce had already been picked up by Tampa and New Orleans and the competition from the parallel road which was part of the New Deal construction projects. The end came when the right-of-way so generously given by the state of Florida in 1905 so that $30 million could be spent building the extension, was sold back to the state for $640,000.

Flagler had already helped create Miami. When the Royal Palm Hotel was finished in early 1897, at the confluence of the Miami River and Biscayne Bay, the press referred to Miami as the "Naples of America." Visions of Italian cities—any one seemed to do—clearly exerted a mystique, since others called it the "Riviera of America," and later Merrick would call his development the "Venice of America."

BOOM TIME

Naples, the Riviera, and Venice—any or all served the fundamental goal of promoting in a grandiose way. That said, it is indisputable that all this early promotion paid off after World War I. New opportunities were opened for a socially mobile labor force and an incipient boom started. At a minimum the newly salaried workers could afford a Model-T Ford and had enough left over to head south. A promised land, "the Riviera of America" was advertised in papers across the US. On paper there were pre-developed plots in well-designed estates. The blueprint was the key since land was sold sight unseen. Certain developments sold out in one day. The "binder"—a legal document issued by the developer—identified your lot. "Binder Boys" gladly took the 10 percent down. But in many cases there was little interest in occupying and building on the plot. Rather, the binder was used for speculation. Many a binder changed hands over ten times. The practice of "flipping" properties established deep roots in Miami's real estate industry.

By 1925 the real estate boom—and its accompanying "flipping"—was in full swing. The numbers of real estate transfers and conveyances for Miami during the boom years were impressive for any city but especially one this new and this small. In the active months of April, May, and June together, real estate moved as follows: 1919, 4,001 sales; 1921, 6,663; 1923, 10,182; and in 1925, 48,904 sales. Aside from the downtown area of Miami, there were other neighborhoods cashing in on the boom. Coral Gables ("The City Beautiful" or the "Venice of America") was foremost among them and deserves special mention.

"Binder Boys" selling real estate, Coral Gables

The origin of that city goes back to 1899 when George Merrick accompanied his father, a Congregational minister from Cape Cod, down to Miami. In keeping with the pioneering spirit they cultivated 160 acres of grapefruit doing all the selling themselves. By the early 1920s, young Merrick had married the daughter of early Coconut Grove settler Charles Peacock and caught the wave of the boom in land sales. As distinct from many of the other land developers, Merrick had a plan of considerable artistic merit which made sense given the boom. The *Miami Daily News* (21 June 1925) called it "an intelligent city plan and artistic design, supervised by experts." It certainly began explosively. Within three and a half years there were over a thousand residences ranging from one-story homes to palatial Mediterranean-style dwellings, four hundred of which had telephone service. Merrick himself described his project to the *Miami Daily Tribune* (3 June 1925):

> We have the greatest known architects in America at work upon the plans of this greater Coral Gables, which is Greater Miami... We have adapted the Spanish architecture at points; but we chiefly adapted the Mediterranean type of architecture as best fitted by the comparison of climate... Everything is designed to be in harmony.

Truth be said, it was a rare case where extravagant rhetoric was matched by performance. There was also philanthropy since he donated 160 acres of land to the University of Miami and pledged $5 million towards its endowment fund.

Naturally, as was customary already in Miami, there had to be some hyperbole coming from the press—a press hardly prone to parsimony in language. Merrick, said the *Miami Daily Tribune*, was building a city of "miraculous age-old beauty," where in "lace of stone their spires stab the skies and with their golden crosses kiss the sun—the perpetual glorious sunshine of Southern Florida, the place where the dreamer's dreams are made to come true."

Merrick's determination to construct water features in various formations led to the building of the world's largest hotel swimming pool, larger even than the spectacular Venetian Pool he had built nearby and which still today serves as a favorite recreation spot. Merrick dug multiple canals reminiscent of the Italian Riviera on which gondolas imported from

Venice carried guests down to the Cocoplum Beach. There was also public transportation. Because Coral Gables had been incorporated as a municipality of Dade County in 1925, that same year a trolley service began from Miami's center to Coral Gables. Under construction were six hotels including a Golf and Country Club with an 18-hole golf course and a polo field. At the center of all this was a magnificent hotel, the Biltmore, designed by Schultze and Weaver who had also designed the Miami News Tower in downtown Miami, today the Freedom Tower. Both buildings were done in Plateresque style inspired by the fifteenth-century La Giralda tower in Seville, Spain. This hotel, which the architects promised would be "the most pretentious in the world," was co-owned by John McEntee Bowman who also owned the Commodore in New York, the Biltmore in Los Angeles, the Biltmore in Atlanta, and the Seville-Biltmore in Havana. The inauguration of the Biltmore Hotel in January 1926 was more than a local affair; it was, according to the *Miami Daily News*, a national event with representatives "from almost every part of the country." One can understand the *Miami Daily News and Metropolis* calling Merrick one of "the most brilliant figures in America's real estate history" and Coral Gables "the most outstanding realty development of the entire United States." If this was not actually the case it certainly deserved to be. Coral Gables remains one of the best designed communities in Florida and just maybe in the United States.

The Biltmore Hotel, Coral Gables

All that praise was true and well-deserved, but Merrick's timing was off. By 1927 the Florida real estate boom was going flat, the national economy was entering into a depression, and tourists stopped coming. In 1929 Merrick's Coral Gables Corporation filed for bankruptcy and this included the Biltmore. It was testimony to the lingering hope that Miami and Coral Gables could withstand the downturn that Bowman and a group which included Al Smith, the former Governor of New York, bought it. The grand hotel fared no better and would not be restored to full occupancy until the War Department turned it into a military hospital in World War II. In 1989, 59 years after its inauguration, the Biltmore was again opened as a hotel, arguably the grandest in Miami.

The other great design for splendid living and the tourist trade was Miami Beach. When Charles Lum of New Jersey visited in the 1870s, this is what he saw, as described later by Miami Beach historian Abraham D. Lavender: "A sand ridge running along the ocean side [which] was covered by a tangled mass of sea grapes. The peninsula that would later become an island was a haven for rattlesnakes, mosquitoes, wildcats, raccoons, 'possums, rabbits, and bears." The Lums enticed others in New Jersey to invest in land for a coconut plantation and in 1885 they planted over 300,000 seed coconuts imported from Trinidad, Cuba, and Nicaragua. Marsh rabbits and rats put an end to that project. Next came John Stiles Collins who started an avocado grove. It was advertised as "the largest in the world" and of course since there was no way to know whether it really was, the claim could safely be made. Alas, the avocado farm attempt also failed. Conditions were not right for intense agriculture on the sandbar. Undeterred, Collins and his son-in-law Thomas J. Pancoast shifted plans. They realized that with Miami already connected by a railroad and growing fast, the sandbar could be used to build a tourist destination. In 1912 they formed the Miami Beach Improvement Company and people began to buy into the opportunity. Once a bridge was built across the two-and-a-half-mile stretch from Miami to the peninsula, that dreamed-of city began to take shape.

The ode paid to Collins (after whom the avenue on Miami Beach is named) by the *Miami Daily News and Metropolis* of 29 December 1925 is typical of what was said of such innovators from the earliest days:

> There was little in the quiet surroundings... of Mr. Collins to call to mind the lifetime of struggle against the forces of wind and sea, the resistance of tropical mangrove swamps... that have made his triumph assume heroic proportions.

The press in Miami called the bridge he had built "the longest wagon bridge in the world." Again, who would know? By 1925 the wooden bridge was replaced by a causeway and people flocked to the hundreds of houses and apartments and the six sizable hotels already established on Miami Beach. Later, responding to the wave of patriotism during World War II, the causeway was renamed the MacArthur Causeway in 1942.

While Collins had been the precursor who "opened up" Miami Beach, it was Carl Fisher who converted that sandbar and mangrove swamp into the favorite playground for Americans, Europeans, and Latin Americans. Fisher was the kind of man who came to Miami and saw opportunity. Like the other pioneers, all men and women with egos as grand as their ideas, Fisher was very conscious of the fact that while Palm Beach was upmarket, Miami was much less so. He was determined to outdo the "snobs" of Palm Beach by doing something different in the Miami Beach which Collins had opened up and which was now connected by a bridge.

Fisher's determination to compete with Palm Beach meant that he had to replicate much of what that established resort town did. First, Fisher did everything to limit his clientele on Miami Beach to white Anglo-Saxon Protestants (WASPs). Jews, and certainly blacks, were not welcome. Secondly, he had to outdo Palm Beach in terms of the sporting activities which would attract a younger crowd. One of these activities was the powerboat races predictably accompanied by what had already become typically Miamian exaggeration. The 1920 Miami Beach Regatta, headlined the *Miami Herald*, was "one of the most brilliant spectacles ever displayed in the world." (What, one must ask, was this early Miami penchant for competing with and out-doing "the world?") To Fisher, it was not enough to build the finest polo field and club in the southeast at Miami Beach; he also had to imitate the exotic "Grand Gymkhana" riders of British India and invited Cuba's national teams—invariably led by the sons of that country's presidents—to compete. These polo meetings were the first ever sports events between Cuba and the US and, again, the event was described with the usual Miami gusto by the *Miami Herald* as "the largest, the most fashionable, and the most brilliant ever assembled in Miami Beach." Part of the fascination, no doubt, was that in an age when dancing was so popular, the Cubans added to the atmosphere of romance by being as skilled on the dance floor as they were on the polo field. Many of the toasts by American and Cubans alike spoke of this event being the forerunner of many more to come.

AGE OF AVIATION

What gave these sentiments a ring of truth was that the age of air travel had arrived and it provided an aerial bridge between Cuba and Miami. As we will describe later in greater detail, commercial aviation was born in Miami. It is an interesting historical coincidence that Miami, being such a latecomer to the history of cities in Florida and the Caribbean, was established just a few years before the emergence of the age of flight. Miami had its first air-show in 1911 and air shows (with planes leaving from Miami) became a standard Miami Beach entertainment. In fact, Miami was the first American city to undertake international air travel. And this explains why Cuba figured so prominently in the early days of Miami and Miami Beach.

On 30 January 1911 J. A. D. McCurdy—test-pilot for Curtis Aircraft—undertook the daring ninety-mile flight from Key West to Havana. His pontoon-equipped biplane, made of Philippine bamboo and spruce, flew for two hours and eight minutes before the engine stalled not far off the coast of Cuba. He was towed into Havana harbor. As Geoffrey Arend explains, such was the enthusiasm in Cuba and the US over an air connection that in 1913 the Cuban government offered a reward of $10,000 to the first person to fly direct from Key West and land successfully in Havana. Augustín Parlá Orduña, a Key West Cuban-American son of parents exiled during Cuba's revolutionary War of Independence, took up the challenge in an 80 HP Curtis with these stirring words which have such a contemporary ring to them: "Today, on the anniversary of the death of Martí, I will depart with no more help than God, with the flag of the Apostle [Martí] which I will carry to the Cuban Coasts, or bury myself with it in the deep."

After flying for one hour and fifty-two minutes he landed in Mariel, Cuba—a seaport which, as we explain in Chapter Four, would later play a major part in US-Cuban relations. The geographical barrier of distance had been broken and the dreams of many, including the two trailblazing railroad Henrys, had come true. In 1919 Cuban entrepreneurs purchased some US Navy flying boats and launched the Compañia Cubana Americana de Aviación. Lacking radios, communication of approximate arrivals in Miami was made by carrier pigeons.

It is good to recount this early history since we later explore at greater depth the roots of the Miami-Cuba link. It explains, in part, why David Rieff's 1993 *The Exile* is subtitled "Cuba in the Heart of Miami," and Claudia Lightfoot ends her book *Havana* with a chapter entitled "Havana North." Havana and Miami, she says, are two cities which yearn for each other. "[T]hey belong to each other and are both inextricably joined and divided like Siamese twins joined at the hip but with their faces turned away from each other." We shall return to this in the final chapter.

One of the significant changes wrought by all this contact with the wider world, whether by wooden bridge or rustic plane, was that the race and class exclusivity of Miami Beach began to change. World War II accelerated the changes in every area except race. First, the ethnic composition changed as wave-after-wave of Yiddish-speaking Jews arrived. They turned the southern part of the peninsula into what Nobel Prize winner Isaac Singer said "resembled a small Israel." The second aspect of the early Beach which changed with the war was the class composition of the tourist trade; it became the first case of middle- and working-class folks in large numbers seeking sand and sun at hotels charging affordable rates.

As all these pioneers dreamed and built Miami and Miami Beach, the Seminole Indians languished abandoned and for all practical purposes forgotten—until they decided in the 1950s to sue the US government over the lands they lost to white settlers, Spanish and American. Once they won their suit and received the millions which came with the judgment, they fought among themselves over how to divide the pie. Eventually they divided into Seminole and Miccosukee tribes and began to negotiate with the federal government as to the nature of their tribal sovereignty. In one of the great ironies of South Florida history, the Indians went from rags to riches at breakneck speed. By the mid-1960s their wealth was augmented enormously by the authority they were given to sell tax-free cigarettes and, fundamentally, to build casinos. The Seminole Tribe, based in Dania, owns the enormously profitable Hard Rock Casino on their lands, and the Miccosukee own the equally profitable Bingo Gambling and Gaming establishment on the border of the Everglades. Both tribes are among the largest contributors to political campaigns and maintain armies of lobbyists and lawyers in the capital, Tallahassee. As we shall see, they are today the most effective opponents of extending legalized gambling to any other group. It is not at all clear that they will manage to keep a monopoly on this pot of gold but if they do, it just might be one of the great historical redresses if not in "the world," then certainly in Florida history.

HISTORY AND MYTH

As one reviews Florida's and especially South Florida's short history one is made aware of an undisputed universal fact: the forces of historical conjuncture create opportunities which only men and women of vision and passion take full advantage of. Just as time (as in "time will tell") is a neutral factor so, more often than not, is geographical location. Spaces can just lie still until "discovered" by humans. It is this which leads us to end this introduction into South Florida history by focusing again on two cases: the story of the man, Henry Flagler, who joined Key West to the mainland and Miami, is the stuff of legend, second only to the building of the Panama Canal. The discovery of Miami's Indian past does have elements of historical fact but what is a tenuous historical legacy has been converted into a largely myth-making operation. In these two stories we see how the grand and the grandiose come together to engender the excitement that is Miami and South Florida.

Unforeseen by Flagler, the beneficiary of the decline of Key West was Miami as new entrepreneurs began to promote it. Few of the tobacco rollers moved to Miami—they went to Ybor City in Tampa—but thousands did leave the keys to settle there. The new road made that easy. Be that as it may, it was all made possible by that grand pioneer, Henry Flagler.

But Miami was still a frontier. The hordes of job-seekers and, frankly, hustlers, who came to make their fortune were "presentists"—the here and now is what mattered. The myths and legends which already existed in North Florida were absent here. It is a revealing fact that while the Bicentennial Commission of Florida Catalogue of 1972 listed eight "Historic Markers" for Alachua County and an equal number for Duval, Escambia Gulf, Leon, and other northern counties, it listed two for Miami-Dade. Eleven Historic Markers were listed for Key West in Monroe County.

Clearly Miami-Dade needed some "markers" to celebrate. The myth of an Indian settlement in Miami's past was one of the most self-aggrandizing efforts made to construct a legacy. How much was history and how much myth?

Juan Ponce de León was the first European known to have landed at the mouth of what is today the Miami River and Biscayne Bay. He had no plans to settle and left no trace. After collecting fresh water he headed north where his deeds became part of Florida history—North Florida that is. He did notice a village of Tequesta Indians on the north shore of the river, the only memorable feature of which was an elevated burial site called a "midden." The Tequestas were related to the more numerous and more advanced Calusa Indians of Florida's West Coast. The fact that the Tequestas were not agriculturalists who accumulated surpluses of food and that they remained for most of known history the only native Indians of southeast Florida is indication that there was little here to attract other tribes. It was, however, suitable to hunters and gatherers, builders of primitive structures which could be easily abandoned as they took off in their large canoes to fish and gather fruits at considerable distances from their village on the Bay—or, as they did once a year in the summer, to escape the mosquito plague. Further proof of the relative unimportance of the southeast area is provided by the puny attempts of Spanish missionaries to establish themselves there. Contrary to the chain of missions in North Florida, only two attempts at establishing missions are known: one in 1567 and another in 1743. The inhospitable climate and the unavoidable swarms of mosquitoes combined with the Tequestas' frank lack of interest in the Spanish god brought both to rapid and unhappy ends.

"Miami" is a Seminole Indian word meaning sweet water and indeed, among the many names by which the river was called over the centuries— Garband River, Río Ratones, and Lemon River—it only became known as the Miami River during the Seminole Wars (1835–1858). Northern Florida had, and has, navigable rivers such as the St. John River in Jacksonville, the Caloosahatchee running east to Lake Okeechobee from what is now Fort Myers on the West Coast, or the scenic Ocklawaha which took tourists to Ocala and Silver Springs, and the Apalachicola River which turned the port city of the same name into one of the busiest in Florida. In the age before railroads, when boats facilitated productive settlement and exports, southeast Florida had the Miami River which served few of those functions. That river, which emptied at Biscayne Bay, ran a short five miles inland and navigation ended there. At that point, "falls" (really rapids given the area's general flatness) were fed by headwaters at the eastern side of the Everglades. It was then, and remains today, the shortest commercial river in the US. There was little reason for the Tequestas to settle up-river since what was there were the Everglades, hardly a place to hunt for fish, manatees, sharks, porpoises, turtles, and snails—all staples of the Tequesta diet. When the British took possession of Florida in 1763, most of the Tequestas left for Cuba with the withdrawing Spaniards. It appears that a previous migration of Tequestas (this time fleeing from Creek Indian slaving parties) had fled to Cuba in 1711. By the time the British ceded Florida back to Spain in 1784 and Spain sold it to the newly independent Americans in 1821, there was no evident trace of the Tequestas in South Florida.

There is no known history of contacts between the early white settlers and the Tequestas. The settlers' contacts were with hostile raiding parties of Seminoles during the Seminole Wars. A US Coast Guard survey map of 1849 does, however, show the Tequesta midden in the same spot where the present and much heralded Miami Circle sits today, on the western side of the mouth of the Miami river on Brickell Avenue. According to the website of the Florida Division of Historical Resources, the Miami Circle is 38 feet in diameter, carved into bedrock. It consists of 24 holes which might have held the columns of a large structure. The carbon-dating of a charcoal sample in the Circle traces it back 1,900 years. It was the efforts of a determined local archaeologist Bob Carr, Director of the Historic Preservation Board, and the Board volunteers' struggle to find support and even more to receive official blessings for their work that put the project on the map. Discovering the Circle in the midst of major excavation groundwork for yet another tower of condominiums and preserving the site was an exceptional accomplishment by Carr and his mostly amateur archaeologists. Public enthusiasm helped Carr take on all the powerful developers. As the *New York Times* put it (15 February 1999), this discovery "stirred the community pride not seen since the [Florida, now Miami] Marlins won the World Series in 1997." The description by the *Times* went further in describing the evolution of the myth: "Supporters of the move to preserve the site staged a candlelight vigil in front of the dig... Surrounded by television camera crews, they danced to American

Indian drumbeats and displayed placards reading: 'Don't Pave our History' and 'Save the Circle.'"

The Circle was saved and Miami acquired its very own "Indian" past, vague and largely speculative but enough for a city on the move, populated by elites who already knew how to construct plausible stories out of minimal facts.

Aerial view of the Tequesta Indian "Miami Circle"

Chapter Two

PROHIBITION, THE DEPRESSION, AND WORLD WAR II

FROM BACKWATER TO OPEN CITY

With the traditional promotion of Florida and Miami as sites for sun and fun, it is easy to overlook the fact that religion played an important role in the city's foundation and evolution. Miami's origins were solidly Protestant and its early citizens all took great pride in the architecture of their houses of worship. Julia Tuttle's innovating energy carried over into her passion for her religion. She had much to do with convincing John D. Rockefeller to contribute towards the building of a church, arguing that she was still holding services of the Episcopal Church at the Hotel Miami, which she owned. She then donated two lots on which to build a church.

In early July 1896 John Sewell was construction foreman for Henry Flagler's magnificent Royal Palm Hotel. He used his position to bring his black workers to lend their vote to the incorporation of Miami as a city. He also found time to organize sixteen other prominent white citizens into the committee which established, and then built, Miami's First Baptist Church. Certainly, the Baptist church was the first to have a permanent building, now called the Central Baptist Church and which still stands in downtown Miami. Similarly, the largely Bahamian sector of black Coconut Grove established a substantial building housing the St. Agnes Missionary Baptist Church. That church still stands on Charles Avenue in what is now called West Grove.

Another denomination with early roots was the Presbyterian Church. By far its most prominent, and deep-pocketed, member was Henry Flagler. He had already built the Memorial Presbyterian Church in St. Augustine in memory of a daughter who died very young and also donated the land and funds for the Miami church which was inaugurated in 1900. That building was torn down in 1940 and in 1949 the present First Presbyterian Church was inaugurated at 600 Brickell Avenue. This attractive building now forms part of the fastest growing and most fashionable area of Miami which we discuss in Chapter Seven.

Art Deco style of the Scottish Rites Masonic Temple

By 1903 the pioneer Mrs. J. N. Lummus described Miami as composed of "three banks, built of marble, brick, and stone, and six Christian denominations." Certainly the most interesting church in the area extending west of Miami was the Union Congregational Church, built in Coconut Grove in 1891 by Ralph Munroe and later George Merrick. It was a non-denominational church which welcomed both whites and blacks to its services. That was the origin of today's Plymouth Congregational Church, a solid stone building still in the Grove.

This was a time when Protestant denominations cooperated with each other to solidify the non-conformist nature of the new settlement. The *Miami Metropolis* newspaper of 29 November 1901 described how the Methodist and Presbyterian congregations dispensed with their normal morning services "in order to unite with their Baptist friends in their first service." Sturdy church buildings were symbols of the community's material standing. The proclivity for building in a grand style is evident also in the Scottish Rites Masonic Temple—no Catholics were members—built in 1924 in the King Tut Egyptian Revival style. It stands today as the first, and still imposing, Art Deco building in Miami.

These Protestant churches were for whites and none made much of an effort to proselytize among the native Indians. This task seemed to have been left to the Roman Catholic Church, dominant in Tampa and St. Augustine but still marginal in Miami. Despite the zeal of the Catholic missionaries, little was achieved as far as enduring conversions were concerned. Similar to the failure of the Jesuits with the Tequestas, initial efforts by a few Catholic families were also frustrated. One of these families, the Wagners, built a small Catholic chapel up the Miami river and had two priests come up from Key West as missionaries. It was all in vain. In a written reminiscence of 1897, Mrs. A. C. Lovelace relates how a Seminole elder told her: "Indian hunt, fish, trap—no learn to read. No want Jesus Christ."

Catholic missionaries were not the only ones ignored. Much later, a determined Episcopal deaconess, Harriet Bedell, traveled in her Model-A Ford among the Seminoles attempting conversions. As related to Ron Jamro of *South Florida History Magazine* (Fall 2001), Ms. Bedell recalled how the Seminoles instinctively shunned any kind of help from the white man or, as in this case, a white woman. "I would talk and they would listen. Then they would return to their sewing, and I to my knitting." Later the Episcopalian Church was enriched by the arrival of many West Indian Anglicans, but the Catholic Church only much later experienced happier returns with the arrival of two groups of immigrants and/or refugees from the Caribbean: Cubans and Haitians.

The first permanent Roman Catholic church was inaugurated in 1930. In 1937 it was moved and services were held in a new, but still wooden, building. It was not until 1955 that another permanent church—built in the Spanish colonial revival style—was erected. In 1958 it was inaugurated as St. Mary's Cathedral of the new Diocese of Miami and served as the seat of Miami's first bishop. In 1968 the diocese received its first archbishop. Still somewhat marginal to the upper echelons of Miami society, the cathedral came into the local, national, and international limelight when it performed final funeral services for comic actor Jackie Gleason. In Miami, even religion needed to be touched by stars to claim some status. Today, as we will describe later, the church sits in the midst of an expanding Haitian community whose members fill its pews.

PROHIBITION AND PROGRESS

Churches were the material manifestations of social position but they also expressed the existing political power. This history of early Protestant religiosity thus explains why both Miami and Miami Beach were "dry" seven years before the Volstead Act and the Eighteenth Amendment to the Constitution formalized Prohibition in 1920. Dade County voted to go dry in 1913, and in 1916 Florida elected the strongly prohibitionist Sidney J. Catts as governor. Consistent with the double standard (hypocrisy might be too strong a word) which usually accompanies such moral strictures, Catts was teetotal in public, but was known to enjoy more than an occasional strong one or two in private.

The double standard had long been established. Henry Flagler, a devout Presbyterian and dry, prohibited liquor among his workers but allowed it to be served in his majestic Miami hotel, the Royal Palm. Indeed, the double standard covered a large number of peccadilloes. Donald C. Gaby, in his informative *The Miami River and its Tributaries* (1993), tells the story of Miami's most select brothel, "Gertie's," which catered to the wealthy businessmen and politicians of Miami, and to some of its wealthy visitors. Among its celebrated customers, says Gaby, was William K. Vanderbilt, who brought a party of his guests there from the exclusive, then and now, Fisher Island. Another was John D. Hertz, owner of many businesses, who on one occasion stayed at Gertie's place for three days. "The cuisine," says Gaby "must have been as good as the girls."

It was evident that in the midst of the fervent religiosity of the southern migrants to Florida there was ample room for some secret high-living. Newly-rich mid-western and northeastern politicians and law enforcement officials soon developed very agile strategies of accommodating themselves to the demands of both the dry and the wet constituencies. Miami, meanwhile, proved to be accommodating to both.

In many ways that state of affairs spoke loudly as to the kinds of populations that settled in South Florida: native, white, Protestant, and mostly rural folk all tenaciously prohibitionist, but with elites which were capable of defying the law, any law that did not suit them. Few of the "wets," i.e. the heavy-drinking new immigrants—Germans and the mostly Catholic Irish, Italians, and Eastern Europeans, who tended to be settled in those urban areas of the American northeast—came to Miami in these early days. There is no evidence that the dry and pious citizens of Miami would have missed them. They were not the type of settlers they wanted, for as Seymour Martin Lipset notes, "To the ascetic small-town Protestants, these cities represented drunkenness, immorality, political corruption, and cosmopolitanism." In the early years it was precisely these ascetic, small-town Protestants largely from the south who settled in Miami, albeit in limited numbers. At least up to the late 1930s, and despite the boom years, Florida was the least populated of the southeastern United States. Palm Beach, where Flagler's hotels and his private residence were located, did not attract "tin can" tourists who came in droves in their automobiles and by train. (The sobriquet "tin can" derived from the practice of these tourists of eating food out of tin cans to reduce their expenditure.) Instead, Palm Beach attracted members of high society from the north and northeast who generally partied at each other's palatial homes. As Florida historian Michael Gannon explains, "The *nouveau riche* preferred Miami, where illegal liquor parties in the hotels and clubs became showplaces for the new fashions and mores of the Roaring Twenties." This was further evidence that Prohibition was changing Miami in ways which meant it was leaving its quasi-rural, Protestant puritan, pioneering origins behind.

Federal agents enforce Prohibition laws in Miami

Alas, if Prohibition was the expression of small-town power in Miami, it would also in time be the movement which shook its social structure to the foundations by creating the exact opposite of what the ascetics wished for: an open, global city. The first impact of Prohibition was to encourage cross-border tourism. The largest flow by far was over the US-Canadian border to Canadian towns such as Victoria, British Columbia, and Windsor, Ontario. However, none of this was comparable to the excitement of a foreign adventure such as a trip to Miami, and from there to, among many other destinations, Havana or the "Bimini Rod and Gun Club" in the Bahamas, both easily accessed by seaplane service.

By 1925 two and a half million tourists came each year to Florida, mostly by automobile and train. The age of the Model-T Ford had arrived, and "tin can" tourists were stopping in large numbers at campgrounds and motels along the way. And there were long distances to travel before arriving in South Florida. The drive from Chicago to Miami took fourteen days; three of them spent traversing the length of Florida itself. This large movement was made possible by the availability of Henry Ford's cars and the road building programs such as the 1916 Federal Road Aid Act and the 1921 Federal Highway Act, all predecessors of President Dwight D. Eisenhower's monumental Federal Interstate Highway initiatives of the 1960s. In 1920 Florida had 1,000 miles of paved roads including US Highway No. 1 (known in the north as the Boston Post Road), and by 1930 paved roads covered 3,800 miles. As elsewhere in the world, roads were the vital infrastructure of expanding real estate development.

In his best-selling classic, *Only Yesterday: Informal Treatment of the 1920s,* Frederick Lewis Allen listed the following reasons why Miami boomed: attractive climate, accessibility to the populous cities of the northeast, the automobile and new roads, a spirit of abundance and adventure, and the persuasive stories of leisure and business opportunities, especially in the real estate business. T. H. Weigall, a British journalist who spent a year in Miami, spoke of "that bedlam that was Miami... utter confusion... an insane chorus" of real estate sales. "Everybody in Miami," he wrote "was real estate mad."

Also serving the new liquor tourism were flights to Havana, and facilitating the movements of the thirsty was the Hamburg-American Cruise Line which made stops in several of the other Caribbean ports, all decidedly wet. As Daniel Okrent relates in his informative book *Last Call: The*

Rise and Fall of Prohibition, ship stewards knew that once out of Miami and beyond the three-mile territorial sea limit, their patrons learned about daiquiri cocktails in Havana, rum swizzles in Trinidad, and rum punches in Kingston. In Havana in particular but also in the western part of Cuba, a booming rum distilling industry made every effort to exploit the Miami-Havana flood of refugees from Volstead, which explains why the new Pan American Airways advertised: "Fly with us to Havana and you can bathe in Bacardi Rum two hours from now."

Predictably, Americans did not need encouragement, much less cajoling, on this score since American soldiers stationed on the island during and after the Spanish-American War were well acquainted with Cuban rum and returned home singing its praises. Puerto Rico's fate was dramatically different from Cuba's, and that difference later revealed itself in the different social, economic, and political positions of both groups in Miami and central Florida. As distinct from Cuba, which as an independent country was "wet," Puerto Rico was an American territory and thus also "dry." Indeed, it soon became a matter of rum against self-rule. Given the ongoing Puerto Rican struggle to expand the areas of self-government permitted under US colonial rule, that process was held hostage by the forces of Prohibition. The implications, says Arturo Morales Carrión, were clear: "[I]f Puerto Rico wanted a larger dose of self-government, the price was to do away with rum-drinking. Rum and home rule could not go together." What a strange irony, noted Morales Carrión, that now suddenly "rum… was the enemy of Caucasian constitutionalism!"

The irony went deeper in its convoluted logic: Puerto Ricans, who up to then had never been given the privilege of a referendum on their political status, were suddenly summoned to a plebiscite on rum in 1917. The ballot showed a choice between a rum bottle and a coconut. Since both home rule and even US citizenship were perceived to hang in the balance, the people voted to expel rum from the island. Predictably, if people of means had their rum and Scotch smuggled in from Jamaica and Cuba, the poor had only their now homemade *cañita* (moonshine). Morales Carrión explained the cultural peculiarity of what Gordon K. Lewis called "the vagaries of the American puritan conscience" as follows: "The rum revenues were lost, but not the taste for rum or whisky. Prohibition became more than a social farce; it became a cultural aberration. It also left its

37

imprint on local folklore. When someone had been fooled, it used to be said that he had been given coconut milk!"

Clearly, none of this open bootlegging and less-than-secret partying in Miami was encouraging to the pious hearts of the supporters of the "Noble Experiment" and certainly not to the "Great Commoner," William Jennings Bryan, the perpetual Democratic Party candidate for the presidency (defeated in the elections of 1896, 1900, and 1908). An avowed "dry," he eventually withdrew to Miami, settling in a waterfront mansion named "Villa Serena." The irony was that the scene he could observe from his domestic tranquillity was anything but serene. Well within sight were the ships coming from Cuba, Belize, Bimini, and Nassau, making contact with the rum-runners of Miami's Biscayne Bay. "Near Miami," says Okrent, "small boats dropped anchor and hung poster-sized price lists over the gunwales no more self-consciously than if they were selling potatoes." It all so irritated Bryan that in 1921 he called for an invasion of British-governed Bimini and the stripping of US citizenship from those arrested for "conspiring" against the Eighteenth Amendment of the US Constitution.

The British government expressed its profound displeasure with the threat to invade one of its colonies, especially since the Eighteenth Amendment had salvaged the Scottish whisky industry and converted Nassau, Bahamas, from a sleepy sponge-diving society into a veritable booze depot. Alcoholic spirits of every origin—Scotland, the Caribbean, France—flowed into Nassau, making the Lilliputian island of New Providence a significant revenue-producing tourist destination as well as a major exporter of the banned product. Naturally, Miami benefitted from it all. "If anyone wants to go to hell in a hurry," a troubled Protestant minister told the *New York Times* in 1925, "there are greased banks aplenty on Miami."

From Miami the imported liquor moved to other thirsty parts of the state and the southeast, while in Miami Beach rum-running contributed to a whole new lifestyle. Residents did not go sleuthing around looking for some speakeasy or otherwise bootleg liquor; they boldly drove their limousines up to the wharf on Miami Beach to receive their supplies from the heavily-laden rum-runners. Both Havana and Bimini were a two-day round-trip sail away, and local authorities showed all the relaxed attitudes proper to the tropics. Rum-running was an important part of the area's new enterprises by those with solid foreign contacts. By "opening" to the world Miami was laying the foundation of its role as a global city. The changing value system reflected the changing economic reality.

Van E. Huff, a long-time Miami resident, relates witnessing the following in his 1982 memoirs, *From Mountains to Miami*:

> Prohibition was in full swing, but if officials took it seriously at all in Miami, I suspect it was probably to get a piece of the action. Only the Coast Guard seemed to take the whole thing in dead earnest, and when Coast Guardsmen killed a popular bootlegger during a chase, the sailors were spirited out of town to calm down the irate citizenry.
>
> The bootlegger's name was Red Shannon, and his customers included some of the "best people." Perhaps considering it a lark, he led his pursuers into Biscayne Bay, zooming right through a motorboat race in progress. Spectators, thinking it was a stunt, cheered until the machinegun bullets started flying, and Red was pulled dying from his boat. If the Coast Guard had gunned down the mayor, the city couldn't have been more scandalized.

No one should be surprised that the then-Commandant of the US Coast Guard would argue in Malcolm F. Willoughby's book, *Rum War at Sea*, that the "Rum War" was largely a Coast Guard story and that it was "a hard, unremitting war with few of the rewards normally accompanying performance of such duty." It was a thankless and hopeless task which would later be repeated in the cocaine wars. If one keeps in mind that the rum-runner boat was usually a shallow-draft, slick-hulled craft propelled by a Liberty aircraft engine, the forerunner of today's "cigarette" speedboat, and that at least for the first years of the "war" the Coast Guard depended on vessels of pre-World War I vintage, one understands why Willoughby highlights the personal heroics of his fellow Coast Guard men. Florida's 3,800 miles of tidal shore lands, dotted with bays and inlets, was a rum-runner's paradise. Indeed, those who knew what was taking place were not shy about letting their views be known. "Florida," said an English traveler, "from my personal experience in it, was the wettest country I have ever known." Such an opinion received a strong second from Fiorello LaGuardia, Mayor of New York—a city which, like Key West, never even made a pretence of being dry. "There are more prohibition law-breakers in Florida," he intoned, "than in my state." Translated: South Florida was urbanizing and taking on the social habits and styles of the bigger northeastern cities.

These are the salacious and anecdotal stories of the impact of Prohibition on Miami. The more structural and enduring story is how Prohibition spawned the explosion in organized crime in the United States—organizations that are operating alive and well to this day—as well as deepening Miami's ties to the Caribbean region. Here the impact of Prohibition varied with the distance between the producer and the American market, especially South Florida. Distant producers such as British Guiana and the eastern Caribbean, including Trinidad, did not fare well. Closer islands such as Cuba and the Dominican Republic and the "bridges" like the Bahamas and British Honduras (now Belize) benefitted.

Geographical proximity to the US allowed the rum-runners to smuggle not only rum but to benefit from the even larger trade in Scotch. It was American Puritanism which made their businesses boom. Imports of Scotch into the Bahamas (a British territory) went from 25,000 gallons in 1920 to nearly six million in 1930. In fact, the "Cutty Sark" brand of whisky was specifically developed for this illicit but wildly popular trade. One can only surmise that there was little romantic glamour and mileage to be gained from calling the smugglers "Scotch-runners."

In all this informal activity Cuba was particularly fortunate because it also picked up most of the tourist trade. Alec Waugh recorded the varying impact of abstention on the tourist trade in the Caribbean and warned quite accurately that "a West Indian island that did not offer its visitors the opportunity of resisting the midday heat with the cool, mellow, and fragrant sustenance of a rum punch, stood little chance of attracting tourist trade." Given the city's size and general wealth, a large assortment of American businessmen, engineers, soldiers, gangsters, and famous writers all began to turn Havana into a lively entertainment center and with that came the drinking and promotion of new exotic rum-based cocktails such as the daiquiri, the mojito, and the "Cuba Libre."

Substantial fortunes were also made in the islands and mainland territories. In British Honduras, Carlos Melhado, once a poor Portuguese Sephardic Jew, came to dominate the warehousing and trans-shipment of spirits. He ended up paying 10 percent of the colony's taxes and was—after converting to Catholicism—eventually knighted. Prior to 1920, British Honduras imported some 6,000 gallons of whisky for local and

Central American use. By 1930, it was re-exporting 200,000 gallons, mostly on Melhado's own schooners. According to a note to the Colonial Office from the governor in 1927, the "penurious and struggling colony" of British Honduras was thus "saved." In the US Virgin Islands, another originally poor Jewish family, the Paiewonskys, accumulated such wealth that a descendant, Ralph Paiewonsky, was elected governor and served admirably (1961–69) as well as becoming the island's most active conservationist. The largest fortunes, however, were made in Cuba. As Tom Gjelten, the historian of the Cuban Bacardi rum business tells it in his 2008 book *Bacardi and the Long Fight for Cuba*, Prohibition was a blessing to the rum business, a real commercial opportunity. Once the liquor was sold to a third party, it was not the Bacardi family's concern where it went. In fact, a commonly listed destination was "Shanghai." "Facundito Bacardi," says Gjelten, "was fond of telling visitors, with a wink and a grin, that boatloads of his family's rum went to Shanghai because 'there are more drinkers in Shanghai than anywhere on earth.'"

Because the number of US tourists going to Cuba doubled between 1916 and 1928 to 90,000 and the sales to "Shanghai" kept growing, reaching 40,000 cases a year by the mid-1920s, Bacardi was the island's largest industrial enterprise by the end of that decade. Frederick H. Smith, author of the authoritative, *Caribbean Rum: A Social and Economic History*, calculates that in 1929 and 1930, Bacardi paid more than $400,000 in taxes, more than half of all taxes collected from Cuba's many distilleries.

GRAND SCHEMES

Of course, money was also made in Miami and South Florida and with that came new initiatives which distanced the city even more from its fundamentalist roots. As already noted, one of the truly grand real estate projects was Coral Gables and one of its most grandiose promoters was the same William Jennings Bryan. In very Miami fashion, he became both a draw for clients and tourists as well as a tourist attraction himself. As reported by the *Miami Herald* (25 November 1920), Bryan had some very positive suggestions for the city's future, to wit: digging a deep water harbor, building many small parks, and establishing boarding schools to attract people from elsewhere in the US and Latin America to settle. As was his wont, Bryan also pushed a puritanical and moralistic agenda which appeared to run counter to the big city model he was promoting and to which Miami was quickly though covertly aspiring. "You cannot build a city by inviting the sporting element," he argued, "The greatest advertisement you can have is to let it be known that Miami is peopled by folks who are interested in virtue and the higher things in life."

Miamians never really bought into Bryan's definition of virtue which meant two things: a stringent version of the Protestant religion and staying dry. No wonder that the investigative journalist H. L. Mencken called him the "Fundamentalist Pope" and that Clarence Darrow, his opponent in the 1925 Scopes Monkey Trial which pitted Darwinian evolutionary theory against Bryan's biblical version of man's creation, mocked him as "the Idol of all Morondom." Clearly, Bryan's efforts to moralize South Florida by keeping it dry was a non-starter, evidence of which was that Carl Fisher and the elite of Miami Beach were just then doing everything they could to attract the "sporting element."

What Miamians did buy into, or let us say, had already bought into, was sustaining the frontier spirit of *laissez-faire,* i.e. keeping the government and its regulation off the backs of citizens. To Bryan this meant, for starters, not being burdened with environmental concerns. Concern about the environment was very late in coming to South Florida. The new settlers—to the delight of real estate salesmen—needed land and, as many including Bryan suggested, that could be accomplished by draining the Everglades. What a boon it would surely be to settlers and small and extensive agriculturalists alike. It was, in fact, an idea shared by virtually everyone at the time. Arguably the most enthusiastic proponent was a former riverboat captain bearing the imposing name of Napoleon Bonaparte Broward. (You recognize his name when you travel north from Miami-Dade to Fort Lauderdale in Broward County.) Despite his general grandiosity of style and intention, there was much that was grand about this American Napoleon. As sheriff in the Jacksonville area he was known for his integrity and courage in exposing grafters and corruption in general. As a gun smuggler to Cubans fighting for their independence he was known for his daring. Michael Grunwald portrays him best in his book *The Swamp:* "He was also a native Floridian, a log-cabin pioneer, a self-made businessman, a reform sheriff, a father of nine, and a brilliant campaigner." With such sterling qualities, it came as a surprise when he was barely elected—by a very slim majority indeed—state governor. The explanation might be that, as a reformer *à la* Teddy Roosevelt, he was opposed by

Henry Flagler and the other railroad and real estate magnates. Undeterred, Napoleon Bonaparte Broward vowed to stop the state's give-away of land to railroads and corporations. Alas, he also had "land fever," which explains why he promised that the Everglades—"that fabulous muck," he called it—would be drained for the benefit of the state and its new class of yeoman farmers.

His ambitious project was put in the hands of Richard Bolles, a Colorado Springs businessman whom Grunwald describes as a "deep-pocketed developer with silver tongue and a gambler's heart." True to this description, Bolles promoted a belief system which appealed to Miamians perfectly. "Money," he would pronounce, "will assuage almost every other grief." Other than the promotion of mammon, he kept his doctrine of success simple and adequate to his surroundings: modesty in a man was not the path to a fortune. In fact, Bolles argued that only three traits were necessary for getting rich: "impudence, impudence, and more impudence." He seemed tailor-made for early twentieth-century South Florida and beyond. Soon the drainage (called "land reclamation") of the Everglades was being promoted in predictably grandiloquent terms: a

Dredging for drainage and land fill

43

drained Everglades would be a "Tropical Paradise," the "Land of Destiny," "Nature's Gift to Florida," the "Poor Man's Paradise." In short, this "Land of Opportunity" was, as the promoters put it, the "Magnet Whose Climate and Agriculture Will Bring the Human Flood."

Even Flagler, who had opposed the drainage project on the grounds that it would adversely affect his own land schemes, was now on board. Grunwald quotes the Flagler company's newspaper, *Florida East Coast Homeseeker*, making fantastic claims about a drained Everglades including its prediction that within a decade the population of Palm Beach County would grow from its then 5,000 to 750,000. "It is hard to keep within the bounds of belief in foretelling the future," Flagler's paper proclaimed, "as the possibilities here are greater than in any other part of the Union. The resources are unlimited and the opportunities unsurpassed." This is how the drainage of the Everglades figured in those freewheeling—and, of course, equally freebooting—years. How the fate of this great aquifer for all of South Florida would eventually be decided is a discussion we resume later. For now, the moral of the story of the feverish rush to drain the Everglades stands as testimony to a society which was so ready to have the government intervene in their private lives (i.e., Prohibition) but was totally resistant to any government action in many other areas vital to the general well-being of the population. Florida during the boom decade of the 1920s anticipated the twenty-first century libertarians and Tea Partiers by wishing nothing more than that "the state" stay out of their private economic affairs. It was—and still is—truly a minimalist government state: no state income tax, no inheritance tax—everything to attract people to the state and to the land auctions that were booming. Helen Muir describes this milieu well and sees it represented in an editorial in the *Miami News* which she quotes: "Miami asks no special favors only that it be free of unreasonable handicaps, that it be given a chance to run its race."

BOOM TO BUST

Miamians were given that chance and they ran it into the ground. Even as the end of the boom was evident, as business failures followed one after the other in the late 1920s—in banking, railroads, housing, and agriculture—the obstinate but highly selective determination to keep the state at arm's length persisted. The belief was unremitting that because they were not a "smokestack" industrial economy they would not share the fate of the northern cities where unemployment, food lines, and plant closings were the order of the day. In fact, many displaced northeasterners streamed into Florida where at least the warm climate provided some relief. The national government of Herbert Hoover supported this general *laissez-faire* philosophy and refused to order direct government intervention. There was a heavy price to be paid.

As magnificent as Coral Gables with its stellar Biltmore Hotel was, and as attractive as it was to travel to Miami and Miami Beach and from there to the Caribbean wet spots, none of this could escape the end of the housing boom and the collapse of the economy. Given that what already existed in South Florida was an economy based on tourism and an explosive real estate market, all fueled by largely unregulated banks, it collapsed even before the Great Depression hit the nation as a whole. Michael Gannon cites the *Nation* magazine's report on the collapse: "The world's greatest poker game, played with building lots instead of chips, is over. And the players are now... paying up." Like so many others, most of George Merrick's 3,000 salesmen headed back north leaving behind bankrupt banks, unfinished buildings, and whole neighborhoods unsold. What about Bolles' Everglades projects? Bolles, like most others, went bankrupt. He had ignored the signs of a downturn, an attitude easily understood when, as Helen Muir says, you are flushed with monetary success by just "dipping into the pot where sand was being turned into gold."

In addition to the man-made disaster, two devastating hurricanes compounded the local depression. On 18 September 1926 the first major hurricane since 1910 caught the population, mostly new migrants from the north, completely unprepared. Hurricane winds drove the Atlantic Ocean clear across Miami Beach and downtown Miami. Ninety-two residents in this area were killed, and in the vicinity of Lake Okeechobee the newly established towns resulting from the "Drain the Everglades" movement were flooded and more than 20,000 left homeless. A typical headline across the country was "South Florida Wiped Out in Storm." To be sure, an exaggeration—and yet in Dade County one hundred died and 854 people were hospitalized. Conditions were so bad that even President Gerardo Machado of Cuba sent a naval vessel loaded with doctors and nurses. Yes, Miami was badly damaged; destroyed, no. Within a week of the hurricane the Miami press showed the kind of bravado the area was known for: "Miami was almost back to normal" it headlined. The idea, of course, was to try to save the upcoming tourist season which, within the national economic circumstances, did not turn out to be great. Miami was lucky when exactly two years later another hurricane hit Florida but not Miami. It entered through Palm Beach, causing the dikes around Lake Okeechobee to breach. In what was a mostly agricultural area settled around the lake, the flood took some 2,000 (nearly all black) agricultural workers to a watery grave. The economic decline accelerated, banks failed, property values dropped, county and municipal bonds defaulted, and those critical lifelines, the railroads, including Flagler's East Coast Railroad, went into receivership.

By the early 1930s it was fair to say that Florida was in a full depression. Had it been a sovereign country it would have truly been down and out. Fortunately for the many new settlers seeking a better future, it was part of a grand nation which in 1932 changed to an administration with a different model of development and new economic programs. Franklin Delano Roosevelt (FDR) won the elections of 1932 carrying Florida with 74.6 percent of the vote. He helped change the reigning philosophy of governance and *laissez-faire* development and dragged a slew of Florida politicians along on his coattails.

Virtually immediately, FDR began his expansive set of reforms known as the New Deal. As John A. Stuart and John F. Stack note in their edited volume *The New Deal in South Florida*, the state responded enthusiastically to the multiple agencies which were attempting to pump-prime the economy. FDR had a formidable Florida ally and Florida and Miami a champion in Senator Claude Pepper who made sure his state got its share of funds for reconstruction. We shall encounter Pepper again further on, but for now let it be known that it was his lobbying which explains why, in the case of the Works Progress Administration (WPA) for instance, Florida received the highest *per capita* federal contribution in the southeast.

There was the Civilian Conservation Corp (CCC) building parks, doing reforestation work, and teaching young men to read and write. One of the parks they built, and which today is one of the most popular spots in Miami, was the Matheson Hammock Park, south of Coconut Grove. The WPA employed nearly 50,000 in public works, and the National Youth Administration and the Federal Emergency Relief Administration employed additional thousands.

Certainly among the most impressive projects was the Overseas Highway to Key West. It was built upon the still-standing railway bridges of Henry Flagler's railroad, destroyed by the hurricane of 1928, and to a large extent on the ideas Flagler espoused. Aside from the monumental feat of engineering, the project was visualized as a significant part of FDR's Good Neighbor Policy towards Latin America. "The fact is," wrote the *Miami Herald*, "this highway to Key West is only the beginning of an even more ambitious and far-seeing highway program... with the ultimate aim of connecting the eastern section of the United States and Canada with Cuba, Mexico, Central, and South America..." As John Stuart argues, this New Deal vision, while certainly not new, helped establish South Florida's physical and ideological position in the region for decades to come. Geography dictated that Texas would benefit from the Pan American Highway which was eventually completed (except for the section of Panama's Darien jungle) all the way down to Patagonia. Miami, Tampa, and Key West required the expansion of the air and sea transportation facilities they already had. These were some of the New Deal's longer-term projects which they interspersed with short-term initiatives.

The veritable "alphabet soup" of federal agencies and programs, together with a rediscovered Miamian "can do" attitude, not only halted the economic downward slide, but also lay the basis for much of what modern Florida would become. One of FDR's reforms was the lifting of Prohibition in 1933. This resulted in another boon: with US domestic production of distilled liquor virtually destroyed after fourteen years of Prohibition, imported liquor was ready to meet the demand. Cuba exported well over seven million gallons and the Virgin Islands 1.7 million gallons of rum. And, in no time at all, Puerto Rico was exporting 6.3 million gallons of rum, much of it produced in the distillery owned by the Cuban Bacardí family who had established it there in 1936. There is an interesting story in this.

The Puerto Rican Serrallés family, who owned a major sugar estate in the south of the island and whose pot-still began making "Ron Don Q" in 1865, had strongly resisted the entry of the Cuban Bacardís into Puerto Rico. A legal battle royal ensued and was litigated all the way up to the US Supreme Court, where, in 1936, the Bacardís won the right to operate a distillery on that American island. All of which goes to say that to understand the formidable later presence of the Bacardís in Miami, one has to understand that once permanently established in Puerto Rico, they were in the US market, duty-free.

Clearly Prohibition, the construction boom, and collapse, followed by FDR's New Deal reforms had changed Miami. It was the years of World War II, however, which not only reinforced these changes but propelled them into the future that would be Miami.

THE WAR YEARS

The start of the war did not occur without trauma, partly because Florida contributed 250,000 soldiers of whom 3,000 died, and partly because events were to prove that post-Prohibition Florida, and South Florida in particular, was not prepared for what the conflict had in store for them. Before the war Florida had only two significant military installations, Camp Blanding near Starke, and the Jacksonville Naval Air Station. If one recalls that what historians came to call "the War of the Atlantic" began in September 1939, that France had fallen to Hitler's forces in June 1940, and that the US entered World War II on 8 December 1941 (the day after the attack on Pearl Harbor), it is astonishing to discover that a Joint Army and Navy Operations Center was not opened in Miami until December 1941... with one naval officer on duty. That the threat was underestimated is evident.

Two trends finally shook Miami, and America as a whole, out of its smug sense of invulnerability. First there were the fears of Axis "fifth column" activities, i.e. subversion both at home and in the hemisphere. By 1940, as war raged in Europe, the US was pushing even harder to secure Latin American support. After all, it was known that important sectors of the Latin American elites and the Roman Catholic Church sympathized with fascism. A much more important development, however, was what Winston Churchill later confessed as "the only thing that ever really frightened me during the War," the "U-boat peril" of German submarine warfare. Rumors were rampant that German submarines were refueling from bases in Mexico, Central America, Haiti, and the Dominican Republic. A release of the Associated Press of 20 May 1942 warned ominously that it was strongly believed that the U-boats had "access to some well-hidden bases" in the Caribbean. While none of this proved to be true, the important point was that an America that was properly proud of the naval and geostrategic doctrines legated by Alfred Mahan, and of the heroic deeds and performances of some of its naval heroes, was totally unprepared for what it now confronted. In fact, what has since been called the "U-boat War" and the "Battle of the Caribbean" came close to being a major calamity. Dealing with perceived subversives was considerably easier than dealing with German U-boats.

By the time the Gulf Sea Frontier was established in Miami in June 1942, 56 ships had already been sunk in its area of responsibility, the vital Yucatan Channel and the west coast of Florida bordering the Gulf of Mexico. A total of 70 ships were sunk in the Gulf before the U-boat threat was brought to an end in mid-1943. The Germans caused havoc to the supply of oil and gas entering and exiting the refineries in the Gulf. And those were the losses in only one of Florida's three sea frontiers. Because of these losses and because thousands were mobilized to patrol the state's long coastlines on foot, known then as "sandpounders," it is a plausible thought that perhaps for the first time Floridians and Miamians in particular became aware that their long peninsula had to defend three sea frontiers: the Gulf, the Atlantic, and the Caribbean. The Atlantic Sea Frontier stretched all the way from Newfoundland to Jacksonville, Florida. The Caribbean Sea Frontier was headquartered in Puerto Rico but affected Miami and South Florida directly, commanding as it did the entry into the Gulf of Mexico.

In the Caribbean there was an additional potential threat: part of the French fleet (carrying France's gold) had made a run to Martinique and was under the command of Admiral Georges Robert of known pro-Vichy proclivities, as anyone remembering Humphrey Bogart and Lauren Bacall in *To Have and Have Not* will recall. With a 22,000-ton aircraft carrier transporting the latest American combat aircraft (which even the US Air Force did not have), an 8,000 ton cruiser and other vessels, the French fleet was by far the most powerful force in the Caribbean. An American carrot-and-stick strategy, as well as appeals to Admiral Robert's vanity and instinct for survival, avoided a bloody battle in the Caribbean Frontier.

The situation in the Caribbean stood as follows in mid-1942 just as the Germans unleashed their U-boat "wolf-packs" in "Operation Drumbeat":

Total Area:	2 ½ million square miles
Headquarters:	San Juan, Puerto Rico
Sector Commands (with great autonomy):	
	Guantánamo, Cuba;
	Willemstad, Curaçao; Chaguaramas, Trinidad
US Naval Strength:	9 destroyers, 3 gunboats, 9 Coast Guard Cutters,
	24 Search/Rescue Craft, 40 smaller craft

This was hardly a force to make the Germans shake in their boots. The "astonishing U-boat war," as Admiral Hoover, Commander of the Caribbean Sea Frontier, put it, was proof that the US was not ready. The threats were not just naval. In fact, even US coasts were no longer impenetrable. In mid-1941 only luck led a coastal patrol to catch eight German infiltrators who had disembarked from a U-boat. They were all condemned to death by a military court. Two other landings of saboteurs in the US occurred in Rhode Island on 13 June 1942 and in Jacksonville Beach, Florida, on 17 June of that same year.

So wide was the choice of targets off the Florida coast, wrote a German commander, "that it was quite impossible to attack them all." One German captain called it the "American Turkey Shoot," while another spoke with astonishment at the "business as usual" attitude of citizens and merchants in US towns, including very much so, Miami. Their refusal to "black out" denied Allied ships cover and encouraged the boldness of U-boat captains even within sight of US shores. According to Gannon, the refusal to maintain a general blackout was proof that "civilian avarice and carelessness must take their places on the list of agents accountable for the U-boat triumphs." There surely was carelessness but also a certain civilian naiveté about the consequences of war. Miami historian Helen Muir in her *Miami, USA* (1953) records seeing a nurse cleaning the tar off a survivor from a torpedoed tanker and asking him, "Is this your first trip to Florida?"

The sad reality is that German U-boats sank close to a total of 600 ships in the Caribbean before a concerted land, sea, and air counterattack brought their presence to an end in the region. By then, the Roosevelt-Churchill exchange of 44 US destroyers for fourteen British bases in the Caribbean had taken place. In addition, British scientists had broken the German communications code, Allied radar and sonar were fully operational, and the coalition of armed forces—especially American and British combat aircraft—had shifted the balance dramatically. Germany's Admiral Doenitz decided to pull his by-then much reduced U-boat fleet out of the Caribbean and concentrate them in the North Atlantic, preparing for an Allied invasion the German command knew was coming but did not know when or from where it would be launched. For the societies of Florida and the Caribbean, the end of the U-boat war was a great relief. Shortages and rationing were still in place, but any threat of direct attack was now over.

What remained and brought about significant changes in the nature of Miami was the formidable presence of the American military. It was evident in many ways but in keeping with our previous discussion of the rum industry in the Caribbean it is instructive to note the changes World War II exerted on this industry and the American market it supplied. By the end of the war, US imports of Caribbean rum surpassed all other categories of imported distilled spirits. Then there were the habits and tastes developed by the thousands of GIs based in the rum-producing islands. It was a profitable exchange all-round. Anyone old enough to remember a Trinidad calypso called "Rum and Coca Cola," whose lyrics contained the words "both mother and daughter… working for the Yankee dollar," will know

GIs train on Miami Beach

that neither law nor religion could stop rum from becoming the Yankee's wartime "comfort water." This song, composed by the Trinidad calypsonian Lord Invader, was brought back to the mainland to the great fortune of Mory Amsterdam and the Andrews Sisters, who made it wildly popular and remunerative. Of course, Lord Invader received no credit, much less royalties, for his famous tune. Music and a taste for new Caribbean rums were just small parts of island influences flowing north.

In Miami and Florida generally, the most evident physical consequence of the war was the tremendous multiplication of military bases. Florida's politics of "bringing home the bacon" unleashed a scramble in Washington to have bases, airfields, and/or shipyards built in the electoral districts of influential politicians. There were 172 bases built one year after the initiation of hostilities.

Miami and Miami Beach were essentially training grounds for American and Allied troops alike. During the war years, one-third of the Army's Air Force officers and one-fifth of the enlisted men had trained in Miami Beach. Florida's benign weather and flat terrain were ideal for aviation training; there were forty aviation installations offering specialized training. Despite the ideal flying environment, Florida historian Michael Gannon maintains that hundreds of pilots were killed in training accidents, many more than the 507 RAF pilots lost in the Battle of Britain. There was also a desperate need for military uniforms, which for Miami and Miami Beach meant manufacturing "fewer tuxedos and more overalls." Helen Muir describes the moment:

> Consolidated Vultee manufactured airplane parts, hiring up to four thousand men and women at its peak. Other small firms converted to wartime manufacturing. Shipbuilding became an important industry. Tantalizingly backward in growing up to its responsibilities, Miami took several giant steps forward as the result of the war. It is doubtful if anything but a world cataclysm could have turned her away from her self-preoccupation and frivolous disregard of proper values.

By the autumn of 1942 more than 300 hotels with 70,000 rooms in Miami and Miami Beach were accommodating some 78,000 servicemen and women. The Biltmore of Coral Gables was purchased outright by the federal government. A war film industry developed.

Even as the war effort kept Floridians and Miamians busy, the conflict did not stop the migration of Americans to Florida. In the 1940s the population of the US as a whole grew by 15 percent; in Florida it grew by 46 percent. Key West, already the residence of writers such as Ernest Hemingway, grew from a sleepy town of 13,000 to a mid-size city of 45,000. In Miami, according to historian Gary R. Mormino, the number of actual residents grew very little between 1940 and 1945: from 173,065 to 192,122, while non-residents, tourists, and soldiers increased in numbers to what the *Miami Herald* calculated were 325,000 people in the city. "Except for the land boom of 1925," noted the *Herald's* Nixon Smiley, "no other event in Miami's history had done so much to change the city as World War II. At the War's beginnings Miami had still had many of the qualities of a small town... the War changed all that."

What had not changed much was Miami's propensity to pretentiousness, occasionally bordering on vulgarity. The following advertisement was placed by the City of Miami in *Time* magazine in January 1942:

MIAMI'S PLEDGE to AMERICA AT WAR

> Above all others, Miami knows how to do one job surprisingly well—to take our God-given warmth and sea and sunshine, and to convert it into rest and recreation and healthful living for the benefit of thousands of visitors
>
> So Miami pledges itself to carry on at the job we really know how to do. We think it's important to keep on supplying the best vacations in the world to those who need and deserve them—and who can work more efficiently for having had them.
>
> And we pledge that our part in "keeping 'em flying" will be to do our best to "keep 'em smiling," too!

This was the kind of tawdriness which got under the skin of fearless observers, and there was no grander and more astute observer of the vagaries of Miami-at-war than resident muckraker Philip Wylie. Writing for the *New Republic* in February 1944, Wylie described the crowds of out-of-towners spending hundreds of thousands of dollars every day at the Hialeah Race Track, and $100,000 a day at the dog races. While the city, like the rest of the country, was formally still under government war-time regulations including rationing, Wylie described how "there are in practice more ways to get around gasoline rationing, liquor shortages, and the officially-mandated rent ceilings than there were ways to get into a speakeasy during prohibition." In his columns in the *Miami Herald* and the *Saturday Evening Post* he excoriated the corrupt and underhanded ways of many Miami merchants and hotel owners, the treatment of blacks, and other sensitive topics. Predictably, he was not popular. Helen Muir put it most clearly: "The flow of lucid, graphic phrases from the Wyle typewriter turned dyed-in-the-wool Miamians apoplectic. The old unspoken rule about hiding Miami's defects away from the eyes of tourists did not hold with this prolific, hard-hitting upstart."

Wylie, in short, described how the greed of hotel proprietors and other merchants had created an atmosphere that was a "national disgrace." He was careful, however, to distinguish between the grand—the decent patriotic natives of Miami—and the grandiose—the thoughtless, get-rich-quick crowds whom he called "wishful, witless self-indulgent" outsiders. The attitude of military personnel toward Miami landlords, said Wylie, "bordered on maniacal fury" over the way they were treated. There was, however, no stopping the maddening pace, not even in Miami Beach so fervently promoted to rich, young, and energetic WASPs. As is usually the case, social change often brings with it unexpected outcomes. It had been the case that explicit discrimination against Jews, blacks, and what was said to be "riff-raff" of all kinds guaranteed that the exclusivist wishes of this particular clientele were met. Such was the determination of certain white groups to insulate themselves from the changes taking place in the area that one hundred wealthy folk who had formed their own beach club in 1935, the Surf Club, then pushed for the formation of a whole new city, Surfside, in order to retain the club's exclusivity. With exceptions such as that of the Surf Club, the Depression and World War II opened up Miami Beach.

Suddenly, as has been noted, there was a need for beds for the tens of thousands of GIs training for war, which meant building at breakneck pace and in whatever style came to hand: West Indian bungalows, stark and austere "depression" architecture, and, fatefully for the future, the sleek Art Deco buildings which aimed to duplicate the streamlined automotive style of the time. Any style was permitted as long as it could accommodate the troops, and not, incidentally, the hordes of tourists who continued to come. Somewhat later, when Arthur Godfrey and then Jackie Gleason declared Miami and Miami Beach "the fun capital of the world," the two places had the space to accommodate the "world."

A middle-class aesthetic was now in vogue, not just in Miami and Miami Beach but in the whole US. Miami merely added a certain tropical flair to the temper of the times. That is when the old dream that Miami would one day become a great northern city transplanted to the tropics turned to reality. "[Miami] has," said Helen Muir, "the lure of a tropical country, but it is strictly American with all the good and bad ingredients that America can produce."

There was one more piece of social legislation that played a fundamental role in post-war Miami and Florida generally: Franklin Delano Roosevelt's Servicemen's Readjustment Act, known as the GI Bill. By assisting with re-entry into civilian life through funding education and housing, the GI Bill had a considerable impact on the quality of the young people who came back to settle where they had trained during the war. These veterans became suburbanites as air conditioning and war-time mosquito eradication programs made South Florida an ideal place to raise a family. There were many old, non-resolved issues, however, which these new residents had to confront, not the least of which were generalized racism and organized crime. World War II did ease access to Miami, and Miami Beach especially, to Jews but did no such thing for blacks. The US armed forces remained segregated and this injustice was not remedied until President Truman did the right thing during the Korean War.

INTERNATIONAL HUB

It is useful to ask, therefore, whether the boom and bust and the New Deal left much of worth in Miami. Aside from the truly grandly-designed Coral Gables—Merrick's "vast and wonder-filled garden"—there were in fact only a few examples that could support the claim that Miami was the much-heralded "city of the future." And yet it was and is part of Miami's capacity to rise after a fall, using with great panache whatever could cast a "magical spell" on many a wealthy outsider. Critical to this attraction was the fact that the war not only sustained Miami as a major base for aviation, civilian and military, but also expanded it. The growth of aviation was a major stepping stone to global city status. Will Rogers put it precisely when he said that "Miami is the jumping-off place of the world." Some history is in order.

It is ironic that Miami's grand entry into the age of international travel took place just as the boom years in Miami and Miami Beach were coming to an end, and years before the Great Depression hit. First and foremost among the pioneers of aviation was Juan Terry Trippe, son of a wealthy investment banker from New York. Trippe beat all other competitors when he organized Pan American Airlines (PAA) in Key West, and secured the contract with the US Post Office. In October 1927 PAA began a mail service to Havana in tri-motor Fokker F-7 planes inscribed "US Mail, Cuban Mail." In January 1928 PAA carried its first passengers to Havana, launching the service which contributed to Miami's growth and reputation as an international city. In the midst of the depression in Miami and the nation, PAA moved its operations to Miami. The airport was called PanAm Field Miami, today's Miami International Airport (MIA). International commercial aviation was born in Key West, Miami, and Havana. Since steamers took up to thirty hours to reach Havana and PAA flying boats

Pan American Airways "Clipper" at Dinner Key base, Coconut Grove

only ninety minutes, the airline was justified in advertising "Breakfast in Miami, lunch in Havana, dinner in Miami." In 1930 PanAm shifted from its Miami airport to Dinner Key, Coconut Grove. The terminal was finished in 1935, designed in Art Deco style by Delano and Aldrich. It now serves as the Miami-Dade City Hall.

Another one of those who recognized Miami's ideal location for air service between North and South America was World War I ace Eddie Rickenbacker. In 1923 he organized Florida Airways and while it had only a short life, Miami's association with the Rickenbacker name did no harm. By the early 1930s, there were thirty flights in and out of Miami every day.

Rickenbacker represented something of a throwback to the pioneering days of Florida. He openly expressed himself as a foe of government, consistently rejecting any of the federal subsidies all the other airlines were accepting. He certainly fought mightily to stop the establishment of the Civil Aeronautics Act passed by Congress in 1938. He hated trade unions, supported Senator Joe McCarthy's actions, and advocated the abolition of the Sixteenth Amendment to the Constitution authorizing a personal income tax. Reminiscent of many contemporary libertarians, he believed that abiding by these principles of absolute *laissez-faire* was the only way to "save the American way of life." By the time he passed away in 1973, Eastern Airlines was a major part of Miami's rise as one of the nation's busiest airports. In 1989 American Airlines bought Eastern's route rights.

Meanwhile, George T. (Ted) Baker founded National Airlines at St. Petersburg, Florida, in 1934. He was outgoing and as flamboyant as he was combative. He and Rickenbacker had a decades-long rivalry which occasionally led to strong words. According to Geoffrey Arend in his wonderfully illustrated *Great Airports: Miami International* (1993), it was National Airlines which gave the Miami Beach hotel industry a lift by promoting its "no frills night fares," year-round night flights from New York. That converted the Beach into an equally year-round operation with cut rates in the summer months. National's habit of calling its planes after stewardesses and then advertising "I'm Dorothy—Fly Me" incited feminist opposition. National took advantage of the rakish reputation of Miami by calling its New York–Miami–Havana route "the Route of the Buccaneers." In 1980 National was absorbed by Pan American Airways which itself disappeared a few years later. It was now the turn of American Airlines, but that is a history for another occasion.

Finally, and lest we forget when talking about conquering the skies, one should mention the role of the German Graf Zeppelin which was based at Opa-Locka Airport for its trips from Berlin to South America. It was only proper that that German grand venture be based in that city. Very much in the tradition of flights of fancy, the city of Opa-Locka was built by Glenn Curtiss to replicate an Arab city and was known as the "Baghdad of Florida." What does it say when new neighborhoods have to be called after foreign places such as Venice or, indeed, Baghdad? Drive through Coral Gables and witness every street named after a city in Spain. The Anglos who originally bought there could not pronounce the names of the streets on which they lived. Today, the increasing number of Hispanic residents has brought correct pronunciation to this great flight of planning fancy. This was very much the legacy of the man who arguably invented the South Florida architectural style, Addison Mizner. He was, in the words of Laurence Leanmer, "the great architectural fabulist" who created magic with "a bit of Spain, a dash of Morocco, a hint of Paris, a flourish of Hollywood, and something of exotic, jungle Florida as well." Too bad that in much of Miami all that is left of Mizner's magic are the foreign place names.

Chapter Three

THE BATTLES AGAINST JIM CROW AND ORGANIZED CRIME

UNFINISHED AGENDAS

As we have already seen, Miami was not yet an established city, in law or population, when Florida seceded from the Union and its citizens eagerly fought for the Confederacy of slave-holding states. This historical fact has led to the generalization that Florida is composed of two states: a northern part identified with the traditions and conventions of the "south," and the part south of Ocala which was more "northern" (as in northeastern). This is true in terms of what is generally considered the "frontier" experience of the northern part of the state, i.e. white yeomen and slave-owning planters fighting wars with the already settled Indians, in this case the Seminoles. No such battles took place in the south of the state.

This conceptualized divide does not hold true, however, in terms of those abominable practices of the southern plantation way of life—segregation, discrimination, and racism. Even without plantations and slavery in the southern part, migration from the plantation south brought racism with it so that segregation was practised throughout Florida. To be sure, there were differences in terms of the historical memories of the plantation society of North Florida which the south did not have. This was part of what could explain the differences in the expression and the intensity and style of race relations between North and South Florida.

RACISTS AND REFORMERS

The question of style of racism should not be dismissed too readily. By style one understands the characteristic way a society responds to its environment—the do's and don'ts that implicitly prescribe and proscribe permissible modes of action (call them "operational codes"). South Florida in fact showed—and still shows—a stronger, though hardly total, resemblance to the Latin American pattern of race relations: strong prejudices and discrimination in private relations such as residence, primary family attachments, and social club memberships, and less abrasive relations in

59

public intercourse. North Florida's fanatical and crude determination to defend segregation did not sit well with a southern part which wished to portray itself in milder tones. This had as much to do with the nature of the south's industry sustained by tourism as it did with any individual or group predispositions. Attempting to convey a more urbane, less parochial style is the best South Florida could manage for the simple reason that political power was centered in the northern part of the state. Of course, it is perfectly understandable that to an American and immigrant black these must have seemed distinctions without a difference. Residential segregation continued, and continues today, to characterize Miami-Dade as we shall describe later.

Even so, the differences were important in a wider political sense. It was the northern politician elites who had the means to enforce not just the official codes of race relations but virtually every aspect of governance for the state as a whole. The misdistribution of electoral districts ensured this system. Therefore, these differences would influence the way race and broader ethnic relations evolved in the north and in the south of Florida.

Historically, residential segregation was the rule in South Florida, even in the tourist industry. As Gary R. Mormino describes Florida tourism, it was riddled with discrimination and not just against blacks. Signs reading variously "Restricted Clientele," "Gentiles Only," "Exclusive," "For Whites Only," or "No Mexicans Allowed" littered the tourism landscape. In 1953 one in five Miami Beach hotels barred Jews and all barred blacks. Further north, in places such as Pensacola and St. Augustine, terms such as "pickaninnies," "care-free darkies," and "mammies" were common. As Mormino notes, "Along rural highways and city streets, middle class Blacks felt the sting of humiliation from routinely denied restrooms and accommodations."

Segregation in housing always meant separate but never equal: it meant bad sanitary conditions and totally underfunded and thus inadequate housing and education for black Americans. "By the early 1930s," says James A. Schnur, "contagious diseases ravaged the unfortunate occupants of the small, dirty shacks that constituted Miami's 350 acre Colored Town, now known as Overtown." Predictably, the "blame the victim" syndrome was alive and well even in the "non-southern" city of Miami. Note an editorial in the *Miami Herald* in 1941: "Negro town has become a den of iniquity with prostitution flourishing, bolita tickets for sale on every hand… [children] grow up under the illusion that crime is a normal way-of-life."

All attempts to allow blacks to move out of this area were met with burning crosses and even bombings. The same segregation held sway in public schools and recreational facilities such as beaches and parks, not to mention private theaters. The greatest and most violently enforced taboo of all, however, was miscegenation. Mixed marriages were constitutionally banned in the Florida Constitution of 1885, a provision not rescinded until the 1967 US Supreme Court case of *Loving v. Virginia* held the banning of "miscegenation" to be unconstitutional. Indeed, such was the atmosphere during World War II that when German prisoners-of-war at a Miami prison camp complained about having to share a mess with black American servicemen, they were given their own segregated quarters, superior in conditions to those of the black American soldiers.

In other words, well past the end of the Civil War and Reconstruction, Florida was a Jim Crow state. The dominant Democratic Party fully endorsed and perpetuated this racist system. A poll tax and other measures successfully kept blacks from voting, and major offices were decided in the segregated primaries of the Democratic Party, not in the general elections. In order to maintain this pattern of racial segregation throughout the state it was important to first keep political power in the "old southern" or Dixie, i.e. northern, part of the state. This explains the fierce resistance to any redrawing of electoral district boundaries (known as reapportionment) which might have shifted power to the rapidly growing populations of the "new" South Florida. Secondly, powerful methods of enforcing the do's and don'ts and instilling fear were essential. This is where the paranoiac style in American politics combined with the racism of contemporary society played its part. And in this the Ku Klux Klan (KKK) had an important role in the 1920s.

The Klan, with its attack on metropolitan "cosmopolitanism" and the more traditional minority ethnic scapegoats, seems to have provided an outlet to the frustrated residents of provincial America who felt their values, power, and status slipping away. In this sense, the impulses of the KKK were similar to those driving Prohibition: Protestant provincials versus big city ethnics, popularly called "metropolitans." Even the "Great Commoner" Bryan, as Richard Hofstadter wrote, was "a provincial politician, following a provincial populace in provincial prejudices"—including Prohibition, religious intolerance, and support of the Klan.

In the 1920s the situation in Miami lent itself to this kind of provincial response to demographic and ethnic changes. Not the least of these was anger at the large influx of West Indian blacks, mostly Bahamian. These black immigrants invested but did not settle in Colored Town, preferring a segregated section of the mostly white, old pioneer neighborhood of Coconut Grove. And they settled in considerable numbers. Of the 29,571 residents in Miami in 1920, 9,259 or 30 percent were black, of whom 4,815 or 52 percent were from the Bahamas and other West Indian islands. Similarly, 8,000 of the 25,000 people in Key West at the end of the nineteenth century were Bahamian. The Bahamians and West Indians brought a different set of behavioral styles and operational codes to the segregated black community of Miami, codes derived from their more international outlook. Many of them had worked on the Panama Canal and after its inauguration in the building of docks and railways in Central America and its banana plantations.

It is this large West Indian presence which explains the success the Jamaican-born Marcus Garvey and his United Negro Improvement Association (UNIA) had in recruiting members in Miami. Predictably, the white community was not happy with these black immigrants. It was not just the "cheeky" or "uppity" attitudes of the West Indians and their open talk of "black liberation" and a possible "return to Africa" (i.e. Liberia); it was also their entrepreneurial, commercial, and real estate speculative capabilities which contributed to suspicion and antagonism. UNIA's ability to collect money allowed the organization to take advantage of the real estate boom occurring in Miami. Its members bought, then rented out many properties to American blacks, or started small businesses themselves in Colored Town. These commercial successes and the organizational skills so evident in their churches and fraternal societies were threatening to the equally-migrant white settlers, mostly from Georgia and other southern states, many not as successful.

All this was reason enough for the KKK to spring into action. Where and when verbally intimidating black leaders did not work, kidnapping, flogging, and then tar-and-feathering were common. This criminal behavior was hardly met with the kind of vigorous response one would normally expect from the authorities including the police. The fact was that many of these police in Miami and other towns were themselves members of the hooded Klan. But how about the federal authorities? Here also one found the "paranoiac" style dominating. The case of FBI Director J. Edgar Hoover illustrates the point. Robert Hill, editor of the papers of Marcus Garvey and the UNIA, describes Hoover's fear of the Garveyites from as early as 1919:

> Hoover had come to believe that the Garvey movement in America was subsidized to some extent by the British Government; another government official voiced the equally far-fetched suspicion that Garvey might have been working as part of an international Jewish conspiracy aimed at fomenting revolution.

As Miami historian Paul S. George notes in several well-documented articles on the "policing" of Miami's black community, the FBI kept up a steady stream of field reports on activities in Colored Town. Kip Vought provides a good summary of the early decades of Miami's black community:

> While these brutal tactics kept [up] the level of fear and intimidation… the political battles for fairness were slowly picking up steam. Since Miami's incorporation as a city, blacks had challenged, usually without success, the racial tyranny afflicting their community. The UNIA's contribution in this struggle lies in the fact that it brought the message and philosophy of Black Nationalism to Miami's blacks thirty to forty years before the civil rights movement.

Eventually the presence of the UNIA in Miami vanished, replicating the nationwide crisis in the organization. Among the various factors which contributed to this decline was a division in the leadership of the black community, intensified by Garvey's ill-advised meeting and meeting-of-minds with the Klan. He welcomed this strange alliance, explained Garvey, because both favored "racial purity through segregation." The whole affair was so shocking to some black leaders that they accused Garvey of being a Klansman. The collapse of most of UNIA's business ventures, especially that of the Black Star Line shipping concern, occurred just as the real estate bubble in Florida, and Miami in particular, burst. Everyone, black or white, who participated in the real estate frenzy, suffered. Finally, there was the arrest and deportation of Garvey to Jamaica in 1927, and so ended one of the most dynamic but also conflictive phases of race relations in Miami-Dade. The races continued as segregated as before and other major battles were still to be fought. A few of these battles brought about marginal gains for the black community, but most did not.

One of these battles involved the determination to defend Jim Crow laws by opposing any redrawing of electoral boundaries. Legislative leaders from North Florida, believing that not only their political dominance but their way of life was threatened by reapportionment, put up ferocious resistance. They suspected (probably correctly) that the crowds of outsiders flowing from northern and mid-western states into South Florida might not have the same commitment to the state's Jim Crow traditions that they had, and that those residents would probably cast some of these traditions aside if they felt their economic prosperity threatened. Thus, to the North Florida segregationists, known as "Dixiecrats," the battle over reapportionment had even greater significance than was first apparent. To the average South Florida politician the battle was simply over democratic representation or one man one vote, not necessarily an attack on their traditional way of life. To the minority of true reformers, it was a battle to dismantle a way of life which had segregation at its core. It took personal and political courage to be a reformer.

This is where Governor LeRoy Collins, the first major grand reformer of Florida, played his part. Collins was born in Tallahassee, the state capital and seat of the "Old South." He was elected in 1934 at the age of 25 to the state legislature. He served three terms and was elected to the Florida Senate in 1940. After serving in the Navy in World War II he was re-elected to the Senate in 1946 and 1950, and to the governorship in 1955. He certainly was no liberal on racial matters. In fact, he joined his fellow southern governors in opposing school desegregation. Locked in a struggle to win the governorship in a special election at a time when the US Supreme Court and the federal government were making pronouncements in favor of desegregation, Collins announced his commitment to continued segregation. He was realistic enough to understand, however, that times were changing. In 1965 President Lyndon B. Johnson asked Collins to represent the US Presidency in the "Dr. Martin Luther King, Jr. Voting Rights" march in Selma, Alabama. Showing great personal courage, Collins accepted. This contributed to his being smeared as a

"Nigger Lover" in the 1968 campaign for the Senate. In an outright racist campaign, the Republican Ed Gurney, part of Richard Nixon's "Southern Strategy," managed to have Collins labeled "Liberal Leroy." Collins overcame all that and won a victory which represented a watershed in Florida politics.

Despite his segregationist inclinations and proclivities, Collins had evolved into someone moderate in style and pragmatic in practice. He believed it important that Florida create an environment that would help the state diversify economically, and he understood that racial militancy, and perhaps even more so, the images that such militancy engendered nationally, could crush his modernization program. It was this program which got him the backing of the new urban parts of the state, a support which led to his victory.

Unsurprisingly, the top political priority for those new urban sections was reapportionment. The data showed why. By 1950, as South Florida continued to grow dramatically and as the legislature remained unreapportioned, 13.6 percent of the state's population elected more than one-half of the state senators, and 18 percent of the population elected more than half the members of the House of Representatives. As the battle over legislative reapportionment unfolded, rural legislators formed what became known as the Pork Chop Gang and took the equivalent of a blood oath to stick together, thereby controlling all legislation, especially as regarded reapportionment. This was what Collins confronted as governor when he introduced reapportionment legislation in each legislative session, only to see it blocked by rural legislators who dominated the Senate leadership and held nearly a majority of the seats in the house.

It is difficult to understand the full nature of this battle for political and civil rights without understanding the travails which faced any politician from Miami who, as distinct from LeRoy Collins, did consider segregation intrinsically immoral. Such reformers had to endure a veritable seething cauldron of political opposition by segregationists still holding office. The situation in Miami was best described by Frank Donner of the *Nation* (22 January 1950) who called it the "Miami Formula": the attempt by the mayor's office, the city council, and the police force to enforce segregation and racism through intimidation, red-baiting, and outright corruption in controlling city politics. Author Melanie Shell-Weiss quotes Florida journalist Stetson Kennedy's description of Miami as an "anteroom

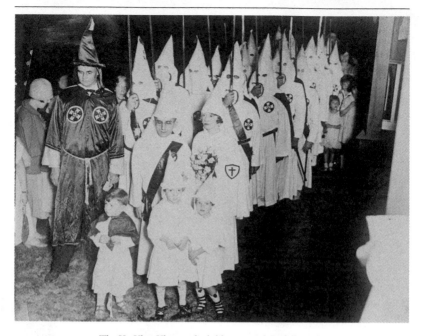

The Ku Klux Klan, with children, march in full regalia

to Fascism," with bombings designed to enforce residential segregation and the chief of police supporting the marching Ku Klux Klan as "an American law-abiding organization chartered by the state of Florida." At least as far as race was concerned, it would be difficult indeed for an outsider to distinguish the behavior of these South Florida authorities from that of the openly Jim Crow North Florida.

Thus, it is evident that post-World War II Miami was hardly the subtropical paradise—the Magic City—it promoted itself to be for one and all. As the *Miami Herald* described it on 22 April 1957:

[Miami] is a young, fast-moving community in our nation's only subtropical region and placed strategically at the aerial gateway to South America. It has large Jewish, Negro, and Puerto Rican groups; its native white citizens are largely of Deep South origin but it has drawn its fifty years of existence from all sections of the United States. The pattern of its race and ethnic relations is currently in flux. Apathy now will permit tensions free play.

As gutsy as the few South Florida reformers were, it is fair to say that they needed outside assistance. Enter the actions of the federal government and the Supreme Court, which removed the civil rights issue from state control. Three major federal policies—because Supreme Court-mandated—represented a major watershed: (1) *Brown v. Board of Education of Topeka* (17 May 1954) which ordered school desegregation; (2) the Civil Rights Act of 1965 which banned segregation in public places; and (3) the Voting Rights Act of 1965 which invoked the "one man one vote" principle, thereby mandating reapportionment. The result was that Florida's new Constitution of 1967 completely overhauled the segregationist Jim Crow Constitution of 1885. Of course, one thing is an institutional and legal watershed; another is a fundamental change in individual and collective attitudes and behavior.

In addition to the edicts and actions of the federal government, the reformist pushback came from several courageous, truly great political reformers. Two in particular, aside from Leroy Collins, stood out: Claude Pepper and Robert King High. Claude Pepper, the enthusiastic New Dealer, was first elected to the Florida House of Representatives in 1929. He would move on to the US Senate in 1936, where he was an ardent advocate of civil and trade union rights. By the late 1940s, however, the spirited progressive atmosphere of the New Deal had fallen victim to the collective paranoia wrought by the Cold War. In 1950 Claude Pepper was defeated by the young, rich, and debonair George Smathers. Smathers was a man with a foot in both northern Florida (as a segregationist) and the new south, i.e. Miami, where his wealthy family resided. He had the kind of credentials Americans admire: good looks, an athletic past (former captain of the University of Florida basketball team), a military record (a Marine in the war), and connections with the elite of the northeast of the US. Not only had he been best man at the wedding of later President John F. Kennedy, but he was a permanent part of the Kennedys' Palm Beach social entourage.

The 1950 Pepper versus Smathers contest was best described by *Time* magazine (17 April 1950) as "the great game of politics being played without benefit of rules in Florida... the knee-action and eye-gouging could be felt from Pensacola to Fort Lauderdale." At every stop Smathers read from an old 1946 newspaper clipping that quoted Pepper saying: "pray for Joseph Stalin because he is the kind of man America could trust." This was hardly the sort of language to which the new vituperative politics of the Cold War took kindly. Red-baiting was "in" and was already being expressed in such violations of civil rights as the actions of the committee of former Governor Charlie Johns (1953–55) who went around the state "hunting for communists." To Johns the National Association for the Advancement of Colored People (NAACP) was definitely a "communist organization" and beyond that he vowed to weed out all communists from the state university system. Where and when communists were not found on the campuses, homosexual faculty members were entrapped and hounded out of the system.

The Smathers campaign adopted red-baiting with gusto. There was a sad irony in this since Pepper had introduced young Smathers into politics and Smathers had long been known as a Pepper acolyte in the Miami Democratic Party. There is no evidence that during that long acquaintance Smathers ever made an allegation of Pepper being "red." But then ambition got the better of him. In the midst of the campaign the Smathers team produced a 49-page booklet titled *The Red Record of Senator Claude Pepper*. The clincher, however, was *Time*'s reprinting of a story which was certainly apocryphal but which became part of the political lore. In the so-called "redneck speech," delivered to an uneducated and prejudiced audience, Smathers reportedly asked:

> Are you aware that Claude Pepper is known all over Washington as a shameless extrovert? Not only that, but this man is reliably reported to practice nepotism with his sister-in-law, he has a brother who is a known homo sapiens, and he has a sister who was once a thespian in wicked New York. Worst of all, it is an established fact that Mr. Pepper, before his marriage, habitually practiced celibacy.

The Smathers campaign always denied (correctly as it turned out) that he had made the speech but, finding that the wit did him no harm, was glad to have it repeated. The hoax followed Smathers to his death, and in fact is now a prominent part of the Smathers display at the Smathers

Library, part of the $25 million he donated to the University of Florida in Gainesville. Predictably, Pepper lost the 1950 election. Not one to be easily counted out, however, Pepper recovered and was elected to the US House of Representatives in 1963. In the House, Pepper labored for the elderly and minorities and was known as the "grand old man of Florida politics" until his death in 1989.

AL CAPONE AND THE MOB

The courageous and principled stances of LeRoy Collins and Claude Pepper made it possible for Florida to accept (albeit in the case of Collins, grudgingly) the reforms brought about by the US Supreme Court's edicts on desegregation. This was one of the battles Florida and Miami had to fight to be considered upstanding parts of America. The other battle was the confrontation with organized crime and its corrupting influences. This confrontation was long overdue and the national muckraking press was saying as much. But even these seasoned journalists underestimated the persistence of the culture of corruption which allowed the Mob to survive one generation after the other. It would outlive and thrive well beyond the tenure of the early reformers.

Journalist Jack Kofoed was one who knew Miami inside and out. He loved the city but thoroughly disliked what he called its hypocrisy and Miami's extreme touchiness "about any fling at her standing." He found distasteful what was already known as Miami's "addiction to boosterism." Putting all pretence aside, he wrote in the *North American Review* in 1929 that "the Magic City has torn itself away from the staid old dream... the real atmosphere has been tinted by the Tex Guinans, Jack Dempseys, Scarface Capones, and by a motley crew from Broadway and the race track." Miami, he concluded, was little different from New York in terms of undercover conditions, "but New York does not pretend morality."

Similarly, Oswald Garrison Villard wrote about "Florida Flamboyant" in the *Nation* in 1935. "There has been," he said, "a general disposition to run a 'wide-open town.'" He described the indictment of a judge, a state senator, the chief of police, and other high officials, indictments which went nowhere. His verdict on Miami was harsh to an extreme. "It is," he concluded, "the harlot of American cities..." How fast this young city had moved beyond its Puritan origins.

Al Capone arrested on tax evasion charges

To understand what journalists like Kofoed and Villard were talking about one must understand just how pervasive the penetration of organized crime was. It had established its roots during the bootlegging days of Prohibition and continued virtually unnoticed by Washington until confronted by the federal government in the late 1950s. No one represented this dark side more dramatically and thoroughly than Alphonse, aka "Big Al" or "Scarface," Capone.

Capone was the first big-time mobster from the US to use Florida and Cuba for bootlegging during Prohibition. Havana was the "in" city. As T. J. English put it, "Booze, gambling and sex—What more could a Yankee tourist ask for?" He could certainly get all three in Miami and Miami Beach, but not legally. No matter: Capone and the underworld provided them in abundance; after all, Capone did not use to say "public service is my motto" for nothing. He was also capable of considerable self-righteous yet utilitarian rationalizations by arguing that since most of the people he knew drank and gambled, "I've tried to serve them decent liquor and square games." Capone's biographer John Kobler estimated that by 1929 Capone's annual "take" included $60 million from bootlegging, $25 million from gambling,

$10 million from generalized vice such as brothels, and $10 million from various other rackets. Despite providing this ample "public service," Capone constantly complained that he was not appreciated, repeatedly griping that "I'm known all over the world as a millionaire gorilla." Certainly it was true that he did not feel welcome anywhere in the US, not even in Miami where he lived, originally in a rented house before buying in to a glitzy neighborhood. While some elites in Miami preferred to keep his presence quiet—scandal being bad for the tourist trade—others wanted him out. One of these was the *Miami News*, which kept up a drumbeat against "the notorious beer and brothel baron of Chicago," hoping that he would leave town. He did not, and Helen Muir who wrote for the *News* at the time quoted the *Kansas City Star* headline: "Chicago and Al Capone both breathe more freely while he fishes in South Florida."

Capone was incarcerated but only temporarily. In 1939 he was released from Alcatraz, where he had served time on tax evasion charges. He purchased a fourteen-room Spanish-style estate at 93 Palm Island off the McArthur Causeway to Miami Beach, originally built by the beer barons of the Busch family. In Miami he spared no effort or money to establish himself as a legitimate citizen, so much so that his son Albert Francis ("Sonny") Capone, Jr. attended St. Patrick's School on Miami Beach. The young Capone was a likeable fellow. At St. Patrick School one of his good friends was a Cuban immigrant's son, Desi Arnaz. Albert Francis married a schoolmate and lived for a while on the farm his father owned in Jupiter, Florida. Hollywood actor Burt Reynolds later bought that farm. But by this time Capone was fading into the tertiary stage of the syphilis he had contracted as a young man. He died in his Miami home in 1947 aged 48. In 1966 Albert Francis decided to leave his father's shadowy reputation behind and moved to California, where he dropped the surname Capone and lived as simply Albert Francis. In an interesting twist, he later sued (unsuccessfully) Desi Arnaz, producer of the TV series *The Untouchables*, for exploiting his father's image and life. He died in 2004.

No matter how legitimate Capone's life in Miami might have seemed, it is good to keep in mind what he told the *Philadelphia Public Ledger* in 1929: "Once in the racket, you're always in the racket." Standard behavior necessarily involved paying officials for protection and for "access" to any place where money could be made, all of which Capone did, and in the process did his part in further corrupting the Miami milieu.

This corrupting influence was amply documented by Senator Estes Kefauver's "Special Committee to Investigate Organized Crime in Interstate Commerce" when it held hearings in Miami in 1950. "Criminal organizations," said the committee, "have succeeded in monopolizing certain of the channels of interstate communication and commerce by means of violence, bribery, corruption, and intimidation." The committee found these criminal groups operating virtually openly in Miami and Miami Beach. The latter in particular was the favorite residence of the racketeers. The Wofford and Boulevard Hotels were the headquarters of the New York gang, while the Detroit gang resided at the Grand Hotel, and the Philadelphia gang at the Sands. They operated "openly and notoriously" in clear violation of Florida law and, said the Kefauver Committee report, with the full knowledge of the entire community, "including the law-enforcement officers." Much of the criminal activity in Miami Beach, for instance, was controlled by the "S&G Syndicate" and operated "with the protection of the Miami Beach Police Department and of the Dade County Sheriff, and apparently under cover of a complacent city council." Predictably, the S&G Syndicate had proven links with the Chicago Capone group.

Given the profits produced by the various gambling and waging establishments, there was enough to spread the wealth among a wide circle of officials all of whom contributed to the popular adage: in Florida a sheriff can retire after one term in office. The Kefauver Committee calculated that the S&G Syndicate was taking in more than $50 million a year. As was the custom, such large sums attracted the greedy interests of other gangs which attempted encroachment. This was the case with William H. Johnston, a known associate of the Capone gang in Chicago. Johnston knew that the game played in Florida was not unlike that played in Chicago. In 1950 he contributed $100,000 to the gubernatorial campaign of Fuller Warren. Johnston was keenly aware that the newly elected governor was under strong pressure from some upstanding members of the community to take action against the increasingly bold criminal interests in the state. Warren appointed C. V. Griffin, a $154,000-contributor to his campaign, as a special investigator. Griffin testified before the Kefauver Committee that his commission was revoked immediately after the mobster Johnston paid a visit to Tallahassee where he had lunch with the new governor. There is no record as to what went on, though Florida historian Michael Gannon admits that Warren's capability as governor was "impaired by charges that he was the tool of aides with links to organized crime." This was known and Warren was lucky to survive an impeachment vote in the Florida House of Representatives. Gannon explains that soon thereafter he "effectively removed himself from office," spending almost all of his time on the road promoting Florida as a place to live and do business. Gannon believes that even as Warren was surrounded by corrupt advisors and friends, he himself "remained incorruptible," dying broke in a Miami hotel apartment in 1973. Evidently, crime did not pay for everybody in Miami.

Whether the governor was himself in the pay of Capone is less important than the fact that organized crime appeared to operate with impunity in South Florida. Public agitation had led to the seating of grand juries in 1944, 1947, and 1949, all finding that the gangs which operated during the rum-running days were still active. The 1949 grand jury noted that it was finding the same patterns as its predecessor juries. "There is present in our community," it said, "a large number of individuals of unsavory reputation. These persons are criminals of national stature."

Nothing effective was done until a residual undercurrent of collective moral indignation—driven persistently by editorials in the *Miami News* and the *Miami Herald*—managed to bring about the election of one of the grandest reformers to ever serve as Mayor of Miami, Robert King High.

High was born in 1924 in Tennessee and moved to Miami in 1944. He graduated from the University of Miami and received his law degree from Stetson University in Deland, Florida. Aside from his firm support of civil rights, Mayor High was best known and remembered for his resolute campaign against organized crime and corruption. As described by his widow Faith High Barnebey in her 1971 biography *Integrity is the Issue: Campaign Life with Robert King High*, Mayor High went after illegal gambling, insurance fraud, and exorbitant electrical and telephone rates, and successfully collected back taxes from the omnipotent Jacksonville-based East Coast Railway. By insisting on the latter, he earned a powerful political enemy. Because he had provided Miami with a rare honest and efficient administration, he was persuaded to run for governor in 1964. In those days, the fundamental campaign was the primary in the Democratic Party. His opponent was the mayor of the northern city of Jacksonville, W.

Haydon Burns.

High and his followers soon discovered just how unreconstructed Florida still was. Predictably, the Burns campaign reflected the majority sentiments which characterized the state. One of the most widely circulated flyers of the Burns campaign played on the pathological fear of miscegenation by portraying a pregnant young black woman with the caption: "I went all the way with Robert King High." Another pamphlet carried a cartoon of High with the caption, "Black Power is with you 100%, Bob, let's march!" Powerful economic interests in the northern part of the state supported the Burns campaign and this explains how he could spend $2.19 per vote received while High's expenditure was 38 cents per vote. Surprisingly, High defeated Burns in the primary. Then, of course, came the election proper. High's opponent was the first Republican to run for the governorship, Claude Kirk, who, like Burns, was from Jacksonville. With Burns' behind-the-scenes support and with similar racist slurs, including accusations that High was a puppet of the architects of Washington's "ultraliberal" war on poverty and the push for civil rights, High lost the election. His wife recalls him saying that he wanted a clean win or no win at all. As always, his slogan was "Integrity is the Issue." The *Miami News* commended him for his integrity in an editorial which highlighted his efforts to create a new mood in Florida politics and for not ducking any of the prickly issues which other politicians swept under the rug. "Our hope," said the *News*, "is that in losing, he prepared the ground for a host of young men who might now get into politics with the noble ideas that made Mr. High's candidacy so attractive."

High died at age 43 while in his fifth term as Mayor of Miami. His legacy included a more honest city government, a racially integrated City Commission, and the bringing to Miami of the National Football League (NFL) franchise team, the Dolphins. When he set $10,000 as the maximum which could be spent on a city election he was perhaps naïve about the way "informal" money operated in his city and state, but it gave hope to the many who admired clean government and the principle of integrity. This he undoubtedly did but his defeat provided ample proof that things had not changed in any fundamental way. In that same vein, High's widow put hope over experience when she predicted that because of her husband's example in Florida, "politics as usual and the usual politics were on the way out." Not by a long shot.

Presenting a picture of clean government and personal rectitude were critically important factors at the time because the issue of image and perceptions went well beyond being purely a matter of public relations. It had a fundamental relationship to the opportunities for attracting outside investments. Florida's economy, while still somewhat dependent on agriculture and the phosphate industries, was changing quickly in line with national trends. Mayor High understood where Miami's present and future economic interest lay: tourism and trade. It can be argued that it was High who as mayor picked up the dream of men like Flagler to exploit the Latin American and Caribbean markets. This international orientation plus his fluency in Spanish helped him and the city advance these ideas and also to cope with the first waves of Cuban refugees fleeing Cuba in 1959.

WALT DISNEY AND THE NEW ECONOMY

Robert King High and LeRoy Collins set the stage for the new Florida economy. As Raymond Mohl and Gary Mormino, two of the most respected authorities on Florida tourism, have noted, post-war Florida "came to embody and in turn radiate the values of American culture: youth, leisure, consumption, mobility, and affluence. Tourism figures prominently in this midcentury culture. Television enhanced the image of Florida as the Sunshine State." Since tourism had already become the beating heart of the economy, keeping Florida attractive meant avoiding the images on TV and in the press of police dogs mauling and water cannons drenching peaceful civil rights marchers—in other words, avoiding the images of a Mississippi or an Alabama. Florida accomplished this, and proof certain was the winning of the grandest prize of all when the Disney Corporation started building its second theme park in Orlando. At that point the nature of the tourist industry changed.

Walt Disney World was based on the success of its predecessor, the Disneyland Park in Anaheim, California. Today Walt Disney World in Orlando is the single most visited park in the world. Walt Disney chose Orlando after surveying a number of potential sites on the East Coast. Planning began in 1959 and continued through 1966, the year Disney died. The Magic Kingdom of Walt Disney World opened in October, 1971, replicating many of the theme rides and attractions which proved

Disney World, Orlando, Florida

so popular in California.

Predictably, the Magic Kingdom is not without its critics. Perhaps the most penetrating, and certainly most read, critique is by an anthropologist at Florida International University, Stephen M. Fjellman in his book *Vinyl Leaves: Walt Disney World and America*. It is—if you judge it in the "postmodernist" genre in which it is written—a brilliant piece of "semiology," i.e. the study of the broader ideological meaning of symbols. To Fjellman, the symbols in Disney World act as muses, representations, or "ideological tokens" of the interests of the capitalist corporate world and of what Florida was betting its future on. As intellectually brilliant as this analysis of "late capitalism" might be, it has not ruffled one single vinyl leaf of the Magic Kingdom in the two decades since its publication. Disney's plan to awaken the whimsy of young and old, with Florida's enthusiastic support, has succeeded totally.

Statistics show that in 1933 perhaps a million tourists came to Florida. By 1950 there were twenty million, and Miami and Miami Beach were the preferred destination. With Disney World open, a new geographical pole opened up with millions of visitors turning this site into the world's biggest tourist draw as a theme park. By 2011, over 87 million tourists visited Florida, 95 percent of whom came to Miami and Orlando, spending over $67 billion. Only New York received more visitors. Fjellman was prescient when he predicted that promoting and keeping the image of a "Sunshine State" became an industry in itself. He was wrong, however, in arguing that it was a narrow pitch since the industry was catering to tourists alone. In fact, Disney World has created a new urban spread, stretching from Orlando to Tampa, settled by young and retirees alike. Clearly, the last thing the Florida promoters wished to see repeated was the likes of Al Capone being quoted in *Fortune* magazine saying that Florida was "the Garden of America."

None of this, however, meant that the eradication of organized crime in the state had been totally achieved. The long tentacles might not have penetrated Disney's Kingdom but neither federal nor state authorities had yet to investigate and successfully convict and incarcerate for any length of time the man considered the brains behind organized crime since the 1930s, Meyer Lansky.

MEYER LANSKY AND THE BAHAMAS CONNECTION

The Kefauver Committee in 1950 called Meyer Lansky "one of the masterminds of modern organized crime." Lansky, originally from New York, settled in Miami Beach after Fidel Castro confiscated his prized possession in Havana, the Hotel Riviera with its enormous casino. The federal authorities considered Lansky so threatening to the integrity of any community that they established an entire multi-agency task force to try and bring him to justice.

On 12 December 1967 the FBI prepared a comprehensive file on Lansky. This file has been accessed through the Freedom of Information/Privacy Act. These were the vital facts on this man who would control the rackets in Miami and the rest of the country: born Majer Suchowlinski, in Grodno, Poland, on 4 July 1902; arrived in New York, 1911; and naturalized as US citizen Meyer Lansky in 1928. During the 1920s he was a muscle man in the alcohol wars in New York and soon controlled, along with Benjamin ("Bugsy") Siegal and Frank Costello, a string of "distilleries" in the city. By the end of Prohibition the FBI described Lansky as the head of organized crime and rackets and as having a record of arrests for a series of crimes including forgery, felonious assault, and homicide. He already had strong contacts with the remnants of the Capone gang in Chicago, which still controlled all forms of gambling in Las Vegas. Sometime between 1946 and 1950 he moved to an unpretentious house in Hallandale, Broward County, Florida. There he controlled the Colonial Inn and the Greenacres Casinos. When the state closed down his casinos, he moved to Havana where he was quickly recognized as the leader of all gambling and, after 1953, became financial advisor to the dictator Fulgencio Batista. The FBI dossier ends by stating that by 1967 "Lansky is associated with practically every known leading figure in organized criminal activity."

As interesting as the FBI findings were, they paled compared to an investigatory series which ran in the *Miami Herald* in late January 1967.

The investigators, Clarence Jones and James Savage, did the kind of in-depth probing and uncovering for which newspaper became known nationally. Their first installation, on 29 January 1967, carried the banner headline, "Mob Money: Silent Host in Beach Hotels," and was a mind-boggling description of how the Mob controlled so many of Miami Beach's hotels on celebrated Collins Avenue. "'The Mob doesn't run this town,' says Miami Beach Mayor Elliott Roosevelt, 'The Mob owns it.'" Fourth son of Franklin and Eleanor Roosevelt and a retired Army Air Force Brigadier General, Elliott Roosevelt was very much the dilettante, but with connections nationally and with no known ties or indebtedness to the Mob, was free to speak his mind during the years (1964–69) he was Mayor of Miami Beach. Taking their cue from Roosevelt, Jones and Savage added their views: "Millions of dollars made from murder, dope, and syndicated gambling have been funneled into ocean front property… Thousands of tourists are guests of a silent, secret host." In the center of it all this was Meyer Lansky and his brother Jake. "Some of the biggest hoodlums in the nation," continued the story, "drop in regularly to the Meyer-owned 'Singapore Hotel' to confer and get their orders." Further installments in the newspaper attempted to trace the "corporate maze" of ownerships and finally on 30 January 1967 it published an article, "Fontainebleau: Mob Money's Beach Prize," describing how the crown jewel of Miami Beach's hotels came into the bloody grasp of the Lansky crowd:

> The transactions involving the Fontainebleau… are typical of what happens when the racketeering element has an interest in a hotel or motel… Some of the best attorneys in the nation are called into to take advantage of intricate tax loopholes and squeeze the last drop of cash out of hotel operations.

This, then, was Meyer Lansky, the South Florida resident kingpin of the rackets, whose personal fortune was calculated at $300 million. It is interesting that virtually every one of his close associates in crime was Jewish. A letter in the FBI file (11 August 1967) notes that he was "the protector of the Jewish element" who organized the gambling industry in Las Vegas and who gave him his entrée into the business he would eventually dominate. Despite that, he was one of the only Jews ever denied residence in Israel and his offers of hundreds of thousands of dollars in exchange for a

Meyer Lansky walks his dog on Collins Avenue, Miami Beach

residency permit in some of the most corrupt countries in Latin America were rejected. Even as he kept his house in Hallandale, he really settled down in Miami Beach, and, according to his foremost biographer Robert Lacey, appeared to be just another "early bird" resident—one of those who took advantage of the discounts given on their meals by Wolfie's Deli on Collins Avenue (now closed). He seemed content to walk his dog and to serenely play golf and cards with his Jewish buddies.

All efforts by the FBI and the IRS to prosecute Lansky on the grounds that he was still involved in skimming money from Las Vegas casinos were for naught. This did not convince English crime writer Lauren Carter, who asserts with some authority that Lansky continued to receive money from Mob businesses elsewhere and laundered it in the Bahamas, an active "offshore" location. Writing about the offshore laundering business, she concludes: "Meyer Lansky, either rightly or wrongly, was reputed to be the genius that had dreamed up the whole scam."

In 1982 *Forbes* magazine listed Lansky as one of the wealthiest 400 Americans. And, according to an investigative piece by Gary Cohen in the

Miami Beach magazine *Ocean Drive* in January 2005, Lansky's wife Teddy's daughter-in-law claimed that he told her that "he still had a couple of million socked away in Switzerland." Alas, to the disappointment of the whole family, Cohen noted that Lansky's will and testament showed a grand total worth of $57,000. Did he really end his days in such relative penury? We should keep in mind that this is the Lansky who was the genius behind the Mob for decades, was the financial brains behind the new casinos in the Bahamas, and also, from 1953 to 1958, Fulgencio Batista's money-man during the thoroughly corrupt dictatorship in Cuba. Hiding millions (or in offshore lingo, "parking" it) would have been a cinch for the "Little Man" of organized crime.

Gus Russo, who studies the Mob, maintains that it is impossible to have a complete accounting of any gangster's resources. The take from casinos and illicit activities was great but so were the expenses: cutting-in politicians, huge armies of bodyguards, and maintaining the casino equipment. Russo's book, *The Outfit: The Role of Chicago's Underworld in the Shaping of Modern America*, (2003) rings true for Miami. For good and for bad, in tolerating it and combating it with convincing vigor, Miami became a part and arguably the most important part of a wider world where the legal and the illegal, in other words the "grey," transcended state boundaries. With Cuba in 1959 in the hands of socialist revolutionaries who began their rule by immediately shutting down the nation's casinos, and Florida still refusing to legalize casino gambling, the search was on for a new location. There were certain absolute essentials for such a location: (1) a place with proximity to Miami having good air and sea links; (2) a native political and economic elite open to dealing; (3) a location attractive enough to be inviting to both tourists and members of the Mob who would be resident and run the casinos; and (4) an English-speaking population with English Common Law tradition and enough trained lawyers to accommodate any "legal" needs.

The obvious candidate was the British colony of the Bahamas. Even before Meyer Lansky and his cronies arrived, the Bahamas was known as a thoroughly corrupt place run by a white establishment which made real money when it graduated from fishing and sponge diving to bootlegging during Prohibition. This establishment's nickname, "Bay Street Boys," stemmed from the fact that they had their offices on Bay Street, Nassau. The key figure in that exclusive white oligarchy was Sir Stafford Sands.

There is no need here to detail how or when Sir Stafford agreed to accept the good services of Meyer Lansky. That was revealed, blow by blow, by the *Miami Herald's* superb investigatory reporter Hank Messick in his 1969 book *Syndicate Abroad*. The broader outlines of the case were already well known. The long-standing hopes of the Bay Street Boys to develop the tourist industry had led them to target Freeport on Grand Bahama Island as the most likely site for their enterprises. The 1967 *Report of the Commission of Inquiry into the Operation of the Business of Casinos in Freeport and in Nassau* spells out the situation:

> During 1962 it became increasingly apparent that the Freeport area was not developing as rapidly as had been planned. Land sales were below the level necessary to justify the enormous investment which the Development Company had already made in that area, and by the later half of the year that company was running into severe financial difficulties.

Casino gambling was the solution. It had brought the tourists to Havana; they would now come to the new Lucayan Beach Hotel and Casino in Freeport. Since Mob involvement was still not a generally popular proposition, however, secrecy was the essence; and if that secrecy had depended solely on Bahamian sources it might have been kept. But the Bay Street Boys had no control over the American press.

First to spring the sordid story of the Mob's role was the *New York Times* of 15 February with a report captioned "Gambling in Bahamas Worries United States Officials." The story described the doings of seven individuals who in the past had extensive relations with Meyer Lansky and his brother Jake. No sooner had Bahamians read that story than the *Wall Street Journal* of 5 October 1965 carried a story by staff writers Monroe W. Karmin and Stanley Penn headlined "Las Vegas East." That report revealed how two Lansky associates ran the Lucayan Beach Hotel and Casino. One of these men, George Sadlow, already eighty years old, had figured in the Kefauver Committee inquest in Miami. All of this was grist for the upcoming political campaign which saw the white oligarchy and its organization, the United Bahamian Party, challenged by a populist black movement led by Lynden Pindling. Just before the crucial elections of 1967, the *Wall Street Journal* (19 April 1967) carried another feature by

Monroe W. Karmin which exposed the whole arrangement between the people involved in the new hotels and casinos and Meyer Lansky. Not surprisingly, the secret meetings took place at the Fontainebleau in Miami and the upshot was that Lansky's people ended up in complete control of gambling in the Bahamas.

After that the Bahamas became fair game for muckraking journalists. the *New York World Journal Tribune* of 23 April 1967 said it all in its headline "Bahamas: You Can't Tell Good from Bad Guys." Given a boost by the foreign press, Pindling and his Progressive Liberal Party won the elections and took the nation to independence in 1973. It was now "payback" time in the Bahamas. No sooner had the Pindling government taken power in Nassau than it began to investigate the use of the Bahamas in the drug trade. Its 1984 *Report of the Commission of Inquiry into the Use of the Bahamas for the Transshipment of Dangerous Drugs Destined for the United States* certainly did not reveal the whole story, but in what it did reveal the name Miami kept cropping up. No one who knew the history of the association of Lansky and his pals and the previous regime was surprised. Casinos were not all they were running and peddling. But it was also "blowback" time in the Caribbean, time for the negative unintended consequences of previous policies and behavior (see Chapter Six for a fuller discussion of this phenomenon). This requires some explaining since the new Pindling government would soon be involved in much the same scandalous activities it had charged the Bay Street Boys with during the political campaign.

During the period of the Cold War, Washington—and to a certain extent Europe—decided to turn a blind eye to any activities that did not threaten the active pursuit of Cold War policies. This was regrettable because there were in fact very serious consequences to Washington's single-minded and tunnel-vision approach to the area, and to the Caribbean's short-term tactical use of this reckless disregard. Among the most serious of these were narco-trafficking and other corrupt activities on the part of national elites. This intentional inattention to crime created a host of unintended consequences, and two in particular—Cuba and the Bahamas—had lasting consequences for the post-Cold War phase.

It is now known that there had been trafficking in morphine and heroin between Medellín, Colombia, and Havana since the late 1940s. Elements of organized crime and corrupt officials of the Cuban government had connections with international criminal networks, especially the American Mafia, who were already well-established in Havana and Miami and were all involved this trafficking. Meyer Lansky and mobster Lucky Luciano traveled to Havana occasionally, and Santos Trafficante (who had been living in Havana since 1946) all had a Miami connection. In fact, Warren Hinckle and William Turner call Trafficante "the Florida Mafia boss" who was behind the Cubans involved in his smuggling network.

When the Cuban revolutionary leaders decided to expel the US Mafia and dismantle its local organizations, these criminals relocated to Miami where they soon took full advantage of the Cold War strategies of their host society. The story illustrates how criminal activities can prosper when there is no will on the part of elites to label and combat them. This turning a blind eye characterized both British and US foreign policy. The result was more than one "blowback" event. The critical aspect of these situations is that Miami was more often than not the city where the illicit deals were arranged. The ghosts of Meyer Lansky and his associates seemed to linger in that city and the wider Caribbean region. This became especially the case in terms of movements of money—legal and illegal—and small weapons.

TENTACLES OF CRIME

The reality was that the actual movement of large amounts of cash throughout Miami and the Caribbean made a mockery of official statistics on the nature of the economies of Miami and of the Bahamas. That said, the Bahamas was not the only place in the area where big money was moving. In fact, it is critical to an understanding of the growth of Caribbean offshore centers to know that in many ways they are part of an international financial network which includes on a very important scale Florida, and Miami in particular.

Far from being removed from the burgeoning money laundering network, by the late 1970s Florida had become the banking center for the Caribbean and perhaps Latin America. As figures reveal, the climate for banking in Florida was clearly propitious. In 1982 Florida banks held 33 percent of all commercial bank deposits and an extraordinary 51 percent of all savings and loan deposits in the southeastern part of the United States. According to Charles Intriago, a former US Federal Prosecutor and now publisher of *Money Laundering Alert*, which specializes in reporting money laundering cases, Miami had become one of the world's premier centers for laundering money. "Miami has all the banking facilities you need," he said, "it has all the non-banking facilities you need; it has all the trades and businesses necessary for laundering money." To Intriago, Miami provided "one-stop shopping for money launderers."

The international press as well as freelance investigative reporters began to associate Miami with international organized crime generally and crime in the Caribbean specifically. Claire Sterling in her fact-filled book, *Octopus: The Long Reach of the International Sicilian Mafia* (1990), maintained that the Sicilian Mafia had its headquarters for Latin America and the Caribbean in Caracas, Venezuela, and made good use of banks in Miami. Two years later, Rachael Ehrenfeld in *Evil Money* (1992) documented the skulduggery and scams which used the Miami-Bahamas connection as a major part of operations. Hank Messick would bring it all together in *Syndicate in the Sun*, a book we will deal with later.

Miami's reach in the Caribbean went well beyond the Bahamas. The case of Antigua, revealed in an Official Commission of Inquiry, "Guns for Antigua" or *Report of the Commission of Enquiry into the Circumstances Surrounding the Shipment of Arms from Israel to Antigua* (2 November 1990), exposed the depth and spread of corruption, indeed its internationalization. The charges were that ten tons of arms were bought in Israel, the end user to be the Antigua Defence Force (fewer than a hundred men already armed by the US), but the weapons ended up on the farm of Medellín Cartel henchman José Rodríguez Gacha. It was proven that some of the guns were used in the assassination of the popular Colombian presidential candidate Luís Carlos Galán.

Among the many terrifying details revealed by the chairman of the Commission of Inquiry, Louis Blom-Cooper QC, are the following: (1) While Antigua had "a heavy moral duty" to Colombia and the world to pursue this matter, its meager diplomatic and police capabilities meant that it could not alone pursue the investigations which had to cover "over four continents;" and (2) Despite the wider conclusions that small Caribbean states could not confront the cartels on their own, "Intellectual collaboration to elicit the truth about Israeli firearms finding their way into the hands of Colombian drug barons was not to be easily achieved." "The British government," said Blom-Cooper, "have turned a blind eye" to evidence that their nationals, operating as skilled mercenaries, "turned untrained killers into trained killers."

On the central role of the city of Miami, Blom-Cooper wrote: "This conspiracy was, in my judgment, hatched in Miami and developed from that city." On the role of the banks: "I find it wholly unacceptable that banks in America, whose services were used to facilitate what can without exaggeration be described as a crime against humanity, should be permitted through the inaction of the American authorities to hide evidence of that crime behind the cloak of confidentiality." Unfortunately, it would take a full-blown "cocaine war" to wake up US and Miami elites to an unfinished agenda and to what dirty money and official indifference had wrought. We shall return to this later.

A Philanthropic Bootlegger

There was and is a big difference between the Lansky types and people with great legitimate fortunes. The latter often engage in philanthropy and community building. The Lansky types did none of that. There is no evidence in Miami or South Florida generally that Lansky or his racketeer associates invested in any community enhancement, whether it was museums, synagogues, or education. If there was any truth to the widely-held belief that cocaine and dirty money had immunized Miami against recession, the fact is that one cannot point to a single major public project (as distinct from banks or condominiums) known to have been built with dirty money. On that score they differed totally from the early settlers. There was, however, one notable exception to this rule: an individual who made his money during Prohibition and had some ties to elements of the Mob, yet contributed to the development of Miami and his legacy is so recognized.

The case of Lewis Solon Rosenstiel, one of Miami's grand philanthropists, is unique. If there is a moral dilemma it is because Rosenstiel was originally a bootlegger and a good friend of several Mob figures, especially Meyer Lansky and Joe Fusco. Yet he also made friends in high—legitimate—places. As Jay Robert Nash asks, "How can Rosenstiel be [FBI Director] J. Edgar Hoover's close friend and have a history of business association and friendships with known leaders of organized crime?" The answer lies in a major paradox of the Prohibition era: when Florida governors and even US President Warren G Harding guzzled illicit hooch in the White House, why would we not expect men like Rosenstiel in the

US and Samuel Bronfman in Canada not to supply the stuff? The paradox is stretched further when one understands, as John L. Smith records, that while men like Lansky remained gangsters all their lives, Rosenstiel cleaned up his illegal business activities after Prohibition and became a mainstream capitalist. The truly grand Rosenstiel School of Marine and Atmospheric Sciences of the University of Miami on Virginia Key is testimony to a moral dilemma resolved, at least for future generations. Alas, Rosenstiel was unfortunately an exceptional case. Gangsters of all ethnicities continued to view Miami as rich pickings for their dastardly deeds and left nothing but bad reputations and bad examples behind. Unfinished business indeed!

Chapter Four

ALEGRÍA TROPICAL
CUBAN NOSTALGIA AND THE CHARACTER
OF MIAMI

Even as the problems of racial segregation and organized crime remained, Miami, as so often in the past, had enough elites who wished to move the place forward. In a city always in a hurry and consequently not much given to historical memory, it is salutary to remember who some of those elites were. This is what Marvin Dunn, a Miami psychologist and black activist does in *Black Miami in the Twentieth Century*:

> Liberal northern Jews like Herbert and Marilyn Bloom of Miami gave time, money, and energy to the movement. Blacks would not have achieved political prominence when they did had Puerto Rican-born Miami mayor Maurice Ferré and Cuban-born mayor Xavier Suarez cared less than they did. Miami institutions such as the *Miami News* and the *Miami Herald*, once enlightened, spread the news and the opinion that change was necessary and morally compelling... [and] (particularly under white liberal editor Bill Baggs) eventually came to champion the aspirations of Miami blacks. This, too, made a difference.

Dunn could have mentioned other liberal Jewish representatives from Miami who did battle in Tallahassee for something very often overlooked, or at best vaguely remembered: the history of the battle to give Miami an administrative apparatus proper to the metropolis it already was. By the end of World War II Miami was but one of 27 cities in Dade County. Like the others it was only semi-autonomous; the rural-dominated legislature in Tallahassee made the final decisions on important matters. "Home Rule" was what the leaders in south Florida wanted. Finally in 1957 the Charter for the Reorganization of Dade County was submitted to a county-wide referendum. With only 25 percent of the registered voters participating, it scraped by with a bare majority of votes (44,404 to 42,620). What the creation of Metropolitan Dade County was supposed to bring was a non-partisan County Manager, non-partisan at-large elections for the County Commission, and a merit-based civil service. With that reform, Dade County now had a two-tier system of government: the metropolitan and the 26 municipal governments. It came just in time before two momentous events shook Miami and other municipalities: the arrival of Cuban refugees after 1959 and the civil rights movement.

It is important to note that it was heavy support in the city of Miami which carried the day for the reforms. Key proponents of the changes were liberal Jewish members of the Florida House of Representatives, the Anglo-dominated newspaper the *Miami Herald*, the Greater Miami Chamber of Commerce, and an Anglo who does not even have a street named after him, Dan Paul. The latter was one of those committed Miamians who invariably made a difference in everything to which he dedicated his energies. To make a long story short, it was Dan Paul who actually wrote the new Miami Charter. In 1957 the plea made by Paul in the Dade County Charter campaign was "Give Miami a chance to be a big city." Upon his passing in January 2010 Miami's alternative investigative newspaper, the *New Times*, noted that in a city without a conscience Paul was the closest thing to being its conscience. The *New Times* carried the headline: "Goodbye, Dan Paul! You made this town." Hyperbole, certainly; but also, to be sure, a statement close to the historical record.

Since 1957 Metropolitan Dade County has grown to contain 34 municipalities. Metro-Dade, as it is called, is governed by an elected mayor and an elected County Commission. They now administer the airport, the sea port, the mass transit system, and Jackson Memorial hospital and, fundamentally, plan and enforce uniform land use and building codes. The freewheeling encroachment into the Everglades and the sloppy construction evident in the massive devastation caused by Hurricane Andrew in 1992 demonstrated that proper urban planning and the enforcement of building codes, now assigned to elected officials, were weakly regulated. Theoretically, at least, when planning and code enforcement functions were not performed as mandated, institutionalized, corrective action was now possible.

Elections for mayor of Dade Metropolitan Government, which has a budget of over a billion dollars and 18,000 employees, are hotly contested. And yet in this megalopolis-in-the-making there is little emotional identification with a body called "Metro-Dade." What continues to engender loyalties and commitments is the existence of the various cities and municipalities. From the very beginning of settlement, these have been the "turfs" residents relate to. And they kept increasing in size and numbers. The arriving Cubans fell right into that pattern, creating their own turfs with their distinctive tone and style, and inspired by their own memories of Cuba. As David Rieff noted decades ago, Cubans took control of the "atmosphere" of their neighborhoods but also eventually of the city of Miami. It is this undisputed fact which led sociologist Lisandro Pérez, in an essay in the book *Miami Now*, to caution that "there is little point... in attempting to understand the Miami of today without a detailed analysis of the characteristics and development of the Cuban community."

Well behind Key West and even Tampa in terms of its contacts with Cuba, Miami strove from its earliest days to catch up in developing a relationship with that island. As we have seen, Henry Flagler pushed his grand railroad over the sea down to Key West in order to take better advantage of the Cuban market. Again, even as Miami took second place to Tampa as a base for US troops moving to Cuba during the Spanish (Cuban)-American War, the city's young leadership lobbied hard to get a share of the action. And, as previously noted, even Andrew Jackson thought of "taking" Cuba after he wrested Florida from the Spanish.

Economics was certainly an important driver in a general sense, but there has always been another feature that attracted Americans to Havana at the more subjective and individual level: urban aesthetics, or the beauty of that major European-style city. There should be no surprise in this; Havana was a city of elegant Baroque architecture which, already in the twentieth century, was crisscrossed by trolleys and connected to the plantations of the interior by a well-developed system of railroads. It was the exotic, tropical, and sensual Havana which exercised such a strong influence on the American conception of not just an ideal urban setting but of urbanity itself. Louis A. Pérez, Jr. put it succinctly: "Miami was a product of the North American infatuation with Cuba in the 1920s and bore distinctive markings of its origins." It was precisely in the 1920s that Cuban governments began beautifying Havana, contracting world-renowned French landscape architects to work with an emerging cadre of Cuban architects on modern city planning. By the end of the decade a large number of parks and other public works had been inaugurated. Carl Fisher on Miami Beach was not the only one enchanted by the results as he at-

tempted to provide a "truly tropical" atmosphere for Miami Beach very much akin to what he saw in Havana, especially its many Art Deco houses and public buildings.

All these efforts to transplant the "tropics" to Miami were, of course, made possible by rapid ferry and air transport links which kept pace with the growth of the city and made frequent contacts eminently feasible. We have already noted how all such links facilitated the rum-running during Prohibition and as a consequence the further enrichment of some of Cuba's rum distillers as well as their Miami distributors. Prohibition also engendered darker sides in both cities, augmenting the roles of the more audacious denizens of their underworlds.

The dreams of Henry Flagler were continued by Miami's mayor Robert King High, who combated the Mob as ardently as he promoted trade with Cuba. His interest in that island—and in learning Spanish—was intensified when as a law student in the mid-1940s he spent a summer at the University of Havana. His widow tells the interesting story of Mayor High taking a delegation of Miami businessmen to Havana in early 1959 after being promised a meeting with the brash young rebel leader, Fidel Castro. Four different appointments with Castro were canceled. A final, definite meeting was set for 4 a.m., which the surprised but determined Miamians turned up for. Yet again, however, Castro was a no-show. High concluded quite accurately that the Cuban leader had no interest in promoting contacts of any sort with the US, much less Miami. The experience of Special US Emissary Philip Bonsal, who was repeatedly kept cooling his heels by Castro, confirmed High's conclusion about the new geopolitical reality in US-Cuban relations.

As it turned out, Mayor High had little time to plumb the depths of Castro's anti-American and anti-Miami sentiments. In no time at all he was dealing with the first wave of Cubans fleeing the increasingly radical Castro regime. Neither High nor any other Miamians had time to be nostalgic about the rich history of Cuba-Miami relations. The fact that most of it had been beneficial to both nations was now irrelevant. Few of the positive aspects of the relationship were remembered. Rather, what was constantly broadcast in revolutionary Cuba was the story of those major periods in Cuban history that revealed sordid tales of Cuban corruption—and Miami's subsequent welcome and benefitting from the proceeds of that corruption. Refugees in Miami were meanwhile recalling, and telling, the exact opposite stories of revolutionary confiscations and political repression.

THE LURE OF THE TROPICS

As true as both contemporary tales were, they certainly were not the whole, deeper history. Pre-revolutionary Havana, and Cuba itself, experienced much more than a series of cyclical phases of disenchantment with dictatorship and corruption. There was an ongoing and deeply-rooted sense of *cubanidad*, which projected a wholesome appreciation of the better things the island and the city had to offer. Cubans called it *alegría*, intrinsic happiness. To understand why and how this happiness attracted so many Americans from early days, one has to do a little comparative ethnology. In play at this time were two very distinct cultures: that of the largely parochial Protestant southern migrants who settled in Miami, and that of the "tropical" Cubans, a blend of Spanish and African styles and rhythms.

Havana, despite its history of slavery and exploitation, was indeed *la ciudad alegre*, the happy city, which Anglos—at least the adventurous ones—desired to emulate. Havana was at once as exotic as it was comfortable, foreign without appearing forbidding. The most frequently used poster by the Cuban tourism authorities proclaimed that the island was "So Near Yet so Foreign." Thus it goes without saying that to understand this Anglo-Miami search for the more sensual, even hedonistic, dimensions of life, one also has to understand something about the tropics in general and Havana in particular. Only that way can we understand how Cubans turned parts of sub-tropical Miami into a city with tropical flair, a Caribbean-like *ciudad alegre*.

It has been the foreign traveler who has often given us insightful descriptions of the sensual and joyful part of Caribbean culture in general. Whether it was Lafcadio Hearn in his splendid *Two Years in the French West Indies* (1890), the American Samuel Hazard in his 1870 *Cuba with Pen and Pencil*, or Patrick Leigh Fermor with *The Traveller's Tree: A Journey through the Caribbean Islands* (1950), all described general stylistic mannerisms—in speaking or walking—characterized with a rhythmic touch. Anthropologist Roger D. Abrahams' *The Man-of-Words in the West Indies* (1983) describes any conversation among tropical people as representing more than the exchange of words; it is a virtual play of gestures and mouth-and-tongue noises which accompany the conversation. Samuel Hazard was especially struck by the Cuban's love of music and of dance, believing this to be characteristic of all "tropical societies." His observation on Cuban dance finds magnificent corroboration in that jewel of a book by Juan Bosch (who was an exile from the dictator Rafael Leonidas Trujillo's Dominican Republic) *Cuba: la isla fascinante*. The Cuban, he wrote, "enjoys dancing to such an extent that it seems as if the music penetrates his bones and veins in a crescendo that makes every muscle tremble."

Critically, as Gabriel Coulthard noted decades ago in his enlightening *Race and Colour in Caribbean Literature* (1958), this phenomenon was not a function of race or "blood" but of aesthetic and artistic sensibilities. The Puerto Rican Pales Matos was white but his Afro-Caribbean poetry had the same cadence as that of the Cuban mulatto, Nicolás Guillén. We might call it tropical *créolité* if we have to call this *joie de vivre* anything at all. It was for this reason that later the general manager of an exclusive Miami country club—for decades closed to Cubans, Jews, and blacks—had to double the size of the club's dance floor once established Cubans were admitted as members in any number. This regional sense of Caribbean *créolité* broke down national and colonial boundaries, allowing the Cuban Guillén to be called a "Caribbean poet" or the Cuban novelist Alejo Carpentier to write on Haiti (*The Kingdom of this World*) and revolutionary Guadeloupe (*Explosion in the Cathedral*). Indeed, both Carpentier and his fellow Cuban José Lezama Lima can justly be considered among the important early contributors to magical realism, the literary genre which Gabriel García Marquez took to new heights.

There is no need to either romanticize or minimize this history. No need, for instance, for the kind of complex parody done by Guillermo Cabrera Infante. For this Cuban novelist who broke with the Revolution and exiled himself, Cuba had no cultural authenticity, but an American-influenced "consumer culture." Cubans, he wrote, merely parroted everything American or European. And yet to read his award-winning 1967 *Tres tristes tigres* (*Three Trapped Tigers*) is to have the nightlife of pre-revolutionary Havana described in all its richness; a city where musicians, dancers, TV personalities, fun-seeking children of the bourgeoisie, and black Cubans from Havana's various ghettoes all mingle and speak in what he calls "degraded" Spanish. One has to wonder how Cabrera Infante

Exoticism at the Tropicana nightclub, Havana

would describe the second-generation Cuban-Americans of Miami who do speak something they themselves call "Spanglish" but who identify as strongly as their parents with their particular *cubania*. The fact is that part of understanding contemporary Cuban-Americans in Miami is to appreciate how deep are the roots of the Cuban community's memories and sentiments, collective nostalgia, myths, and all. To know that Cuban presidents paid for (and Cuban architects, artisans, and even materials built) the San Carlos Institute in Key West in 1922 and in 1925 the Villa Paula Cuban Consulate building in Miami perhaps explains what Paula Harper means when she argues in the *Journal of Decorative and Propaganda Arts* in 1966 that "the style of the Villa Paula, like that of the San Carlos Institute, sent a message about the cosmopolitan civilization enjoyed by Cuba in contrast to the relatively provincial tastes of Miami."

Similarly, Vicki Gold and Steven Heller (*Cuba Style*, 2002) called prerevolutionary Cuban culture "commercially exuberant and artistically electrifying," a culture which in manifestations such as the world-famous Tropicana Club catered to the "fantasies and desires of North Americans." These, of course, were also catered to by a well-developed network of prostitution. It is interesting that such a small island should have, culturally speaking, later radiated out to shape the social and aesthetic tastes of the new city across the Strait of Florida. David Rieff was neither the first nor the last to assert that the "atmosphere" of Miami had a distinctly Cuban content. In fact, Rieff goes as far as to claim—incorrectly as it turns out—that such is the Cuban dominance of what is fundamentally "their town" that they are "probably the only people who really feel comfortable in Dade County."

In an article "Going to Miami" published in the *New Yorker* in 1987, Rieff called Miami "the second Havana." But the influence went both ways. So strong was the American influence on Havana that Lisandro Pérez argues: "In many ways [Havana] resembled a city you would be more likely to find in the US than anywhere else in Latin America." Running all through those historical contacts and interactions, Pérez continues, "was an insidious Americanization of Havana soon to be followed by a Cubanization of Miami that continues unabated." The insidious American contributions to Havana were but a minor part of the larger picture, yet given that there was much of an illicit nature, these were always given prominent space in the newspapers. They included much of what we have already described, to wit: the control by Meyer Lansky and his associates of all casino gambling and major rackets in Cuba. But there was also insidious Cuban influence on Miami which preceded by many years the flow of refugees beginnig in 1959.

MONEY AND POLITICS

There had always been a trickle of Cuban money entering Miami, usually around times of political strife, though never in great amounts. We know of the cigar-makers, but there are no records, for instance, of Cuban money in the speculation in real estate which led to the boom and bust in the 1920s. However, Cuban tourists did begin to arrive in Miami in relatively large numbers after World War II. Between May 1 and August 15, 1948 an estimated 40,000 Cubans visited Miami spending on average $100 each during a four-day stay. Interestingly, according to *Newsweek* (4 July 1949), vacationing in Miami was cheaper for Cubans than in Cuba's Varadero Beach. A roundtrip airfare "costs only" $34.50 and a vacation in Miami meant a complete change of scenery, different food, and the opportunity to walk and swim along miles of beach without charge… as long as you were white. Since Florida and Miami were regularly advertised in the Cuban press it is not surprising that in 1949 Cuban tourists left an estimated $70 million in Miami and Miami Beach. The summer might have been the off-season for US tourists but it was the tourist season for Cubans in Miami. Even Fidel Castro traveled through Miami on his honeymoon. *Newsweek* described an active Cuban presence in 1949:

> The Cubans are leaving their mark on Florida. Last summer it sounded as if as much Spanish as English was being spoken on Miami streets. Shops hired Spanish-speaking clerks and the city broke out with a rash of signs reading "*Se habla español*" (Spanish spoken). Even movie theaters put the word *hoy* (today) over their announcements. A recent Havana cartoon showed a Cuban asking a Miami policeman: "Can you tell me where I can find an American? I want to practice my English."

And this was 1949! The 1940 census showed 4,607 Cubans in Florida, but only 1,318 Cubans in Dade County. Most of them were already settled in a small neighborhood already known as "Little Havana" (*Pequeña Habana*), a quite well-established community. The women were an important part of an infant garment industry in a city where the population had reached about 50,000 by 1959.

Suddenly the trickle of Cuban capital investments in Miami became a torrent. At one point in the late 1940s the largest holder of real estate in Miami was the Cuban Minister of Education, José Manuel Alemán. Cubans on the island were well-informed about Alemán's investments, both in Cuba and in Miami, because the popular magazine *Bohemia* (2 April 1950) had summarized a series on this "Cuban affair" written by Bert Collins of the *Miami Herald*. Alemán had accumulated substantial holdings in Cuba—an airline, multiple plantations, and houses, all calculated at $50 million. In 1946 he decided to diversify into Florida and did so in one fell swoop: he arrived at Miami airport with suitcases stuffed with $20 million. Within a short span of time he was said to be worth between $70 and $200 million. Was the original $20 million part of the $174 million stolen from the Cuban National Treasury or money stolen from the Cuban Ministry of Education? We will never know. What we do know is that Alemán began a wild purchasing spree in Miami. Aside from a magnificent house on Pine Tree Drive in Miami Beach located on a canal with access to the ocean, he bought over 500 acres on Key Biscayne (now the Bill Baggs Cape Florida State Park), six hotels on Collins Avenue in Miami Beach, and the large McAllister Hotel in downtown Miami. He acquired a large extension of land in southwest Miami, which the state of Florida assessed at $2.5 million, and a group of buildings in downtown Miami for which he paid $4 million. His real estate firms were so busy buying and selling property that they hired a total of 1,500 employees. Naturally, it helped that he was a good friend of then-Governor Fuller Warren whom we have already introduced as a man with contacts with the Mob. Most extravagant and costly of all Alemán's doings, however, was his decision in 1947 to build a big, modern stadium in order to attract a Major League baseball team to Miami. This, of course, endeared him to the community. He and his partners formed an association called the Magic City Baseball Club and proceeded to purchase a team they named the Miami Sun Sox.

If Fisher could enhance the image of Miami Beach by bringing in the Cuban polo team, why would Alemán not try to do the same for Miami by bringing in a popular Cuban baseball team? After all, Cuba was playing serious baseball before Miami became a city. Louis A. Pérez, Jr. describes

baseball being brought to Cuba in the 1860s by Cuban students returning from North American colleges. By 1872 Cuba had its first professional
baseball team and many others soon followed. Again, Miami was not only
far behind Cuba, it was also far behind Key West, which in the 1880s had
four teams recruited from Cuban immigrants, and Tampa, which had
formed a team one year after its incorporation as a city in 1886.

The first game played by the Miami Sun Sox (31 August 1949) was
against a Cuban team, the "Havana Cubans." It drew over 13,000 fans.
With typical grandiosity, the *Miami Herald* called it "the greatest single
event in local baseball history." If it was the greatest, it was also the last
great event in that stadium, given that subsequently it drew fans in the
hundreds, not the thousands. Alemán died soon after making all his Miami
purchases. He was 46 years old. His widow, Elena Santeiro Alemán, sold
the Key Biscayne property for $12 million in promissory notes to Arthur
D. Dessler, an associate of Jimmy Hoffa, a man with well-known ties to
the Mob. Dessler finally defaulted. She then put the property in trust with
the Miami Beach First National Bank, owned by the George Smathers
family. In 1965 Elena Alemán deeded the southern tip of her Key Biscayne property to the state of Florida for what became the Cape Florida
Park. She made $8 million on other sales. Alemán's son, José Alemán, Jr.,
was not so lucky. He sold the stadium to the city in 1954 for $850,000 and
then, according to Hinckle and Turner, went into a deep depression when
he failed to secure a loan from the Mafioso Santos Trafficante. Legend has
it that he eventually went insane, cloistered in an aunt's home. In 1959 the
Castro government brought an end to the Alemán empire by confiscating
all its Cuban properties. No one really knows how many Miamians became
rich on Alemán's stolen Cuban money.

Despite the collapse of Alemán's dreams, Miami's elites did not give
up on maintaining a Cuban baseball connection. After purchasing
Alemán's stadium in 1954, the Miami City Commission renamed it the
Bobby Maduro Stadium in honor of the renowned owner of the "Havana
Sugar Kings" baseball team of pre-Castro Cuba. The City Commission
had even less success with it than Alemán had had. Miami's fickle fans
simply did not come. Although it did not become another of the city's
white elephants because it was used for neighborhood sports, it was demolished in 2001. Today, in its place stand apartment buildings with
neither physical trace nor historical memory of what had stood there

The Miami Stadium under construction

before—another case of the collapse of grandiose dreams built with ill-gotten gains.

The importance and deep roots of Cuba and Cubans in the history of Miami are further demonstrated by the friendship of President Richard M. Nixon and Charles ("Bebe") Rebozo. Rebozo was born in Tampa to Cuban parents but came to Miami in 1935 to enter business. He began with a gas station, then a tire retreading operation, all the while dabbling in real estate. In 1950 George Smathers introduced him to Richard Nixon. Eventually Smathers sold Nixon three lots in Key Biscayne—directly on Biscayne Bay right next to Rebozo's house. That is where Nixon built the "Florida White House." The Nixon-Rebozo friendship survived all of Nixon's political ups-and-downs as well as the various FBI investigations of Rebozo and his Key Biscayne Bank. Although nothing ever came of the many suspicions and rumors surrounding the allegedly underhand dealings of Rebozo and his bank, according to Kirkpatrick Sale (*Yankees and Cowboys: The World Behind Watergate*, 1973), many of Rebozo's real estate deals were done with people associated with Meyer Lansky. Again, it is still not known what truth there was in that allegation. It is known, however, that in 1962 Nixon invested in a major Rebozo real estate venture—Fisher Island—and doubled his money in five years.

Real estate was only one part of Rebozo's decades-long relationship with Nixon. Walter Isaacson's highly regarded book, *Kissinger: A Biography*, is especially insightful on this score including the revelation that Nixon and Rebozo tended to engage in heavy drinking during Nixon's frequent trips to the Florida White House. Similarly, Anthony Summers (*The Arrogance of Power: The Secret World of Richard Nixon*, 2000) calculates that Rebozo was at Nixon's side one day in ten for the duration of the presidency. "The friendship had grown so close," says Summers, "that Rebozo effectively had the run of the White House and his own phone number there." He flew on Air Force One and cruised on the presidential yacht with Nixon and Kissinger.

Certainly, judging from his autobiography, *The Memoirs of Richard Nixon* (1978), Nixon himself spoke of Rebozo as if he were a member of the immediate family. They spent Thanksgiving together, and the decision to throw his hat in the ring in 1967 was made at Rebozo's house. At Christmas, Nixon invited his Cuban valet Manolo and his wife Fina and Rebozo, "all of those who basically are our family..." Rebozo gave crucial support during the investigations into the Watergate break-in and what Nixon called his "Impeachment Summer." Four of the five men caught breaking in to the Democratic National Committee headquarters in Washington were Cubans from Miami. In other words, Nixon was surrounded by Cubans and eventually he concluded that he must use them to save his presidency; not the last time Cubans would be used for Republican Party purposes. In this particular case we witness Richard Nixon in his most transparently Machiavellian mode when he conspires to use Cubans for political gain. Nixon describes the scheme with remarkable *sang froid*:

> I called Haldeman. When both he and Colson had mentioned the Bay of Pigs that afternoon, they had stimulated my thinking, and I told him about my new idea for handling the public relations aspect of the Watergate incident. I suggested that if the Cuban explanation for the break-in actually caught on, I would call Rebozo and have him get the anti-McGovern Cubans in Miami to start a public bail fund for their ar-

rested countrymen and make a big media issue out of it. If they used it to revive the Democrats' inept handling of the Bay of Pigs and to attack McGovern's foreign policy ideas, we might even make Watergate work in our favor.

Alas, the ploy did not work, the "Watergate Five" were convicted of breaking and entering, and the Nixon presidency began to sink. When Nixon enquired of Rebozo whether his account in the Key Biscayne Bank had enough funds to cover the legal expenses of Haldeman and Erlichman, Rebozo rejected the idea of using Nixon's own funds; he promised that he and their mutual friend Bob Abplanalp "could raise two or three hundred thousand dollars." This, of course, would have to be in cash and privately donated. No wonder Rebozo was being investigated by the Internal Revenue Service, the Government Accountability Office, and the Miami State Attorney in addition "to being scandalously hounded by the (Congressional) Ervin Committee staff," as Nixon put it. It should surprise no one that Nixon listed as one of his major problems "the Rebozo thing."

Again, it is not known what influences on specific foreign policy generally, and on Cuba in particular, Rebozo might have had. Certainly he must have reinforced Nixon's already intense dislike of Fidel Castro, since Rebozo did have close contacts with important sectors of the exiled Cuban community and helped many of them start their own businesses by extending loans from his bank. As if the constant companionship of Rebozo was not enough, Nixon was never far removed from Cuban affairs since he had close, indeed daily, contact with his valet, Manolo Sánchez and Manolo's wife, both Cuban exiles and who, as we have already noted, were very much considered family. Even as one can only speculate on the constant anti-Castro invective coming from this informal source every morning, it is good to remember that Nixon had disliked and mistrusted Castro since he first met him in 1959. Castro, Nixon told President Eisenhower, was most probably a communist. Hindsight shows him to have been prescient.

The point is that Cuba and Cubans have never been far removed from the Miami scene. Up to 1959, Cubans such as Alemán and Rebozo were what one could call "exotics," not unlike the Cuban polo players and dancers who fulfilled an American idealization of the Cuban *macho*. It was critical that these exotics were white, well-off, and, fundamentally, few in

Desi Arnaz and his conga drum

numbers. They threatened none of the established communities since they often entertained and enriched others. They presented no competition for jobs, housing, or political power, and offered no offense to the sensibilities of the segregated community. White Cubans fit nicely into the Miami elite's search for tropical flair. Music and dance played an important part in this relationship. A case in point was the Cuban band leader Pupi Campo whose band members were all white. He became known as "The Rumba Maestro" and played for the Jack Paar *Morning Show* on television from 1954 to 1958, and also at the Deauville Hotel in Miami.

Even more illustrative is the case of Desi Arnaz, band leader and later husband of Lucille Ball of the famous TV series *I Love Lucy*. His family fled the political violence of Cuba in the early 1930s which followed the fall of the dictator Gerardo Machado whom Desi's father supported. The family settled in Miami. Desi was musically inclined and much influenced by a "Cubanized" Spaniard, Xavier Cugat. The by-then popular Arnaz formed his own band, Siboney, and played at the Top o' the Columbus Hotel, one of the few nightclubs in Miami. Before long, Arnaz had Miamians and Americans generally dancing in a conga line. How many Americans knew, however, that when they heard and sang the theme song of Arnaz' band, "Babayú-Alé," they were chanting to the Afro-

Cuban *Santería* god of medicine represented syncretically in many a Cuban household as San Lázaro? The conga drum which Arnaz hung from his neck was a secular version of the sacred *bata* drum used in *Santería* religious rituals. Those of a certain age will remember the 1949 film *Holiday in Havana* in which Arnaz appears as "Cuban Pete," the "King of the rhumba beat—the dance of Latin romance." What possible threat, religious or otherwise, could come from an exotic, good-looking white Cuban? That the music was of Afro-Cuban origin—who knew? What was telling was what the great Cuban ethnologist Fernando Ortiz once said: "With our music we Cubans have exported more dreams and pleasures than with our tobacco, more sweetness and energy than with all our sugar." If not absolutely true, it was at least a plausible sociological statement, as the Cuban presence in Miami would prove, with one caveat: in the 1940s and 1950s that music had to be delivered by white Cubans. Exoticism had its limits in those segregated days. The most celebrated of Afro-Cuban entertainers of the 1940s, such as Rolando LaSerie, Arsenio Rodríguez, and Benny More and his Banda Gigante, were never invited. Even when in the mid-1950s New York was hosting famous bands such as La Sonora Mantancera with its singer, Celia Cruz, Miami was off-limits. Later, when Celia Cruz decided to go into exile, Miami's Cuban community elevated her to a quasi-deified status. Her funeral in Miami was one of the great apotheoses in the city's history.

In those days, the small Cuban presence did not represent anything more than an exotic touch. If there was any unease at all in the Anglo community, it was with the post-World War II pace of change and the sense that the "old" standards of morality and lawfulness of the pioneer days were eroding. This partly explains why established resident historian Helen Muir felt compelled to insist in 1953 that Miami "is definitely a member of the Union." We can only speculate what she might have concluded when only a decade later the flow of Cuban refugees began to change the character of the city. Muir could certainly not have repeated her 1953 assessment that Miami "had no character at all." Only six years later, a Cuban revolutionary would become the great agent of major changes, in Cuba and Miami.

THE CASTRO GENERATION

What occurred in Miami in 1959 with the Castro revolution was as monumental as it was unprecedented. It was unprecedented in three ways. First, the extraordinary numbers involved. Second, these new arrivals were not just temporary exiles, they were refugees. The fact was, the movement of Cubans was a one-way street which differed from the previous custom of Cuban exiles returning to their country after the fall of the dictator from whom they had fled. Third and critically, the Cubans were a now significant element in the global geopolitical game known as the Cold War.

Cubans arrived in the United States at a time when the Cold War assured them a warm reception. The strident anti-communism of this group fell on receptive ears at both national and local levels. As the quasi-hysteria of anti-communism among the non-Cuban population began to abate, Cubans kept up the agitation while also showing great strategic flexibility. They were able to move smoothly as a Cuban-American minority group in the new climate of ethnic revitalization, calling on their anti-communism as needed. Haitians, as we shall see later, lacked that anti-communism advantage but drew on other sources of American sympathy for the oppressed.

The arrival of the Cubans after 1959 took place in a steady stream but with certain periods of accelerated movement. The first group, which included many adherents of the defeated Fulgencio Batista dictatorship, began to arrive right after the fall of the dictator on December 31, 1958. Within a year there were approximately 50,000 other arrivals, still only 5.4 percent of Dade County's population. Most of the new arrivals settled in what was already called Pequeña Habana, a section between SW 8th Street (today called Calle Ocho or *la saguacera*) and NW 27th Avenue and I-95.

A new surge took place in 1965 fueled by the "Freedom Flights," an agreement between the Cuban and US governments to airlift large groups who were ready to attempt the dangerous crossing by boat across the Straits of Florida. By 1970 the Cuban population of Miami had increased dramatically and had spread beyond Little Havana into Hialeah, West Miami, and Westchester, all areas north and south of the now iconic Calle Ocho. Again, it should be remembered that these travelers were never immigrants but were exiles and refugees, predominantly white and educated. Miami was gaining what Cuba was losing: an entrepreneurial middle class.

According to the US Census, by 1970 the demographics of Metropolitan Dade County and of the city of Miami were as follows:

	In Dade County	% Living in City of Miami
Whites	1,071,662	23.92
Black	189,666	40.15
Cuban	217,892	56.38
Puerto Rican	17,425	38.22

Clearly, Cubans (as well as blacks) clustered in the city, and Calle Ocho was its geographical center. The basic and persisting characteristic of the Cuban community has come from the fact that they constituted what Alejandro Portes in an innovative 1987 essay called "an ethnic enclave." He describes an enclave as "a distinctive economic formation characterized by the spatial concentration of immigrants who organize a variety of enterprises to serve their ethnic market and the general population." Such groups are defined by having a division of labor, a highly differentiated professional class, and the highest (on a *per capita* basis) concentration of Hispanic-owned businesses. This definition describes *la saguacera* perfectly.

This pattern of arrivals changed dramatically between April and September 1980 in an episode now known simply as "Mariel." In Havana, with the economy already stuttering, thousands of Cubans sought refuge in the grounds of the Peruvian Embassy. Castro's government declared that whoever wished to leave could do so by boat from the port of Mariel. As if out of nowhere hundreds of boats of every size departed from Miami, Tampa, and even New Orleans bound for Mariel to pick up relatives or friends, and, as tends to occur in the Caribbean where a culture of migration exists, Haitians followed their example. By September over 125,000 Cubans and some 12,000 Haitians had arrived in Miami. Many among the new arrivals were strikingly different, not just from the established Cuban community but also from the majority of the other Mariel refugees. Among these "strange looking" refugees from Cuba's Mariel were over 5,000 criminals who had been freed from Cuban prisons and others who had been released from the island's mental institutions. Anglos, Cubans, and black Miamians went into a state of collective shock. Even the venerable *Miami Herald* had difficulty establishing a balance between humanitarianism and self-interest. Notice the following sequence of *Miami Herald* editorials in 1980:

April 24: "Every freedom lover sympathizes with Cubans and they certainly will be welcome here."

May 15: "Where is the humanitarianism in opening America's gates to
all comers and then telling local taxpayers: Here they are—you
take care of them."

December 11: "What is needed is a camp of some sort. No other American city is expected to accept the prevailing conditions of a
Haitian or Cuban slum. Miami shouldn't be either."

Initially, the Cuban-American elite in Miami lobbied to have the
Jimmy Carter Administration sponsor an airlift similar to that of 1965. An
influential group of Cuban-Americans traveled to Washington to press
their case in person. When Secretary of State Warren Christopher refused
their request, they stormed out of his office. It was a demonstration of
Cuban emotions and political self-belief best described as hubris. There
was real apprehension about what the *New York Times* (18 May 1980) said
might turn into "bombings and riots in Miami." Meanwhile, Florida
politicians, at first so receptive because they saw the mass migration as a
blow to communist Cuba, were now in a state of agitation. "It's hard to
overstate," protested Florida Senator Stone, "the social upheaval and backlash that have developed over this problem."

Interestingly, as Alejandro Portes and Juan Clark point out, it was the
already-settled Cuban community which eventually responded the most
negatively to the new arrivals, soon referred to as *Marielitos*. Three years
after their arrival, 26 percent of Mariel refugees believed that Anglos discriminated against them, but 75 percent believed that it was the older established Cubans who discriminated the most. Race had much to do with
this result but there was also the fact that by 1980 Miami Cubans formed
a solid middle-class enclave while many of the *Marielitos* showed the "wear-
and-tear" of two decades of Cuban "socialist" hardships and material dep-
rivation.

Despite the veritable collective panic of all communities in Miami,
the Mariel refugees—except for those criminals awaiting deportation back
to Cuba—did not take too long to be accommodated by a Cuban community which by 1985 had grown to 750,000 or 43.3 percent of Dade
County's total population. The early waves of crimes subsided so that the
term *Marielito* began to lose its association with criminality and other

deviant behavior. By the 1990s Cubans comprised 50 percent of the population, and there was a surprising new receptivity towards the many *Marielitos* who showed great artistic and literary talents. One of these talented *Marielitos* was the novelist and poet Reinaldo Arenas. He had suffered imprisonment in Cuba for his openly gay lifestyle and his ridicule of the Castro regime. While all his books deal with Cuba, he seemed always to be in a battle with life, and he soon began excoriating the Cuban community in Miami for what he termed racism, homophobia, and vulgar materialism. According to Achy Obejas of the *Chicago Tribune*, "when Reinaldo arrived, there wasn't really anywhere for him to hang his hat. Being a bad boy in Havana was one thing, but being a bad boy in Miami had different implications: Nobody in the exile community really wanted to hear about his sexuality, and nobody wanted to hear his anti-Castro speeches in the gay one." He moved to New York, already in the terminal stages of AIDS, and committed suicide in 1990. Arenas' most successful book was his autobiography, *Antes que anochezca*, translated in 1993 as *Before the Night Falls*. It was made into a movie that same year, but that film carried little of the power of the written word. It is doubtful that a film can capture the totality of the human tragedy that the Arenas case represents.

Another Cuban poet who arrived in 1980, though not with the Mariel boat lift, was Heberto Padilla. Like so many other intellectuals, he originally supported the Castro revolution but then turned against it. He was imprisoned in 1971 and finally allowed to leave Cuba in 1980. Padilla was fond of Miami though he could not make a living there. In 1985 he told *Time* magazine (8 July), "Florida, Floreeda, Ponce de Leon christened it and in Coral Gables the streets have Spanish names. So we deserve the place. Whenever we had trouble in Havana, we went to Miami, and Miami is very, very important to us. We don't feel like immigrants." He died of a heart attack while teaching at Auburn University in Alabama in 2000. Several editions of his poetry were published in English as well as a book, *Self-Portrait of the Other*. Neither Arenas nor Padilla wrote about Miami. By the 1980s, it was critical that there was land available for the more established Cubans to spread all through Central Dade, Hialeah, Westchester, and points south and west. However, the thirty-block Calle Ocho remained—as it does still today—the sentimental heart of Cuban identity in Miami. Size alone makes this Cuban community the point of com-

The espresso machine for the indispensable *café cubano*, Little Havana

parison with trends in general and trends for other ethnic groups in particular. But size is only one dimension of the dynamics of this group. A respected Florida International University-Cuba Poll shows that a mere 22.6 percent plan to return to Cuba when Castro falls but also revealed a community living on memories of the "real" Cuba before communism. Nostalgia among Miami Cubans is a multigenerational phenomenon and it is fueled by equal measures of fact and legend.

The late Miguel González-Pando (1998) spoke of the "consuming nostalgia" of the exiles. They strived continually to retain as much of Cuban culture and the Spanish language as possible. This explains the thirty or so Cuban schools teaching bilingually and emphasizing Cuban history and culture. The children of the Cuban-American elite study at Belen Jesuit, Columbus, Loyola, and La Salle—all schools prominent in pre-Castro Cuba. Indeed, Fidel Castro graduated from Belen in Havana. In Miami, these schools, where teaching is by priests expelled from Cuba, reinforced the cultural persistence that is already a formidable part of Cuban identity. There is enormous such persistence even among those of

107

the younger generation who listen, with great respect, to their parents, their teachers, and to specific highly identifiable "reference" individuals.

Prominent among these was Jorge Más Canosa, leader of the powerful Cuban American National Foundation, who once said: "I have never assimilated. I never intend to. I am a Cuban first. I live here only as an extension of Cuba." Or there is former Cuban politician Lincoln Díaz Balart, who advised his sons to always be "Cuba-centric." It is precisely these kinds of statements that have sometimes left the Anglo community angry at the "ingratitude" for the acceptance and inclusiveness it had exhibited in absorbing the Cuban exile community. These assertions of Cuban nationalism are undoubtedly true, but it is a paradoxical yet historical fact that Jorge Más Canosa, for instance, after many years of political stridency became one of Miami's grand leaders when he, and his foundation, decided to forgo all forms of violence and take up American-style lobbying. The change of strategy might not have been a sign of full acculturation and assimilation but it was close enough to make significant changes in a city living on its nerves. Más Canosa proved that he did not have to stop "feeling" Cuban to operate and live according to the mores of the US political system. His and the community's growing economic and political power had much to do with this change of tactics if not of heart.

Another community leader was Luís Botifoll. He once asserted forcefully that before the 1959 revolution Cubans "thought Cuba was better" than the US. Rieff notes that in an interview in 1993, Botifoll was as nostalgically adamant as Más Canosa and showed the same kind of contradictory sentiments:

> It will always be difficult for you Americans to understand the realities as we Cubans in Miami see them… even though this country has been very good to me, even after thirty-five years, I don't feel comfortable here. And the reason is simple. I would rather be in Cuba.

The successful *Miami Herald* Cuban-American journalist Fabiola Santiago echoed such sentiments: "Technically, it took me 10 years to become a citizen. Emotionally, it may take me forever." When Juanita Castro, Fidel and Raúl's sister in exile, finally decided to become a US citizen, and was asked what that signified, she answered: "I do not concern myself with irrelevant things." US citizenship was strategic and instrumental, not emotionally fundamental to many of the Cuban-American elite.

So how does one explain that someone "not comfortable" in a given society turns out to excel in that society? Political scientist Dario Moreno cuts through the emotional contradictions and concludes that it is the lore of their transcendent historical success as a group in America which "lies at the very core of Cuban-American identity." Note how grandiloquently Juan Silverio describes this version of Cuban success in his aptly titled 1996 book, *Greater Miami: Spirit of Cuban Enterprise*: "In less than a hundred years Miami has gone from a plot of land located between marshes... to a fascinating cosmopolitan enclave... a deep transformation that is generally acknowledged would have never taken place without the advent of the Cuban exiles..."

Silverio attributes the "decisive turning point" of Miami to "Cuban-ization" which brought "a special form of entrepreneurial individualism" and "Latin culture" to the city. A major part of the explanation, he says, lies in the fact that the "community" experienced great economic success— what the popular press and what Cubans themselves call the "Cuban Miracle," and *Fortune* magazine (October 1966) spoke of as "Those Amazing Cubans."

THE CUBAN MIRACLE

In fact, this success story needs to be studied in terms of two levels of Miami's growth as a major commercial center: the small firm and family-run business, and the growth of corporate Cubans. Both were successful. Cubans point with justified pride to the achievements of families who had their property expropriated in Cuba only to restart with enormous success in Florida. A case in point is that of the Fanjul brothers who went into exile after their family sugar plantations in Cuba were expropriated, and remade their fortune. The sale in London of sugar giant Tate & Lyle revealed a real irony that this author explained in the *Financial Times*:

> One of the two US corporations that bought [Tate & Lyle] is American Sugar Refining, owned by Cuban-Americans Alfonso and Pepe Fanjul of Florida. Their Cuban sugar plantations were confiscated by the Castro regime.
>
> With the acquisition of [British] Tate & Lyle refineries in London and Lisbon, the Fanjuls will now be capable of producing 6 million tons

of sugar per year, five times what Cuba produced in 2008. The old Cuban adage "*Sin azucar no hay país*" (without sugar there is no country) still holds, except no longer in Cuba [but in Florida].

Most social science scholars argue that the successes of those small Cuban businesses which line Calle Ocho in Little Havana and are present throughout Hialeah are founded on the high degree of cooperation within the Cuban family. We will deal with this issue further, but it is instructive to travel into that bustling municipality, Hialeah, and notice the dozens of small shops and businesses on each block. These businesses owned by Cubans tend to be small, family operations with few or no employees. As Boswell and Curtis explain, of 30,336 Cuban firms in the United States (but primarily in Miami-Dade County) in 1977, 24,748 or 82 percent had no employees with the remainder employing only 2.2 percent of all Dade County workers. By 1987 the number of Cuban-owned businesses in the US had grown to 61,470 but only 10,768 or 17.5 percent had paid employees, while 82.5 percent did not—almost exactly the same as in 1977. Fully 83.2 percent of those firms that did have paid employees had fewer than four paid workers.

There can be no arguing with the fact that there is a Cuban ethic of hard work, cohesive families, and a capacity to grasp opportunities. There is evidently a burning ambition to "make it" again and, if possible, "better" in America. One is reminded that many of these Miami Cubans were children of the Spanish immigrants who populated Havana after Cuba became independent in 1902. The creative energy of these Cubans is evident in areas other than commerce. In the early 1960s, a first Cuban radio station began operating in Miami, today called *La Cubanísima* (WQBA) just as it was called in Cuba. Celia Cruz used to sing the station's jingle: "I am the voice of Cuba, from this land, far away... I am liberty, I am WQBA, the most Cuban! (*Yo soy de Cuba, la voz, desde esta tierra lejana... soy libertad, soy WQBA, Cubanísima!*)." By 2010 there were thirteen other Cuban or Spanish-language radio stations and four Spanish-language TV stations operating, including one (Mexican-owned Univision) which has the largest audience in Miami-Dade County. Aside from two established newspapers, *El Nuevo Herald* and *Diário de las Américas*, there are many more small papers Cubans call *periódiquitos*, little shopping center-style newspapers but with editorials which spit fire as if the Cold War had never ended.

Cuban success in politics despite the fact that the highly concentrated residential pattern of the Cuban-Americans gives them a majority in fewer than 5 percent of the electoral precincts in Miami-Dade County has been nothing short of astonishing. By 1982 there were seven Cuban-Americans in the Florida House of Representatives and three in the State Senate. Cuban-Americans were mayors of Miami, West Miami, North Miami, Sweetwater, Hialeah Gardens, and Doral, and some years later even Coral Gables elected a Cuban-American as mayor. A key contest, however, was the one for the US 18th Congressional District in 1989, encompassing Miami, Miami Beach, Coral Gables, and Hialeah, which together was 50 percent Hispanic, 13 percent black, and 36 percent Anglo (including Jews). That congressional seat had been held by the indomitable Claude Pepper for 28 years. The electoral victory of Iliana Ros-Lehtinen in 1989 was the first true demonstration of Cuban voting power. This included a well-oiled Republican Party machine and turn-out-the-vote mobilization as well as some of the old red-baiting accusations such as the charge that Fidel Castro himself had endorsed the Democratic candidate (a Jew, Gerald Richman). Five radio and two television Spanish-language stations supported Ros-Lehtinen. Even the *Miami Herald* endorsed the Republican when publisher Dick Capen overruled his editorial board's support for Richman. Ros-Lehtinen has proven to be a formidable politician, very much in a Cuban populist style. As of 2011 she was chair of the important US House of Representatives Committee on Foreign Affairs.

Before we believe the self-serving Cuban-American claims that they achieved all this political influence strictly though their own efforts, it should be pointed out that one of the most effective skills of the Cubans has been their ability to lobby and to piggyback and use benefits secured by other minority groups. In this they have taken a page from other successful ethnic lobbies. In 1975 when Miami mayor Maurice Ferré (a Puerto Rican) launched the American Coalition for Hispanic Action, he specifically mentioned the Jewish Anti-Defamation League and the National Association for the Advancement of Colored People (NAACP) as models. The National Association of Cuban-American Women is clearly modeled after the Mexican-American Women's National Association. Whether it is the Forum of National Hispanic Organizations or the League of United Latin American Citizens (both with Mexican-American leadership) or any of the other lobbying and civil rights groups, the Cubans have

Early Cuban-American agitation for citizenship and language rights

had ample examples to use as models. The critical point is, of course, that they have used them well. A Washington correspondent put it precisely when discussing the launching of the Washington-headquartered National Coalition of Cuban-Americans: "Forming a lobbying group and swarming around Capitol Hill is something of a rite of passage into the American political mainstream. After 17 years in the United States, the Cuban-born immigrants have taken the step into that mainstream… That is the American way."

By the mid-1980s, with ownership of four major banks in Miami-Dade, several major radio and television stations, newspapers, and major insurance companies, the Cuban community hardly seemed like a minority to some of the others. Already in 1979 Cubans enjoyed the highest median income among Hispanics ($14,000 as against $11,742 for Mexicans, $7,972 for Puerto Ricans, and $9,563 for African-Americans). While 39 percent of the Puerto Rican families, 19 percent of the Mexican, and

21 percent of Hispanic families as a whole lived below the poverty level, 15 percent of the Cuban families were so characterized; the American national average was 9 percent.

More and more, it is the Cuban who provides the point of comparison to other Hispanic groups in Miami. The Cuban community's virtually independent "foreign policy," evidenced in its direct negotiations with Cuba over the release of political prisoners and the massive boatlift from Mariel in April 1980, now converts the lessons learned from others, into providing other groups with their own lessons in political organization and minority ethnic bargaining. Cuban leaders have learned to use to their advantage the presumption that there is a homogeneous "Latin" community, both Cuban and Hispanic, just as their reputation for volatility tends to come in handy in delicate situations. To cite but one case, when the local newspaper called for punishment against Cubans who hijacked a boat from Cuba as an example that the law against hijackings should be respected, the president of the Cuban Patriotic Junta expressed his disagreement and then reminded the editor that he spoke for 206 Cuban organizations and "half a million (Cuban) sons and daughters in the city where your newspaper is published." Substantially irrelevant to the point was the question of what US law mandated.

The latter point brings the story around to what the US, including Miami society generally, contributed to this Cuban "miracle." One has to begin with the largesse of the federal government. As sociologist Alex Stepick has noted, the Cuban exiles were the beneficiary of more US government assistance "than any other group in American history." According to Sylvia Pedraza-Bailey, between 1961 and 1976 the Cuban Refugee Program provided over $1 billion in assistance housing, health, education, food stamps, and outright cash allocations, and $130 million to bilingual education assistance for the Dade County schools. This was a period when targeted "minority" set-asides for contracts took hold. It is calculated that approximately half of all Federal Small Business loans granted in Dade County went to Cuban start-ups.

After the dramatic Mariel boatlift took place, a specially created Cuban-Haitian Task Force provided $400 million to settle 125,000 Cubans and some 8,000 Haitians. Although smaller in scale—but important, as Didion and Rieff point out—newly declassified CIA records show how the CIA funneled money into the Cuban community. In the

1960s and 1970s there were approximately 12,000 Cubans in Miami employed and receiving biweekly stipends from dozens of CIA "front" businesses. This money was "seed" money for many a Cuban business which entered the commercial life of the city once the CIA money dried up. Meanwhile, Cubans were starting other businesses closely associated with their ethnic preferences and the way those preferences were met in prerevolutionary Cuba. Such a case is the delivery of health care. Historically, there were in urban Cuba a series of *Centros Medicos* run by Spanish regional groups, the most architecturally spectacular of which was the Centro Asturiano (now an art museum) and other centers, Gallego, Andaluz, and Catalan. These were replicated in Miami, albeit with much less imposing architecture. As the Dade County Conditions and Needs study of 1972 explained, the reason there were 23 "Cuban Clinics" concentrated in Cuban areas was that "For cultural and ethnic reasons, many Cuban families… prefer medical care as it was provided in Cuba…" By 2010 two major providers, Leon and Pasteur, had 62 clinics between them. The Leon family started their clinics in 1964 and in 2011 sold their holding company to national health insurer Cigna for $3.8 billion. As the Business Section of the *Miami Herald* (25 October 2011) put it, "Cigna is buying into a model of clinics traditionally favored by Cuba-Americans with an emphasis on primary care, along with *cafecitos* and *pastelitos*." The story forgot to mention the free transportation, English language classes, and help in preparation for the naturalization process. These clinics represent successful assimilation without total acculturation.

The Cubanization of Miami reveals a multifaceted history with money coming from many sources and the Cuban family-oriented community knowing well how to use it and leverage it. As such, an exiled banker such as Luís Botifoll could reasonably tell interviewer Miguel González-Pando in 1996 that the "unprecedented levels of prosperity" of the city can truly be called the "Cuban Economic Miracle."

Clearly not everyone in Miami cheered on the Cuban community. The substantial "Anglo-flight" to cities to the north of Miami-Dade was evident in the declining presence of that community: Anglos represented 80 percent of the Miami-Dade population in 1960, falling to 32 percent in 1990, and 20 percent in 2000. The resentment was visible in bumper stickers calling on the "last American to leave to bring the flag" or "Anglos—an endangered species." As early as 1976 the *Miami Herald* noted that the exodus of non-Latin whites was "large enough to almost offset the number of non-Latins moving into the county." Anti-Hispanic feeling was found to be strong. A survey conducted by the overwhelmingly Anglo membership of the United Methodist Church of Dade found that "more than half" the Anglos in Dade County would move out "if they had an opportunity"; nervousness over the growth of the Hispanic population was cited as a major reason (*Miami Herald*, 2 February 1979). A *Miami Herald* survey of 609 Dade County voters during the November 1980 elections indicated that 65 percent of the non-Latin whites responding would move out of Dade County "if it were practical."

Miami Herald columnist Bob Resnick responded to the news that Cuban Roberto Suárez had been made president of the Miami Herald Publishing Company in 1997 with this bitter final column: "Well it is finally over!… It's time to move on. Maybe I'll go back to the US. I still remember some English. I'll get by." Cubans were too busy "making it in America" to pay much attention to any such lamentations. They had already changed the character of Miami.

What lessons might be drawn from Miami-Dade's experience with Cubans? Because the vast majority of Cuban refugees had few involuntary ethnic traits, i.e. they were white, they used their ethnicity strategically. This is what Pupi Campo and Desi Arnaz did. This is what a Haitian black or dark mulatto cannot do. This is why white Argentinians, Colombians, Venezuelans, and Brazilians move to and will continue to move to Miami-Dade County, and why dark West Indians move further north to cities such as Miramar and Plantation in Broward County.

In a plural, multiethnic society such as Miami where strategic ethnic lobbying is the standard method of advancing group interests, it pays not to acculturate entirely even as you assimilate into the economic and political system. Stressing ethnic exceptionalism, including retention of Spanish language and historical memories, helps integrate the group. Any antagonism to such ethnic exclusivity only helps increase the in-group feeling. The consequences can be readily seen in Miami today: a highly racially and ethnically segregated city. And yet Miamians are not only getting along, they have created the first truly "Latin" city in the US. Despite the mostly latent tensions, the city exudes an atmosphere which can best be described as tropical and which continues to attract those who seek just that kind of *alegría* or tropical happiness. This attraction extends to the many adventurous Anglos who enjoy and can adapt to such an atmosphere.

In all its advertising, Miami, sitting plainly in the sub-tropics, promotes itself as "tropical" and no doubt has succeeded in selling two myths about the tropics: that everybody has rhythm and everybody has abundant sexual energy. This is not new. Guillermo Cabrera Infante in his *Tres tristes tigres* conveys a conversation between friends in pre-Castro Havana: "And he explained that rhythm is natural, just like breathing... Everybody's got rhythm, just like everybody's got sex."

Let us not be too hasty, moreover, in dismissing existing theories about the aphrodisiacal benefits of rhythm and sex in the tropics as mere myths. In 2012 condom-maker Trojan carried out a scientific sample of sexual behavior and Miami came out as America's "most sexual city." Credit the warm weather, said sexologist Dr. Logan Levkoff. "Miami," he told the *Miami Herald* (15 June 2012) "has this amazing blending of communities that is really built on a culture of socializing, which may lead to more relationships blossoming." Miami must be happy to see their already grand image of themselves confirmed by a flamboyant theory of rhythm and sex.

Chapter Five
WORLDS APART
PUERTO RICANS AND HAITIANS IN A RACIALLY UNSETTLED CITY

Societies that experience rapid quantitative and qualitative changes often take a while to develop a sense of community, what sociologists call *Gemeinschaft*. In many ways the politics of such societies, even in advanced states, are more akin to those of multiethnic "new nations" than to the established patterns of the broader state and society to which they belong geographically. While much attention has been given to Cuban settlement in Miami, less is known about three other established groups in Miami— the Puerto Ricans, the Haitians, and the American black community.

To be sure, Miami-Dade County has always had pockets of ethnic, religious, or regional minorities. Thus, in the 1940s and 1950s there was a substantial Greek community clustered around St. Sophia's Orthodox Church on Coral Way, not far from Brickell Avenue. There were Lebanese and even larger Jewish communities. Allapattah and Shenandoah neighborhoods were strongly southerner, mainly made up of Georgia whites. By the late 1960s those neighborhoods had changed and large southern Baptist, mainstream Protestant, and fundamentalist churches moved mostly south in Miami-Dade County. Eventually these white groups all merged into the broader "Anglo," i.e. non-Hispanic white society. Today Allapattah is 73 percent Hispanic and 18.3 percent African-American. Working-class blacks have never had such mobility. In fact they were much less mobile than the working-class Puerto Ricans and Haitians. Educated, middle-class blacks have traditionally moved out of Miami and even out of Florida to cities such as Atlanta. This has made it difficult to maintain a considerable black elite in the city.

We have already seen the dramatic shift in Miami-Dade's population size and ethnic composition. The growth has been as rapid as it has been varied. By the end of the twentieth century Miami-Dade County (representing 17 percent of Florida's population) was the most ethnically heterogeneous part of the state. The overall statistics, however, tend to hide some very pertinent facts. The new natural increase of Miami-Dade's population in 1978 was less than 1 percent; the overall growth was due to a 3.3 percent increase in net in-migration (in-migration versus out-migration). And this was in 1978, a slow year for new arrivals. The fact is that since 1975 virtually all of Miami-Dade's population growth has been due not only to net in-migration but specifically to net in-migration of Cubans and other people from the Greater Caribbean.

In 1972, 27.4 percent of the Hispanics in Miami-Dade had lived elsewhere before moving to that county; by 1977 the figure had increased to 34.6 percent. When the county's name was formally changed in 1997 to what was already commonly known as "Miami-Dade" County, the new name reflected the truly spectacular demographic (and with that, spatial) changes taking place. Formerly nondescript outlying areas began to be added to the older parts such as Coconut Grove, Coral Gables, Hialeah, Downtown Miami, and an older section of Little Havana. Given the tendency to ethnic grouping, the new areas soon developed authentic ethnic identities of their own: Little Havana, Little Haiti, Little Managua, and, in Miami Beach, Little Buenos Aires. The decisions to immigrate were then, and continue now to be, grounded in each group's primordial attachments and contributed mightily to the intense in-group ethnic feelings. Language was, as it always is, a key part of this process of attachment to the ethnic turf. Not surprisingly, in 1977 fully 93.2 percent of Hispanics intended to remain despite that year's economic recession and despite the fact that Miami-Dade registered a higher unemployment rate among Hispanics (10.1 percent) than the rate for Hispanics nationwide (9.0 percent). Additionally, once in Miami-Dade, the remarkable permanency of marriage among Hispanics eliminates divorce as a cause of out-migration. These trends among Hispanics take on additional weight since they reflect social behavior and attitudes quite distinct from those of non-Hispanic whites. The latter's high rates of mobility are reflected in their decisions to move out of Miami-Dade.

The exodus of Anglos to Broward, Palm Beach, and counties to the north has been accelerating. Between 2002 and 2007, 151,000 mostly white (including Jews) middle-class residents left Miami and were replaced by 238,000 new residents, mostly from the Caribbean and Central America. The out-migration of whites combined with the phenomenal growth of the Latin sector virtually guarantees the trend towards Cubanization and, more broadly, the Caribbeanization and Hispanicization of Miami-Dade County. By the year 2000, Miami had the largest proportion (51.4 percent) of residents who were foreign-born of any major US city. All this explains why Joel Garreau, in his best selling *The Nine Nations of North America* (1989), argues that Miami is only physically attached to the rest of the US. He argues further that it is more akin to a Caribbean island in terms of values, "tropical" values, which explains why he locates Miami among "The Islands."

It would be highly a-historical, however, to present this evident Caribbeanization of Miami without describing the ethnic sequencing which took place. Just as it was necessary to understand pre-revolutionary Cuban society to understand Miami's Cuban-American culture, so it is necessary to understand the islands from which the migrant Puerto Ricans and Haitians came. Migration certainly involves changes, but never the complete erasure of existing culture. Puerto Rican migration demonstrates this reality. If there has been a Caribbean island where US colonial rule has, initially at least, attempted to change the cultural traditions, it was Puerto Rico. And yet such efforts to make cultural transformations, including a change of language, have failed. The resistance of those colonized and the appointment of more enlightened American rulers assured cultural conformity. The majority of Puerto Ricans arrived in Miami as Spanish-speaking migrants. The Puerto Rican upper class, however, arrived as bilingual migrants and in many ways culturally flexible. They were, like all other Puerto Ricans since 1917, US citizens, but they, as distinct from many of the others from their island, knew how to derive full advantages from that citizenship.

Thus in the late 1940s and early 1950s, when Miami's population was slightly more than a half million people of whom perhaps 2 percent were Hispanic, there was a small but significant Puerto Rican presence at both poles of the social structure. The working-class migrant struggled to survive, while those in the upper class were content to mind their businesses and participate in the city's high-society life. Neither class had much to do with each other, nor did they have an impact on the life and culture of the general population. In other words, in many ways Puerto Rico's stratification system was replicated in Miami-Dade and Florida generally. Neither immigrants nor refugees in any legal sense, they were all fleeing the island in search of better opportunities; the upper classes fearing for their privileges in Puerto Rico, the working class seeking the privilege of a decent wage and housing. Political events and social conditions on the island—American since 1898—explain both types of flight.

When Franklin D. Roosevelt's Secretary of the Interior, Harold Ickes, visited Puerto Rico in the mid-1930s, he was scandalized by what he saw. The slums, he wrote to the president, "are the worst that I have ever seen." To Ickes the cause was evident: it was the large estates' constant search for more land and cheap labor which pushed the peasants off their free-held but small plots, into the slums as urban paupers. Similarly, when Rexford G. Tugwell, a member of Roosevelt's Brain Trust who would later be made governor, first arrived on the island he was, he wrote, "shocked, as all Northerners are, at the squalor in which the island's workers live." His subsequent book, *The Stricken Land: The Story of Puerto Rico* (1947) was a clarion call for change because, he warned, the situation was "ripe for class warfare." What Puerto Rico needed was structural change of the type being wrought on the mainland by the New Deal. Especially urgent was reform of the land tenure system. Once Governor Tugwell found a local champion of reform named Luís Muñoz Marín, "the better element" as Tugwell put it, went into "a panic." As Thomas G. Mathews notes in his well-documented book *Puerto Rico Politics and the New Deal* (1960), important

Poor *guajiro* children in their slum hut, Puerto Rico, 1942

leaders of the island's plutocracy, such as José Ferré, considered the proposed reforms tantamount to "communism" and accused the American governor of planning "socialist experiments." Clearly, both the landless working class—because of poverty—and the land-rich upper class—apprehensive of Tugwell's and Muñoz's reforms—had reason to flee. Miami was a natural haven for the rich; New York, and later to a much lesser degree Miami, a haven for the poor.

Many of the Puerto Ricans who went to New York later joined the migration of Caribbean labor, organized in the late 1940s and 1950s, to pick apples in Michigan and other fruits in New York state, and who then began following the "vegetable circuit" in the south. "Stooping" work in the vegetable fields of Florida's Homestead and the Redlands brought them to the area in south Miami-Dade County. Some of these migrant agricultural workers found "off-season" work in the new, growing hotel industry in Miami Beach, washing dishes in restaurants, as hotel maids, as janitors, and in other menial jobs in Miami Beach. In other words, they anticipated what the much better educated Cubans would do in the early 1960s. Melanie Shell-Weis in her informative 2009 book *Coming to Miami* calculates that at one point Puerto Ricans represented half of all workers in the Miami area's garment industry. There were, of course, no living quarters for workers in what had been a segregated Miami Beach. At day's end they traveled west across the Bay to find rooms for rent, and then houses on the mainland in the then-decrepit neighborhood of Wynwood. Wynwood, located east of US Highway 1 (Biscayne Boulevard), south of black Model City/Edison, and north of Overtown (black downtown), became the Puerto Ricans' turf. Their living conditions were terrible but still a step above the distressed abodes they had left behind on the island. Shell-Weis quotes the *Miami Daily News* as remarking that conditions in the Puerto Rican "slum" in Miami were "worse than in the central district for Blacks." They had to be bad indeed.

In a pathological twist, it was in fact because of their residential proximity to the Miami black community that the Puerto Ricans became objects of concern in an age of repeated "red scares." Accustomed to keeping the native black population cowed, the white elite in Miami did not have any experience with Spanish-speaking labor. Since they were US citizens and thereby enjoyed a minimum of rights, they appeared to be even more threatening to Hoover's FBI. Again, as Shell-Weiss cites in the

121

Miami Daily News, Puerto Ricans and other Latins were said to be "the center of subversion in the United States," which "had shifted from California to Miami." Fearful that they were planning a "Negro revolt in the South," the FBI and Miami police kept them under tight scrutiny. It is not known whether this had anything to do with the futile and feeble attempts at revolt in Puerto Rico by a pro-independence movement led by Albizu Campos. Given the way the FBI suspected the West Indian followers of Marcus Garvey, this would not be surprising though equally misguided. The independence movement in Puerto Rico was an urban phenomenon, but working-class Puerto Ricans in Miami were *jíbaros,* peasants from the plantations or mountains.

As the flow of Cuban refugees increased in the 1960s some of these Puerto Ricans were joined, first by Cubans and then by other ethnic groups, but many others began to move out of Miami, heading south to Homestead, and many more north to Orlando where Disney World was busy recruiting. By the 1990s there were approximately 500,000 Puerto Ricans in Orlando. In due course, a mere 20 percent of Wynwood remained Puerto Rican. In the process of ethnic succession, Wynwood in 2000 was settled by mostly Central Americans, Dominicans, Cubans, and some Haitians. As we shall see later, that same community is now being transformed by a process of gentrification linked to the revival of downtown Miami.

Quite a different Puerto Rican migration to Miami was composed of the wealthy upper- and upper-middle-class elites who, as we have noted, were fleeing from clearly reformist, though hardly radical, Puerto Rican politics. The upper-class Puerto Ricans who settled in Miami had access to a world to which very few others—Hispanic and non-Hispanic—had access and, indeed, knew anything about. But these Puerto Rican aristocrats were not in Miami as idle self-imposed exiles; they invested and expanded opportunities in general with the wealth they brought from Puerto Rico. Miami welcomed them as well as many middle-class professionals such as medical doctors, professors, and businessmen. As members of an educated, white elite they had neither social barriers nor psychological complexes and anxieties to overcome, and certainly had no financial needs. They believed, realistically, that the capitalist grass was greener in Miami and Florida. Land was cheaper in Florida and the state's politicians and laws were substantially more receptive to capitalist investments than those they anticipated would exist in their island's future under a reformist Muñoz Marín government. Thus when the sugar aristocracy began to migrate to Miami, they were not there for the sun and surf; they had plenty of that back home. They came, as many others did before and after, looking for a more welcoming political and economic climate in which to invest and expand their considerable fortunes. In this they differed from the majority of the Cuban bourgeoisie, who had to leave before they had time to get their capital out of their island.

As former Mayor of Miami Maurice Ferré tells it, in the mid- and late 1940s Senator Pedro Juan Serrallés, scion of the family which owned the largest sugar estates in Puerto Rico (and distillers of Don Q rum which competes with Bacardí rum), and his uncle, head of the family Don Juan Eugenio Serrallés, bought mansions on what was then Miami's posh millionaire road, Brickell Avenue. Serrallés also formed the Pan American Bank, which by 1960 was Miami's third largest bank, and the Serrallés' Everglades Farm, a major landowner in south Okeechobee County which was rapidly becoming an important sugar producing area. In that they anticipated by many years the Cuban entry into Florida sugar. The Serrallés

Puerto Rican-owned real estate: Douglas Entrance apartments

were soon followed by J. Adalberto Roig and Doña Asunción Lluberas, both major sugar landowners in southern Puerto Rico, and later, an even larger Puerto Rican sugar landowner, Don Jacobo Cabasa. Cabasa began buying sugar land south of Lake Okeechobee. Cabasa's Everglades Farms became one of the largest land holdings in the south Okeechobee area and subsequently the basis for Ambassador William Pauley's Talisman Sugar Corporation and Okeelanta Sugar. The latter was a sugar venture put together by Puerto Rican senator Miguel Angel García Méndez, who along with the Ramírez de Arellano family was among the largest sugar barons of western Puerto Rico.

Al Roig and his brother, former Puerto Rican senator Antonio Roig, had an incipient sugar mill with large surrounding properties in Fellsmere, west of Vero Beach. He was also a successful *rentier*, dabbling in income-producing properties mostly in Miami, including the Douglas Entrance apartments, one of the architectonic marvels of Coral Gables founder and visionary, George Merrick. In the Okeelanta Group was Luís A. Ferré, an MIT graduate and founder of Puerto Rico's pro-statehood Partido Nuevo Progresista (PNP), who married into the Ramírez de Arellano family. That party won the elections of 1968 and Ferré became Governor of Puerto Rico (1968-72). Similarly, in 1953, Joe Ferré and other members of his family purchased the American Stock Exchange-listed Maule Industries Inc. It soon became Florida's largest rock and concrete company, importing bulk cement by ship from Puerto Rico to serve the post-war building boom in Miami. The Ferré family lost ownership of Maule Industries when the collapse of Florida's building boom led to its bankruptcy. Again, Ferré, like so many others, also bought many properties on Brickell Avenue, the DuPont Plaza building and other downtown properties. Not since the days of Cuba's Manuel Alemán had any outsider bought so much property in Miami-Dade. The Ferré purchases included 1,500 acres along Flagler Street, all now a residential development known as Fontainebleau Park.

The Ferré family became arguably the first major Hispanic "anchor" family in Miami-Dade, evidence of which was that in 1966 Maurice A. Ferré was the first Hispanic from Miami elected to the Florida House of Representatives and in 1967 the first Hispanic Commissioner of the City of Miami. In 1973 he was elected as the first Hispanic Mayor of Miami and was re-elected five more times. He held that office until 1985, presiding creditably over the difficult years of the Mariel boat lift, Haitian migration, and race riots.

The Puerto Rican aristocrats also bought prime residential properties, once the homes of the Anglo elite. Interesting but hardly surprising is that while their working-class compatriots were living in slums and being kept under strict vigilance by the authorities, these Puerto Ricans grandees were taking over the Anglo elite's mansions and breaking down the barriers against Hispanics in Miami's most exclusive clubs. Again, in this they facilitated the acceptance of the white Cuban bourgeoisie who arrived later as refugees. While all this was going on in Miami, back in Cuba the sugar elite were doing very well economically, staying out of the island's politics and understandably little interested in migrating. One of the few Cuban sugar barons to leave Cuba and join the Puerto Rican group in Miami was Billy Sánchez. An illustration of the modest but still existent rate of social mobility in the new city is how so many of the grand properties in the very narrow and exclusive sectors of Miami circulated among each group of rich individuals next to arrive. Even more modest was the entry into the Anglo-dominated social clubs. The Puerto Ricans were the first to gain access.

A few examples of the Puerto Rican social *adelantado* or path-breakers will suffice. Pete Serrallés joined the exclusive La Gorce County Club and, along with Al Roig, also joined the then super-segregated Riviera Country Club. Following the example of their fellow Puerto Ricans, the Ferré brothers joined the Surf Club, the La Gorce Country Club, and later what was arguably the most racially and class restricted club of all, the Bath Club on Miami Beach. Jacobo Cabasa joined the "Miami old families" in the Biscayne Yacht Club. Billy Sánchez, like his Puerto Rican cohorts, was a member of both the Surf Club and Miami Beach's most exclusive club, the Indian Creek Country Club. In 1952 José A. Ferré (Joe) purchased Dr. James M. Jackson's house at 1627 Brickell Avenue. Dr. Jackson had founded what is now Jackson Memorial Hospital, Florida's largest public/private hospital. Jacobo Cabasa bought a mansion on Brickell (now Villa Regina). Al Roig had purchased one of the Addison Mizner-inspired houses, close to James Deering's Vizcaya, which is now one of Miami's landmark properties and a museum of Italian Renaissance art. Roig's house was later purchased by the CEO of Miami's First National Bank and also of National Airlines, who then sold it to the new star of stage and TV, Madonna.

Despite, or perhaps because of, the Puerto Rican upper classes' heavy investments and ready access to the Anglo elite social life, they had minimal wider cultural impact. Miami remained very much an Anglo city. Throughout the 1950s, for instance, there was only one "Spanish" restaurant, El Minerva, and that was Cuban-owned. Other than the Top o' the Columbus there was only one Latin night club, El Toreador. Quite evidently, the upper-class Puerto Ricans arrived before the large Cuban migration had started. Once again, Miami was being affected by changes in the Caribbean. Because the US felt threatened by the Cuban revolution, it became more involved in Puerto Rican development. As the Cuban upper and middle class fled to Miami, the Puerto Rican upper class returned to a now much more prosperous island. The reforms they had fled from had paid real dividends. The reforms the Cubans fled from did not, and still have not. Miami had served as the safe haven in both cases.

THE HAITIAN EXODUS

How very different was the arrival and settlement of another island people who, similar to the Puerto Rican working class, represented the other, most deprived pole of the Haitian social structure. This group arrived dispossessed and, at least at first, had additional strikes against it in Miami. The Haitian bourgeoisie had a long history of receiving US "Green Cards" or alien resident visas, which meant that they had sponsors already in the US or sufficient funds to start with. The Immigration and Naturalization Service (INS) calculates that between 1968 and 1980, 72,000 such visas were issued to Haitians. No information on the number of exile admissions is available. These well-off Haitians tended to migrate to New York, where there was less race prejudice and where a significant Haitian community had developed. In Miami they had the capabilities to settle where ever their finances and the area's notorious racial proclivities allowed. The working class was not so fortunate. They came from a country governed since independence in 1804 by a repressive, corrupt, and obscurantist political elite which if anything benefitted from their flight. The abusive nature of the society from which they took flight, dominated since the late 1950s by the Duvalier dictatorship, is aptly summed up by the celebrated Edwidge Danticat in her 1991 book of vignettes, *Krik? Krak!*: "In Haiti when you get hit by a car, the owner of the car get out and kicks you for getting blood on his bumper." Danticat now lives in Miami and her many admirers await a book from her on that part of the diaspora.

Both the Puerto Rican and the Haitian migrations arrived as important parts of Miami were "Cubanizing" and the incomers had to settle in black areas where they were not exactly welcome. Would any native community, economically depressed and socially segregated, welcome a large number of equally dispossessed people?

Newly arriving Cubans had a large enclave, an established community in Miami's Little Havana and in Hialeah, from which to seek assistance, albeit often hesitatingly given. Haitians had no such "turfs" and consequently they tended to cluster in what had slowly become known as "Little Haiti" in the northeast quadrant of the city's largely African-American community of Edison-Little River. So small was the number of established Haitians in the early to mid-1970s that a significant demographic study by three sociologists mentions Cubans, Puerto Ricans, even Mexicans, but not Haitians. Haitians were counted in as part of the black community. Spatially that might have made sense but not culturally. From the very beginning, the Haitians had a distinct sense of group identity, perhaps even stronger than that of the Cuban migrants. To understand how these Haitians have managed to settle and prosper in one generation, one has to understand several things about that migration. First, the Haitian migration was never of one type. As with the Cubans, geography facilitated the movement of Haitians from their island. They headed west across Cuba and up the Bahamas chain. In 1979 Dawn Marshall in a major study entitled "The Haitian Problem" described a situation in the Bahamas where the authorities had been deporting on average 1,332 Haitians each year between 1957 and 1970. Even so, she calculated that there were 40,000 Haitians in the Bahamas in 1974. This represented approximately 20 percent of the total Bahamian population of 170,000 in 1970. Since they were largely concentrated in the capital Nassau, Haitians represented approximately 40 percent of that city's population of 100,000. They did the hard physical labor, especially in agriculture, fisheries, and construction, building the hotels and casinos then so much in demand. Upon each drop in construction work or in tourist arrivals, pressure was exerted on the government to deport the Haitians. Once again, Miami was a safe-haven. This group, then, can be considered to be the origin of the "Haitian refugee" population of Miami which by 1977 had already become the "established" refugee community. Secondly, since only 35 percent of this pre-1980 community appeared to have come directly from Haiti, the Bahamian origin of the majority explains why the majority of the youth spoke English and did well in school. Third, because of black American hostility and their own sense of identity, they did not wish to—or could not—stay in black-settled Liberty City, Overtown, or largely Cuban Allapattah. Haitians began to move into those sections of formerly white working-class neighborhoods such as Lemon City and Little River, occupying houses being vacated by the departing whites. These are the areas now called Little Haiti. Finally, and crucially, the Haitian communities' sense of identity and determination to make it were reinforced by having to confront a truly malignant campaign of stereotyping and labeling which no other immigrant or refugee group had ever faced: the perception that they were collectively diseased. Marvin Dunn outlines the broader context of this widespread stereotype that Haitians exposed Americans to a number of communicable diseases:

> During the period of greatest influx at the end of the 1970s, a hysterical scare swept through south Florida that tuberculosis was endemic among Haitians and was likely to spread through the general population. Those businesses most likely to employ low-skilled Haitians, the hotels and restaurants, were the most concerned that their employees might harbor a communicable disease.

The 1980s were years in which the hysteria of HIV-AIDS was defined in terms of the "3-Hs": hemophiliacs, homosexuals, and Haitians. Unjustified prejudice handicapped all three groups, but the Haitians were the most vulnerable. Dunn also reports how Haitian students were subjected to verbal abuse and ridicule from their African-American peers at Little Haiti's Miami Edison Senior High School. "Such views," he says, "were expressed by black as well as white established residents." It is fair to say that of all groups migrating to Miami, the Haitian poor had the steepest hill to climb. This makes the strides they have made all the more remarkable.

The community still faced the legal hurdle. The issue of whether the Haitians who had been arriving in South Florida in relatively small numbers since 1972 were political rather than economic refugees has always been a complex issue given present national and international interpretations of what being a refugee means. Is the humble man or woman who is hit by a car, the driver of which gets out to kick him or her, and that injured person has nowhere to turn for compensation or retribution, not a potential political as well as an economic refugee?

The first step in legalizing the Haitian community and putting them on the path followed by other immigrants took place on February 15, 1977. That is the date when one of the truly grand figures to act on the Miami scene, Federal District Judge James L. King, ordered that Haitians—who up to that point were being incarcerated prior to deportation—should be allowed to resubmit requests for asylum. The court also decided that while that process was taking place, those Haitians who had local sponsorship could secure temporary work permits. Additionally, the court ordered a full investigation into the matter of the "refugee" claims of the Haitians and promised a definitive decision in 1980. How was Judge King to know that in mid-1980 15,000 Haitian "boat-people" were to arrive more or less simultaneously with 125,000 Cubans coming from Mariel, Cuba? Judge King had to render his decision in the midst of a genuine "immigration" crisis. His decision came on July 2, 1980, after the March 17 signing of the Federal Refugee Act of 1980 which redefined "refugee" as any person who had a "well-founded fear of persecution" if returned to his country. This led to the federal government's decision to provide both Haitian and Cuban boat-people who had arrived prior to June 19, 1980 with a new status: "entrant."

The path now appeared clear for a full push for "refugee" status for virtually all Haitians arriving in the United States. By 1980 a group called the Haitian Coalition had taken a significant step in that direction when the Congressional Black Caucus openly supported its cause. A clue as to the direction that defense would take came when Representative Shirley Chisholm of Texas pushed the issue beyond the theme of political repression in Haiti to "racist" treatment of Haitians as compared to Cubans. The Haitians deserved "refugee" status, she maintained, because in Haiti "you cannot separate the economic factors from socio-political factors. They are all interconnected." Judge King had already concluded that Haitian economics was a function of Haitian (and specifically Duvalierist) politics; as a consequence, "their economic situation is a political condition."

It was important for the Haitians arriving in 1980 that the Miami Catholic community had already been activated by the arrival of the

Cubans. Although the direct contribution of Miami's Catholics to the Haitians was small, the Church's local influence was enormous. Much of this can be attributed to the efforts of one of Miami's grand figures, Msgr. Bryan O. Walsh, director of Catholic Charities of the Archdiocese of Miami. Walsh was an indefatigable and persuasive advocate of an open policy toward Cuban and Haitian refugees and exercised a decisive influence on the legal proceedings in Judge King's court. He would be quoted at length by Judge King in his decision of 1980. Msgr. Walsh saw to it that the Church's charities included the Haitians, a fact especially important for the Haitian "entrant." Not only were the new Haitian arrivals the poorest in Miami-Dade County, but these new arrivals, some bereft of education, deficient in English, and quite out-of-their-league when competing with the also "entrant" Cubans, were very hesitant to apply for federal and state welfare benefits. Philip Kretsedemas found that fully a decade after 1980, only 5 percent of the Haitians applied for social welfare benefits even though 80 percent were eligible. These Haitian boat-people would have to make it very much on their own… and it is one of the important stories of Miami-Dade and Broward Counties that most of them did in fact make it. Evidence of this success was that they began to move out of the ghetto and out of Miami's city center as their economic situation improved.

Other ethnic groups had made similar moves. Haitians, however, had moved out of Miami-Dade County. According to the 2000 Census, the 63,000 Haitians who moved to Broward County, just north of Miami-Dade, had a median household income of $31,041 compared to $27,284 for those who remained in Miami-Dade. An even more impressive sign that there was an incipient Haitian middle class was that the 5,000 who live in Miramar, Broward County, had a median household income of $43,128. Much of this progress was due to their own efforts to grasp the greater employment opportunities in Broward, but also because Haitians had learned from the Cubans how to lobby, how to use the racial and ethnic card. The Haitians had not waited long to take a page from the Cuban book, just as the Cubans had borrowed a page from the Mexican-Americans, who in turn had done little different from the Irish, Jews, or Italians before them. The demonstration effect of the route to success tends to spread rapidly. By mid-1980 the whole question of refugee status, as defined by national and international law, was being articulated in terms of generalized ethnic bargaining and lobbying. Some of the negative effects of this debate were felt in the Miami-Dade area where the racial situation, unsettled since the inception of the city, was now turning ugly.

RIOTS AND RESENTMENT

An atmosphere of racial defiance was heavy over Miami-Dade in 1980. It was not only Cubans and Haitians who were in the courts and the streets; 10,000 Nicaraguans were now organized and marching, thousands of Salvadorians, growing groups of Guyanese, Jamaicans, Guatemalans, and many other nationalities appeared to be waiting in the wings. The claim to refugee status appeared to have become a popular pitch of ethnic lobbies, some legitimate and some not, but all equally impassioned. Lost in the ebullient mood of "victory" following Judge King's decision was his warning that "it would certainly be inappropriate to conclude that all poor Haitians are entitled to political asylum. Virtually the entire country could make such a claim."

Main commercial street in Colored Town, now Overtown, c. 1920

By the late 1970s, even before 1980, two groups were reacting negatively to the large influx of refugees: Anglos, who began to move out, and American blacks, who had no alternative but to stay put. Both seemed to agree that the changes they would like to see made in immigration policy—greater restriction—could not be accomplished quietly either in Congress or the Executive Branch because of what they considered the vociferous and well-organized ethnic lobbies for continued and expanded immigration. Some form of countervailing force began to emerge. There was no agreement on what the agenda of that force should or could be— at least none that was articulated—but it was patently evident that by the beginning of 1980 an explosive racial atmosphere was coming to a head in Miami-Dade, centered largely in the frustrations of the native black community. While the issues of Cuban and Haitian settlements (and the federal assistance they received) were definitely contributors to the fermenting anger in the black community, it would be to ignore the wider historical context to argue that that was the main source of black discontent. Be that as it may, the explosion which eventually took place defined Miami's image and reputation from the 1960s to the 1980s.

Few in Miami remember that black Overtown, sitting on the northwest of Miami, used to be a vibrant Afro-American community with many decent family residences as well as swanky nightclubs and restaurants catering to blacks and whites alike. Renowned blues and jazz musicians made it a must-stop and aficionados of all races attended the sessions of the various authentically black musical traditions. Visiting entertainers included Count Basie, Ella Fitzgerald, Josephine Baker, Billie Holiday, and Nat King Cole. The Lyric Theater—now a historical marker—hosted vaudeville shows and showed silent movies nightly. There were newspapers, grocery stores, even a small hospital. All this changed dramatically when the City of Miami broke ground in 1965 for the extension of the north-south expressway, now Interstate 95. Predictably, it was the only community through which the planned expressway could be run without a major outcry. Virtually overnight Overtown ceased being grand. That highway cut the black community off from the rest of Miami, and—it has to be said—Overtown has never recovered from this isolation and resulting poverty. The Dade County Community Development Program's *Profile of Metropolitan Dade County* (October 1972) noted that the clearance of over 4,000 units, residential and business, to accommodate the I-

95 Expressway, was "the primary contributor to overcrowding in the downtown area." With the removal of the units, few moderate-cost housing units were then built to accommodate the need.

The story of black Miami, which includes much of today's Haitian Miami, has to be told in racial, but also demographic terms. According to the already mentioned *Profile of Metropolitan Dade County*, in the 1960s Dade County's population increased by 36 percent but its new areas of developed land increased by only 19 percent. Increasing population density was the result. The barriers to further land expansion were, and are, set by the Atlantic Ocean, Biscayne Bay, and the Everglades National Park. Expansion tended to occur by draining and filling lowlands, which explains the enormous number of man-made lakes (more like ponds, really) that dot the landscape and are so visible to anyone arriving in Miami by plane.

What is fundamental to any understanding of contemporary Miami-Dade, therefore, is to trace the expansion of new settlements and ask: did Miami's blacks have the opportunity to settle in these new areas? Even a brief historical review of Miami-Dade's urban growth answers that question. Except for small areas north of Miami International Airport (MIA), the answer is in the negative and the fundamental reason was racial, i.e. enforced segregation and ghettoization. Contributing to this problem was the bias of a real estate industry which derived benefits from keeping communities racially homogenous and thereby "defending" property values. The Dade County *Profile* termed it "historical racism." Both the official authorities and the Ku Klux Klan saw to maintaining the bias during the Jim Crow years, and the generalized poverty of the black population reinforced the trend after that. To appreciate how black Miami became "corralled" one has to recall that between 1960 and 1970 Miami-Dade expanded in three main directions. The largest area of development was along the Palmetto Expressway (SR-826), opened in 1960. This connected with the Airport Expressway (SR-836), giving this western area access to MIA as well as to downtown Miami. South of MIA, prime industrial sites as well as single family residential areas were heavily Cuban, as was Hialeah which developed northeast of the airport. Residential areas such as Hialeah Gardens are nearly totally Cuban. Neat rows of modest houses with well-kept gardens of mango and avocado fruit trees and wrought-iron secured windows and doors all present a sense of permanence and comfort. Another large area of development which is nearly all Cuban is the southwest section bordered by Tamiami Trail (SW 8th Street/US Hwy 41), the famous Cuban Calle Ocho stretching westward, Bird Road (SW 40th Street), and North Kendall Drive. Later, a six-lane artery brought about a significant suburban development popularly known as "the Kendall Area." This is fundamentally a white middle-class Anglo and Cuban expansion containing two of the county's largest shopping malls, Dadeland Mall and the Mall of the Americas which, Lisandro Perez reminds me, is also known as the "Mall of No Americans." In the 1990s the Metrorail connected Dadeland with downtown Miami and by 2012 it extended to Hialeah and then was linked by the MetroMover to MIA.

In south Dade expansion took place primarily along US 1 (South Dixie Highway), moving east along Old Cutler Road towards the Bay. Many new upscale gated communities with access to the Bay sprang up in that area. There residence was, and is, determined by wealth not ethnicity. How different the area north of MIA and further east of Hialeah where one comes upon the nearly totally black and officially labeled "poverty areas" of Model City, West Little River, and further north, Opa-Locka. This, therefore, is the story of how a proud neighborhood called Overtown, or even less benignly Colored Town, went from being a lively, culturally vibrant community to being known informally and formally as a "slum." The latter is how it is referred to in a study of the City of Miami Community Renewal Program Technical Report of 1965.

The definition of "slum" used was one then-popular in the academic literature, much of it driven by federal legislation such as the Federal Housing Act of 1949 aimed at the prevention of "slums and blighted areas." The slum, wrote urbanologist Professor C. J. Stokes, "is the home of the poor and the stranger." Within the slum, says Stokes, are those who one might logically expect to "break out" and be socially mobile but they are blocked by social barriers of various sorts. Unfortunately, much of the literature did not pursue what the nature of these barriers was and focused instead on the persistent behavior of the poor—what one urbanologist called "lower class culture." This notion became virtually axiomatic in the theory of "the culture of poverty," thought to be a cultural milieu characterized by fatalism, resignation, and idleness, all antithetical to personal advancement. Poverty is in these terms a "trap" passed from generation to generation, especially where there is a predominance of families headed by single women.

Simultaneously, according to the Dade County study, the construction of luxury condominiums further contributed to the overcrowding of black areas in central Miami and "[was] a case of going from bad to worse." Overcrowding then spread to Opa-Locka and Edison-Little River where 86 percent of black families lived in poverty areas. The median family income was half that of white families and $3,000 below that of Hispanics. Infant mortality in the black community was double the rate in the white community, and while the median age of death of white males in Miami-Dade County was 70.2 years, for black males it was a shocking and shameful 51.9 years. Also shocking was that 22.3 percent of black deaths resulted from violence and accidents, while the figure for whites was 8.4 percent. (And 96.5 percent of these blacks were US citizens.) The dramatic upshot of all this city planning and general expansion was that the majority of black Americans in Miami were worse off than when they were stuck in more or less the same area in 1896: west of the tracks of Henry Flagler's railroad. The best they could do later was to move north of Miami International Airport.

Should anyone be surprised by the explosion which came in August 1968? The riots in the grossly misnamed ghetto, Liberty City, had an element of "copy cat" dynamics to them. That year there had been black rioting in Washington, D.C.; Baltimore; Chicago; and Kansas City in April and in Louisville, Kentucky in May. The 1968 Miami Riot also coincided with the strife surrounding the Republican National Convention being held in Miami Beach. The year 1968 was a year of rage, whether it was by blacks or white students protesting the war in Vietnam. That said, there was no concealing the anger that had been building up in Miami's ghetto. Eric G. Tscheschlok's 1995 thesis at Florida Atlantic University (FAU), "Long Road to Rebellion: Miami's Liberty City Riot of 1968," spells out the black community's grievances very clearly: slum-like housing, unemployment, resentment at the privileges they perceived Cubans were given, and, critically, terrible relations with the Miami police. The majority of the new members of this police force had been hastily recruited from whites of South Georgia and was hardly sympathetic to minority feelings. According to Paul Eddy, Hugo Sabogal, and Sara Walden in *The Cocaine Wars* (1988), then-Mayor Maurice Ferré described them as people who "don't like Jews,… don't like foreigners, and they don't like blacks." Among moderates in Miami they had a reputation of being brutal and were called "headknockers" in much of the press.

It is true that the 1968 riot can be interpreted as part of the nation-wide sense of rebellion, but the spark was local, as Marvin Dunn explains. A seventeen-year old black was arrested for carrying a knife. Two police officers decided to teach him a lesson by tying him and hanging him naked by his heels from a bridge over the Miami river. The rioting which followed was only controlled when the governor called out the National Guard. Order was restored but the anger remained and exploded again in 1970 over a trivial incident at a food store which became known as the "Rotten Meat Riot." Once again, police managed to contain the rioting to Liberty City. Between 1970 and 1979 there were thirteen outbreaks in the colored ghettos.

In early May 1980 the *Miami Herald* conducted a major survey of attitudes toward the new Cuban and Haitian refugees. What problems did each group contribute to the area? The data indicated that there was hardly a difference between the way Cuban and Haitian refugees were perceived to affect the community, tending to refute the theme propagated by pro-Haitian lobbies that opponents were invariably racist. In fact, black Miami-Dade residents appeared to be equally, if not more, intolerant of refugees (Haitian as well as Cuban) than non-Latin whites and certainly more so than Latins. But even the Latins appeared worried about jobs, housing, and schools. This empirical data on interethnic tensions was corroborated by the concerns expressed by community leaders. "We have more ethnic polarity at this point than at any other," said Merritt Stierheim, Dade County Manager. Marvin Dunn put it in even stronger terms: "We are in for a very intense period of interethnic and intercultural conflict. People are going to stop [just] feeling about this thing. They are going to start acting." Dunn then predicted more public outcries from American whites and blacks against Cuban refugees. As the data show, non-Latin whites and blacks seemed most worried about there being "enough" blacks and Latins, but remarkably, fully 41 percent of the Latins also felt that there were "enough" Latins. It is noteworthy that the results of this survey were published just *one week* before the outbreak of the most destructive race riots in Florida history, riots which took eighteen lives and destroyed $200 million of property in Miami-Dade County. That riot is best explained by Marvin Dunn in his important book, *Black Miami in the Twentieth Century* (1997). We draw heavily from it here.

In 1979, after a police chase, a black motorcyclist, Arthur McDuffie, surrendered and then was beaten to death by four Miami policemen. The four were initially indicted on a manslaughter charge but, given that the presiding judge believed that black Miami was "a time bomb" ready to explode, the trial was moved to Tampa in 1980. After less than three hours of deliberation, the all male, all white jury acquitted the accused policemen. The very next day, under pressure from the Miami Fraternal Order of Police, the city reinstated all four policemen to their posts. All hell then broke loose in the black ghettos of Overtown, Liberty City, and Brownsville—and in the black neighborhoods of Coconut Grove. Despite the calls of the popular governor Bob Graham for calm, rioting, looting, burning, and much sniping continued. Even with over 3,000 National Guardsmen deployed, rioting continued for three days, taking fifteen lives and wounding 165 people. It was one of the deadliest and most destructive riots in the riot-prone history of the United States.

It is not that there were no warnings that Miami's black community was boiling over with anger. The only black-owned newspaper, the *Miami Times*, had been warning that the mood was worse than it had been before the 1968 riots in the city. Predictably, as in the rest of the country, black anger was directed against the largely white, but increasingly Cuban, police force. The Bahamian-born publisher of the *Miami Times* was adamant: "You are not going to have any real peace in this town as long as black people feel Hispanic officers have hunters' rights on their lives." The fact that only one of the four police involved was Cuban says a great deal about the selective focusing on Cubans, the group towards which most of the black anger was directed. After the riots, in a full-page editorial, the *Miami Herald* (3 November 1980) confessed that "Miami is sick." The editorial claimed that the riot, which left Miami "disoriented, in agony, and in danger of destroying itself was borne by fire and water"—fire in the black ghettos and water because the 125,000 *Marielitos* and the 18,000 Haitians had arrived by boat.

But the editorial admitted that the *Marielitos'* presence might have been a straw man, their contribution to black resentment very much secondary to the fact that black Miamians had never been more than "pawns in the hard-nosed [white] game of prosperity" and to the truth that "the fundamental causes of Blacks' seething discontent had barely been addressed since the riots of 1968." *Time* (2 June 1980) acknowledged that not a central city in the US existed where the mood of the black community was not the same as in Miami, and then noted what it called the "uneasy fact" that the Justice Department had received more complaints of police abuses from such cities as Philadelphia, Houston, and Memphis than it had from Miami. What, then, made Miami different? *Time* had an answer: "its huge Cuban population." But *Time* equivocated, asking whether Cubans had indeed taken housing and jobs from blacks or whether they merely represented "just a handy current issue." In other words, was Miami not an ethnically and racially segregated and unsettled city before the Cubans arrived?

The 2000 Census showed that US blacks had a higher rate of high school graduation (64 percent) than Cubans (61 percent), Nicaraguans (58 percent), and certainly greater than Haitians (47 percent). Haitians held the lowest paying jobs in the county, yet their median household income was just a bit lower than the $28,617 of US blacks. The reason for this is that while the Haitians and Cubans had households with several wage earners, the working-class US black household tends to be run by a single wage-earning mother. The latter is often held back by poor education, but she is also discriminated against on three other grounds—race, gender, and the general constraints of the "slums" created by historical racism.

Though no direct causal relationship has been established (nor indeed is implied here) between virtual uncontrolled in-migration and the actual violence, there is no way to avoid concluding that the influx of refugees had contributed to the general malaise in society. One month after the riots the *Miami Herald* conducted another poll, this time of 444 Miami-Dade County blacks. One question sought their response to the statement: "A lot has been said about Cuban and Haitian refugees, and the effects these people may have on the Black community." Four percent felt that the established Cuban community had "helped Black chances," 85 percent felt that it had "hurt" those chances; 2 percent felt the new (Mariel) refugees helped, 87 percent that they had hurt black chances. In the case of Haitian refugees, only 3 percent of the American blacks felt that either the established or the new refugees had helped, while 47 percent felt that they had hurt these chances, and 40 percent perceived no particular effect. In the black community, where the lack of jobs and housing along with bad police-community relations were perceived as the main social problems, massive new arrivals, no matter what race, would hardly be welcome. According to the *Miami Herald*, blacks ask a logical question: why provide all this assistance to "entrants" when the settled domestic community is hurting?

The situation four months after Mariel was described quite accurately by Florida Senator Stone when he noted, "It's hard to overstate the social upheaval and backlash that have developed [in Dade County] over this problem." In April, just five months earlier, Stone had signed Andrew Young's letter to President Carter requesting asylum for Haitians. By November the entry of Haitians had become a flood, and the issue was on the voter's mind. Stone was feeling the pressure.

The fact is that in a plural, multiethnic society and in an era of ethnic revitalization there is no single policy that will receive a general approval and acceptance from all the established groups, and less and less from established immigrant groups. Attempts to placate specific group grievances by opportunistically amending general policy and law can only lead to further pressures and conflict. Exceptions to the rule of law, as distinct from fundamental changes of that law, tend to engender less regard for the law and more searches for successful ways to breach it. Miami-Dade County is a striking example of that fact. It stands as a case study of the costs to community bonds and harmony, of the virtually unrestricted bargaining and lobbying along purely ethnic lines seeking exceptions; in other words, privileges. There can be no substitute for comprehensive federally-mandated reform of immigration laws which attempt to do justice to all claimants.

By the mid-1980s it was unclear what the future held for Miami. Urban segregation and, very specifically, the fate of black Miami represented major unfinished agendas of the city. Were more race riots likely to occur in the future? The drug trade seemed unstoppable and had unleashed a violent crime wave on the citizens of Miami which added to the rash of murders, robberies, and assaults committed in many cases by some of the *Marielitos*. Was the much heralded "City of the Future" ever so out of control? Was it any surprise that *Time* and a whole generation of crime novels began to speak of "paradise lost?"

While the media and novelists were likening Miami to Casablanca for its aura of intrigue and its drug-trade, other groups kept demonstrating that the city was very much a part of an America where opportunity was the operational dynamic. Haitians, arguably the most uprooted and even most despised of all migrants, were concentrating in North Miami and would soon make their presence known. Witnessing their extraordinary rise, economically and politically, a white North Miami Councilman exclaimed, "Ah Oh! They're here." Indeed, they were. It was the newest addition to Miami's potpourri of ethnic enclaves or turfs. The legendary Haitian artistic acuity with painting and sculpture was in incipient stages, but showing real potential, as we will describe later.

If Little Haiti was prospering in the midst of all the turmoil, so was Little San Juan—Puerto Rican Wynwood—north of downtown Miami. Also known, as in New York, as *El Barrio*, working-class Puerto Ricans began settling there in the 1950s and others migrated from the island and from the northeast. They created a vibrant community, but from the mid 1990s large numbers began to migrate to the Orlando area. According to the 2010 Census, Orlando is now second only to New York in terms of Puerto Rican inhabitants. Again, as we noted above, Wynwood was by now quickly gentrifying into a dynamic art and fashion district. The black communities, stripped of virtually all the artistic and cultural riches which once made it a vibrant, albeit segregated, neighborhood, seemed stuck and angry.

"House of Lies"

It was this general state of constant ethnic anger, punctuated by destructive rioting, which prompted the white elite into action. Two men in particular became the powerbrokers of the community: Alvah Chapman, publisher of the *Miami Herald* and chairman of its parent company Knight Ridder, and Harry Hood Bassett, CEO of Miami's largest bank, Southeast Bank. They created the "Non-Group." With a membership believed to have never exceeded forty, the identity of the members was kept secret and they declined to show their hand in politically obvious ways, making it difficult to research this group. More open was the agenda of another creation of the Anglo elite, the Beacon Council, specifically charged with promoting Miami as a place to establish corporate headquarters. They succeeded beyond what anyone who experienced the violent 1980s would have expected: headquarters of dozens of multinational corporations and over seventy branches of banks authorized to engage in international transactions were established. Coral Gables became their favorite location. At least at that level it all spoke well for the Anglo elite who were the ones who still ran Miami.

At this time and with the exception of Bacardí, Cuban Miami had not yet produced any business with over $200 million in annual revenue. Much of the Cuban leadership was still largely concerned with returning victorious to Cuba. This explains why one of the most prominent leaders of that community, Jorge Más Canosa, created much publicity about hiring conservative economist Milton Friedman to design a master plan for the role of the exile community in a post-Castro Cuba. Apparently Friedman never produced any such plan but, as Latins say, the intention was there. The younger Cuban generation had other, more local, plans.

Earning its credentials as an investigative newspaper, the *Miami Herald* ran a series entitled "House of Lies." It was not just that a small circle of developers benefitted enormously from the corruption in City Hall, but it was especially sad that the funds they were stealing were meant to build housing in the black community. The body assigned to that task was the Miami-Dade Housing Agency. It had a budget of $270 million and 700 employees. As one of the "House of Lies" columns stated, speaking of the well-funded HOPE VI Program of building for the needy, millions were spent while "hundreds of public housing units stood wrecked and empty [as] thousands of families waited for a decent place to live."

Unfortunately, it is such activity which engenders a city's reputation and, as we see next, provides ample material for the novelists of the sleazy side of the city. Every ethnic group had its tragic story to tell. Certainly this was a phase of Miami's history when many a white official was indicted. Such a case was that of former Miami City Manager Donald Warshaw, who shamelessly stole from a children's charity. Nothing seemed to be off-limits to those cold and greedy hearts.

Few sections of Miami suffered more from corrupt leadership, however, than the black community; precisely the community in Miami-Dade which desperately needed great leadership. In September 1996 the US Attorney and the FBI in a sting called "Operation Greenpalm" indicted two of the most prominent elected black officials and the past City Manager on bribery charges. Most shocking of all, however, was the fall of Dr. Johnny L. Jones, first black Superintendent of Schools. Miami-Dade County schools were not desegregated until 1960, and Jones had risen steadily until in 1977 he was voted Superintendent of Dade County Public

Schools. With that he became an influential powerbroker for the black community. The white power structure invited him to membership in virtually all the important civic associations. Tragically, two years after assuming the position of superintendent, Jones was charged with using school funds to furnish his vacation home. He was later indicted for taking bribes from textbook suppliers. It was a sad ending for him and a setback for the black community. As Marvin Dunn notes, "To many blacks, Jones's stature had reached almost messianic proportions… He was the epitome of the black fallen star."

Unfortunately, there was still one other shock to come. It could well be said that of all of the personal failures, that of Arthur E. Teele, Jr. was the most disappointing because he had been the most promising. Miami City Commissioner Teele was a rising star. In 1996 he raised $1.2 million in an unsuccessful bid for the Miami mayoralty. Secure, he felt free to hold forth repeatedly on the "racist conspiracy against black businesses" in Miami. His five-year chairmanship of the Community Redevelopment Agency was supposed to revive black businesses in the deteriorated Overtown area. Despite spending $10.6 million, not only did he do nothing of the sort, but he blocked others from doing anything. In 2005 the US Attorney charged Teele with 26 counts of mail fraud, wire fraud, and money-laundering. This followed earlier criminal charges brought by the Miami-Dade State Attorney's Office. The latter were those that caused his denouement because they were the type of allegations over which the press salivated: bribery accompanied by sleaze including male and female prostitutes, cocaine, and extortion. Hounded by the press and, in an act of desperation, on July 27, 2005, Teele entered the foyer of the *Miami Herald* building and ended his life by shooting himself in the head.

The one-hour digital film, *Miami Noir: The Arthur E. Teele Story*, is all that remains of this tragic case. Not even the purveyors of the prolific "Miami *noir*" genre of fiction have dealt with the subject. They had even more salacious plots to weave.

To be sure, there were also many honest and stalwart black politicians to celebrate: Athalie Range, the first black to serve on the Miami City Commission; Carrie Meek, the first black from Dade Country elected to the US Congress; Wilkie D. Ferguson, Jr., the first black from Dade County to serve as a federal judge; and many more. Unfortunately, the plight of a community which had been devastated by a highway system for a city growing so fast it could hardly catch its ambitious breath, needed everyone to carry their load. This did not happen.

Whether the bar was set higher for black leaders than for all others is, of course, a historically relevant question. Unfortunately it is a question for academics to ponder. Polyglot cities in a hurry such as Miami do not tend to pause for sociological analysis. Too many immigrants or refugees who once lost everything—even their countries—are now focused on not only remaking their lives but on making them better. It is a fact that once these groups achieve their goals, they produce new leaders with community-wide concerns. Alas, by the end of the twentieth century, Miami was not yet there.

Hotels on Miami Beach, 1970s: the backdrop for *Miami Vice*

Chapter Six
MIAMI VICE AND MIAMI NICE
FICTION AND REALITY

In 1953, before the Cubans and other migrants from points south arrived in large numbers, Miamian Helen Muir argued that because of its many faces the city had "no character at all... some say the faces are wicked and the world looks at these faces and says: there—that is what Miami is."

Whether she was well informed and prescient or simply placing a probable bet, she was describing how Miami would be portrayed by author after author just two decades later. The oft-repeated theme was Miami "vice" rather than Miami "nice," and even academic historians saw only the former. How to explain the "grandiosely proclaimed Magic City?" asked Florida's foremost historian, Michael Gannon. "Among the answers," he concludes, are "drug murders, home invasions, and corruption of public officials... wasted public money... choking traffic gridlock... the final paving over of paradise." In Miami, says Gannon, it is hard to untangle all the interwoven connections of criminality and intrigue because "secrecy punctuated by tall tales envelops aspect after aspect of Miami... call it Casablanca." It was not an entirely original metaphor since David Rieff had already announced in his 1985 "Letter from Miami" in *Vanity Fair* that "Miami, everyone agrees, is a modern-day Casablanca."

LITERATURE OF NOSTALGIA
This is not how it used to be. Few of the serious early local Florida writers, of fiction or otherwise, dealt with crime, at least not of the type which described virtual rivers of human blood. The concern of these pioneer writers was with the quickly disappearing nature and environment, the "paving over" of Miami and its surroundings. Important among them was Marjorie Kinnan Rawlings, who lived in the middle of Florida's woods, and who had won a Pulitzer Prize in 1938 for her book *The Yearling*. This is an enchanting story set in the 1800s, which describes the relationship between a boy and a tame fawn in the backwoods of Florida. In the words of a reviewer, it portrayed "an era of rough subsistence and sweet survival." Another reviewer wrote that Rawlings captured the yearning for a pre-im-

South bank of Miami river shown flowing into Biscayne Bay, c. 1900

migrant Florida that was rapidly disappearing. It was, said the reviewer, a "glowing picture of life that is far and refreshingly removed from modern patterns of living because universal in its revelation of simple courageous people and the abiding beliefs they live by." Indeed, it was reminiscent of the "paradise lost" complaints of those hardy individuals who settled Miami. Much later, a critic writing in the violent year of 2006 noted that *The Yearling* might seem dull because "it lacks sex, extreme violence, aliens, or *risqué* humor."

Another significant work written before the 1960s was by Rawlings' good friend, Marjory Stoneman Douglas. Her 1947 gem of ecological description, *The Everglades: River of Grass*, was an environmentalist's plea which in sparkling prose described the western one-quarter of South Florida. Not a river and certainly not a swamp as it was conventionally described, it was and is a "natural ecosystem" fed by the waters from Lake Okeechobee. It was and still is the sole source of fresh water for the Biscayne Aquifer which lies under the city of Miami and supplies fresh water for all of urban South Florida. Stoneman Douglas wanted to make sure that every aspect of this natural resource was preserved, above and below ground level. This aim was by no means assured given all the interests (described in Chapter One) that preferred to dismiss the Everglades as a mere swamp: legions of urban builders, sugar and vegetable planters, and sundry developers all wishing to encroach on it. Stoneman Douglas' passionate and incessant lobbying held them all at bay, or at least some of them. Critically, this fighter who always described herself as a "little old lady" managed to stop well-advanced plans to build a new international airport in her beloved Everglades. She lived to the ripe old age of 108 and to the end kept a hawk's eye on any backsliding on the preservation of the river of grass. In the final paragraph of her 1947 book, she warned of the Everglades becoming a victim of ignorance and raw greed: "Cattlemen's fires roared uncontrolled, cane field fires spread… Training planes dropped bombs… the sweet water the rock had held was gone…"

Thanks largely to Marjory Stoneman Douglas the Everglades National Park is now a World Heritage Site and an International Biosphere Reserve. It is one of South Florida's most treasured parks, visited by millions every year, and its continuing importance to the supply of fresh water to South Florida is incomparable.

Both Stoneman Douglas and Rawlings, each in her own way, wished to preserve the "old" Florida. Nostalgic certainly, but both authors were grand and magisterial in their capacity to inspire people to appreciate and then preserve parts of a state which were being steamrollered by the most materialistic forces of the modern age. Their efforts received great support and national attention when Rawlings' *The Yearling* was made into a movie starring Gregory Peck. It would not be the last time Hollywood would support what was grand about Florida, even as it mostly dished out grandiosity in miles of celluloid.

MIAMI *NOIR*

All of the sex, murder, and even humor missing in pre-immigrant Miami books were amply supplied by the next generation of writers on the city. Sex, murder, and black humor were the essential ingredients, the very literary core of the first school of writing of the post-immigrant generation. They can justly be called the "Miami crime" or "Miami *noir*" school. It was not an unexpected development, but the sheer volume and popularity of the genre was and continues to be amazing.

Miami's vice environment was given much ink and air time by the popular press and media so it makes literary sense that a series of "pulp fiction" works would appear. Maurice J. O'Sullivan and Stephen J. Glassman have compiled much of this literature in their anthologies, *Orange Pulp: Stories of Mayhem, Murder and Mystery* (2000) and *Crime Fiction and Film in the Sunshine State: Florida Noir* (1997). There were the descriptions of pre-immigrant Miami illustrated by the high-jinks of detective Michael Shane in Brett Halliday's two dozen crime novels. Since Halliday lived and wrote in California, Miami was just a conveniently exotic setting with the kind of reputation fiction writers could profitably draw from. This is patently the case, for instance, in his 1946 *Blood on Biscayne Bay*, a novel that reveals only a tourist's knowledge of local conditions.

Quite different, however, were the 21 novels with a philosophical-environmental bent by John D. MacDonald, who was a quintessential product of his immediate Miami environment. In his next-to-last novel, *Cinnamon Skin* (1982), MacDonald exuded nostalgia over an early Miami which would be traumatized by the crime wave brought on by the 1980 boat-people from Cuba and Haiti. To him, Miami was now a place gone sour. His protagonist, private eye Travis McGee, warns of the "exodus" of presumably decent Anglo citizens:

> Florida was second rate, flashy and cheap, tacky and noisy. The water supply was failing. The developers were moving in… pleading new economic growth… Miami was the world's murder capital… wary folks [should fear] the minority knife, the ethnic club, the bullet from the stolen gun.

It was the kind of lurid description which went a long way towards explaining what became known as "Anglo flight." Less philosophical but always showing a sharp class perspective was Charles Willeford. For Willeford, American capitalism was invariably predatory and destructive of any artistic inclination or search for the aesthetic. In what is considered his breakthrough novel, *Miami Blues* (1984)—originally entitled *Kiss your Ass Goodbye*—Willeford presents a Miami in transition towards "Latinization of the area's population." Marshall J. Fisher, in an informative piece in the

Atlantic Monthly (May 2000), calls him "the progenitor of the modern South Florida criminal novel," the writer who sparked the modern South Florida "mystery craze." Fisher quotes Mitch Kaplan, Miami's most knowledgeable literary critic (and most successful bookseller), to the effect that: "There is a direct line from Willeford through just about everyone writing crime fiction in Miami today." There have been many of them not least because the local crime scene has produced a constant stream of scare stories for Miami's citizens and, for the same reasons, more grist for the creative mills of what might be called the second generation of Miami crime writers.

Miami, as we learned from investigative journalist Hank Messick, had lived with and occasionally hosted many criminals well before it engendered the emergence of a literary school. Was it because none of these early syndicate criminals was perceived to be as violent and dangerous as those criminals who, from the 1970s onwards, provided enough mayhem and bloodshed to sustain a whole literary genre? The new criminals made Miami their killing field unlike the Mob, who tended to settle their scores in Chicago, New York, or Las Vegas. The perception was that Miami had become a much more violent place.

By the late 1970s, a new roster of Hispanic names made an appearance on the Miami scene: Pablo Escobar Gavíria, Jorge Luís Ochoa Vásquez, Carlos Lehderer, and José González Gacha. Violent to an extreme, they terrified not just Miami but the whole country. Perhaps the most sanguinary of all was Griselda Blanco, known as the "godmother" of the cocaine trade in Miami, where she actually lived. When revenge-seeking competing criminals in Medellín, Colombia put three bullets in her head in 2012, such was the lurid interest in her career that she had already sold the rights to several films and documentaries. Miamians, well accustomed to gangsters, could not recall the likes of Al Capone or Meyer Lansky ever presiding over such bloodshed, at least not in Miami. By the 1980s these Latin names were on the Most Wanted lists of every international, national, and local law enforcement agency. They were the "kings of cocaine," moving over fifty metric tons of the wildly popular white powder each year into the US, 80 percent of it through Miami. The city found itself inundated by drugs, dirty money, and criminal gangs from virtually every Caribbean island, the Jamaican "posses" (known as "Yardies" in Canada and the UK) being among the most bloodthirsty. Predictably, death—in Miami and in their native islands—always accompanied their presence. The $2 billion this criminal trade earned annually subverted police, lawyers, and politicians all along the route from Medellín, up the chain of "stepping stone" islands to Miami and the US generally. Foremost among these islands, within spitting distance of South Florida, were the newly-independent Bahamas. Formerly the playground of the Mafia that had been kicked out of Cuba and which had been refused casino building permits in Florida, this archipelago became an important transhipment point. A reader interested in even the minutest details of the continuity in criminal links between the white colonial "Bay Street Boys" and the black independence government of Lynden Pindling can do no better than to read that indefatigable investigator Hank Messick's 1969 book, *Syndicate Abroad* (1969).

Here, then, was the raw material for the pens of the new genre of writers who produced the second generation Miami crime novels. The most successful were written by working journalists of the only newspaper in town, the *Miami Herald*. This paper already had a well-deserved reputation for tough investigative journalism, earning in 1951 a Pulitzer Prize for its series on organized crime. On staff was the truly grand Gene Miller who won Pulitzers in 1967 and 1976 defending wrongly-convicted persons. The 1976 award recognized the part played by his sensational 1975 bestselling book *Invitation to a Lynching* in the final pardoning of two blacks who had sat on Death Row for twelve years accused of murders they had not committed. Under the Knight Ridder CEO Lee Hills and the editorship of John S. Knight, who won a Pulitzer himself for his hard-hitting editorial writing, the *Miami Herald* cultivated and rewarded keen and courageous investigations such as those of Hank Messick and Gene Miller. The *Herald* was well positioned, therefore, to take on the new and terrifying type of criminal who was littering both city and county with dead bodies. These new perilous times required nothing less than the best and most courageous reporting.

The public did not have to wait long for reporters to deliver. Soon two superbly researched books probing the dark corners of the world of Miami's new drug mafias were on the shelves. These were the kind of books from which the writers of fiction could draw both facts and inspiration. First in 1988 came *The Cocaine Wars,* the product of a team of mostly English journalists who spent three years in Miami. The main authors—

Paul Eddy, Hugo Sabogal (a Colombian), and Sarah Walden—were assisted by another group of investigators committed to serious research. This team produced an extremely detailed account of the complex network of criminal groups in Miami and of the law enforcement authorities which were simply overwhelmed (or in some cases co-opted) by the intractability of the problem. They rightly coined the term "cocaine wars," for not even when President Ronald Reagan sent Vice-President George W. H. Bush to Miami to set up what was essentially an interagency "war room" could the authorities get a handle on the flow of cocaine and the crime wave it engendered. As good as that book was, there certainly was a need for a great deal more. And it was not long in coming. Whatever facts were missing in the Eddy, Sabogal, and Walden book were provided a year later by two *Miami Herald* reporters, Guy Gugliotta and Jeff Leen. In their informative and frightening *Kings of Cocaine* they described most of what even the most astute investigators had not been able to uncover regarding crime and corruption in the city. The fact that they wrote in a breezy and entertaining style as they recreated many real-life dramas enlivened by corresponding dialogues gave it a fictional feel. All the major characters, national and international, are in this book: Panama's General Manuel Antonio Noriega, US embezzler and fugitive Robert Vesco, a slew of corrupt Bahamian officials, CIA-supported Contra fighters in Nicaragua, and Miami "white powder" lawyers, straight and crooked. It is a page-turner about a city under siege from the outside with a "fifth column" on the inside. Upon finishing the book, one is left with the impression that there are mighty few honest leaders in the geographical space between Medellín, Colombia and Miami, Florida. This, as we shall see, would have been a false impression. That said, it is a truism that bad news is good news for the press and also suits the crime novelist's purposes precisely.

COPS AND ROBBERS

Beyond these books, and since a picture is worth more than a thousand words, nothing introduced the dark side of Miami to the world more dramatically than the television series *Miami Vice*. From 1984 to 1989 it was broadcast in five series to more than sixty countries including France, where people were known to postpone that quasi-sacred ritual, dinner, in order to catch the program. The scenes filmed from Biscayne Bay of the skylines of Miami and Miami Beach, of "cigarette" speedboats and fancy

Miami Vice, the remake

cars speeding past palm-fringed streets bordered by palatial mansions, and of the chasing and killing of bad guys, encouraged the perception that this was all that Miami was—and is, since the series is still in re-runs around the globe. Such has been the success of this series that in 2006 a new film (*Vice*) brought it all back to life and enjoyed great box office success. There was a big difference, however. The TV series was done in pastels and filmed with Miami Beach's Art Deco hotels as background. The newer film is in dark shades, filmed in the haunts of Miami and the Miami river so as to reveal a much seedier, less romanticized version of the city. It is factual that the two central characters of the original TV program (and the later film), the white Sonny Crockett and the black Ricardo Tubbs, were modeled on two Metro-Dade undercover detectives. In the TV series they worked together but in real life the Cuban-American Luis Fernández had the white and Cuban neighborhood of West Kendall as his beat and the black Prestout Lucas worked the black neighborhood of Perrine, south of Miami. In sharp contrast to the glamorous architecture of Miami Beach, significant parts of the Perrine portrayed are a ghastly ghetto mired in poverty.

Pure fiction also underlay the gratuitous violence portrayed in the series. The *Miami Herald* reported that the real detectives never shot anybody, while in the TV series the two detectives shot no fewer than sixty people. Not that there was no violence in Miami. In 1998 Rick Navarro, Broward County's crime-fighting sheriff, wrote *The Cuban Cop*, which he thought could be one of those titillating narratives that might end up as a film or TV script but in reality reads more like a police precinct blotter. Be that as it may, very relevant is his account of taking actor Al Pacino to do "the rounds" of Miami's crime-infested areas in preparation for his role in the blockbuster film *Scarface*. Like *Miami Vice*, *Scarface* contributed to Miami's reputation as a drug-infested hellhole. In 1983 *New York Times* film critic Vincent Canby described *Scarface* as "a relentlessly bitter, satirical tale of greed, in which all supposedly decent emotions are screened for the possible ways in which they can be perverted." And there was more to come (Messick's description of Miami as essentially "amoral" comes to mind). Evidence that violence in Miami continues to sell is the remake of *Scarface* in a 2011 high-definition transfer. It is also evident in two new and very popular TV series filmed in Miami and with Miami as backdrop, *Miami-CSI* and *Burn Notice*. The plot of the latter seems to have been taken out of Miami's ongoing reality: the CIA cancels an agent's front and freezes his assets. He then spends his life in Miami attempting to discover who "burned" him and in the process unravels much of the city's underworld and its Mob bosses.

Here, then, were two books, several TV series, and a movie—and their remakes—which served as fillips and useful sources for those with less investigative experience but the literary talent and ambitions to write the great novel which they hoped would land a Hollywood contract. These novelists did not write from a safe distance: they experienced the reality and were well-acquainted with the documentation describing this cauldron of violence, human greed, and misery which had earned Miami the sobriquet "Casablanca." Naturally, as novelists as distinct from journalists they had the time and space and the freedom for imaginative creativity or poetic licence.

No one paved the way for this new genre more thoroughly than Edna Buchanan, crime reporter for the *Miami Herald*. Her determination not to leave any Miami stone unturned is best conveyed by the epigraph which introduces her 1994 book with the self-evident title, *Miami: It's Murder:* "Nothing is covered up that will not be uncovered, and nothing secret that will not become known. *Luke 12:2.*"

Her authority on the subject, she says, comes from years of investigating the Miami scene and the over five thousand violent deaths she covered for the *Miami Herald.* It all resulted in her writing eighteen books of both fiction and nonfiction. Taken together, it led one critic to describe her writing as "an endless production of crime." In her 1987 *The Corpse Had a Familiar Face,* Buchanan related how she visited Miami from Patterson, New Jersey, on a two-week vacation "and fell in love." Why? "Everything is exaggerated in Miami," she writes, "ugly is far uglier in Miami, but beautiful is breathtaking, it hooks you for life." Everything was indeed different in Miami, even the pizzas she proclaims with evident ethnic confusion and exaggeration, "probably because most of the pizza chefs were born in Havana or Port-au-Prince." "A stroll down Flagler Street," she continues, "is a journey to some exotic foreign capital, Miami *is* Casablanca."

As we have seen, this theme of Miami as Casablanca had already caught on in fiction, journalism, and in the sociological literature. Predictably, Buchanan's portrayal of Miami as a place "gone crazy" through contamination from the drug trade runs consistently and seamlessly through her fiction and nonfiction. The already-mentioned quasi-fictional *Miami: It's Murder* is typical. "Miami," she writes, "is a city tainted by the illegal drug trade and awash in its riches… Drugs are the great corrupter, and Miami's largest growth industry." How things had changed in just the few years since Hank Messick had been busy hunting for the links between the illegal numbers game *Bolita*, prostitution, and official corruption, Edna Buchanan was now chasing down an even bigger and more violent commodity: cocaine. What better theme for writers attempting to hit a rich literary vein, hoping to graduate from the sensational novel to TV or the big screen? As we shall see, many did.

Buchanan kept a keen journalist's eye on the ongoing reality, alternating investigative writing with pieces of fiction. Her first books of nonfiction, *Carr: Five Years of Rape and Murder* (1979), *The Corpse Had a Familiar Face,* and *Covering Miami, America's Hottest Beat* (1987) were followed by two novels, *Nobody Lives Forever* (1990) and *Contents under Pres-*

sure (1992). And so it went for the next thirteen novels she produced. In a recent book, *A Dark and Lonely Place* (2011), she traces criminality in Miami from the early twentieth century to 2010 and, not surprisingly, described it on her website as "a sensual and dreamy saga of love, passion, and violence." Buchanan waxes philosophical when she attempts to introduce an existential note by concluding that Miami is not, as it is so often portrayed, "paradise lost." Miami is rather "simply being itself, over and over." A tautology, no doubt, but it is also an accurate description if not of Miami, then certainly of the perceptions behind the plots of the Miami crime novel. The plots occur over and over again but no one complains for one evident reason: violence and sex in the hot and humid tropics is entertaining.

CARL HIAASEN: "AMIABLE DEPRAVITY"

No one has provided this brand of entertainment more often and in a more scintillating way than Carl Hiaasen. This son of Scandinavian immigrants has worked for the *Miami Herald* since 1976 and has excelled in conveying two of the critical strengths of that newspaper's reporting: environmental concerns *à la* Stoneman Douglas and crime investigations *à la* Messick and Buchanan. Hiaasen has brought both concerns to life in his dozen books which have reached an enormous reading audience having been translated into forty languages. His style is a blend of outlandish plots, prodigiously endowed characters, chilling terror, and black humor all delivered through a fast-paced narrative. Clearly this combination appeals to more than just Americans for the simple reason that much of the world has been historically fascinated with the crime novel and with Sherlock Holmes-like detectives. Hiaasen's first three novels were co-authored with another superb *Miami Herald* correspondent, the late Bill Montalbano. Their most popular novel was *Powder Burn* (1981), very much a thriller in the tradition of the Miami crime genre.

Hiaasen's first single-author novel, *Tourist Season* (1986), kept up the pace and the style. In just the first two pages the reader is witness to two murders, but only one of consequence: it involves Starky Harper, president of the Greater Miami Chamber of Commerce. This unfortunate grandee is found with his legs chopped off, stuffed into a fancy suitcase—and, oh yes, he had a toy rubber alligator stuck down his throat. Hiaasen then outlines all the probable culprits one would expect to find in multicultural

Miami: Haitian voodoo practitioners? Cuban murderers using *santeria* rituals? The drug mafia sending some cryptic message? Not that Hiaasen believes the victim did not deserve his horrible fate. "Starky Harper," he says, "takes the cake… the perfect mouthpiece of the hungry-eyed developers, hoteliers, bankers, and lawyers who have made South Florida what it is today: Newark with palm trees." In Hiaasen's opinion, no one except these loathsome Miami types will miss Starky's main duties: composing snazzy new bumper stickers every year, viz. "Miami: too hot to handle," "Florida is… Paradise Found," "Miami melts in your mouth!" By far the favorite, however, because Starky composed it one month after the 1980 bloody race riots which scared the city, was "Miami: The Most Exciting City in America!" And so, in novel after novel, Hiaasen reveals what he really thinks of Miami. He did so with acidic candor in a 2001 collection of his *Miami Herald* columns entitled *Paradise Screwed*. A few years later he reiterated his harsh view of Florida when he told the CBS television program *60 Minutes* on April 17, 2005: "The Sunshine State is a paradise of scandals teeming with drifters, deadbeats, and misfits drawn here by some dark primordial calling like demented trout." Then, to forcefully bring home what appears in so many of his novels, he added, "And you'd be surprised how many of them decide to run for public office."

Hiaasen was even more lyrical in his own inimitably sarcastic way when he told an NPR audience in April 2012 that Miami could be described as "amiable depravity." Of course, one has to admit that Hiaasen had much to draw upon. Scandal after scandal hit the pages of the *Miami Herald* regarding chicanery in the Port of Miami, the airport, the hospital, the school board, the building inspector's office, and, in the center of it all, various city managers. How could Hiaasen or any other proponents of Miami *noir* miss noticing that some of the corrupt showed burlesque-like flaws? This was, for instance, the case of Miami City Commissioner Humberto ("Smirkin' Bert") Hernández who was charged with falsifying and inflating loan documents to get over $8 million in property in Key Biscayne. While on trial, he called for a mistrial on the grounds that his wife was having an affair with his lawyer, José Quiñon. He never won the mistrial, and was later suspended by the governor and disbarred in 1999 for registering deceased people to vote for mayoral candidate Xavier Suarez.

Tragic was the case of Art Teele, discussed in Chapter Five. To be sure, Teele was probably not the worst offender, if the pages of the *Miami Herald* and the considerable documentation which S. L. Croucher put together in his 1997 book, *Imagining Miami: Ethnic Politics in a Postmodern World*, were correct. Miami became equated with a "banana republic" and every year up to the present the largely Anglo-run "Mango Strut" Festival in Coconut Grove has a field day poking fun at the politicians and city administrators. An irreverent group in the 1997 Mango Strut Festival did not hide its target, Miami Mayor Xavier Suarez. Hiaasen had been calling him "a babbling fruitcake… either certifiably nuts or seriously under medicated." Predictably, this Coconut Grove team, calling themselves the "X Generation," picked up the theme. Their skit carried a poster reading:

> The Miami Herald treat me mean
> It says I need Thorazine
> I'm into total domination
> This is the X (for Javier) Generation

It is a totally different Hiaasen, however, who has written three novels for children. His most successful has been *Hoot*, about a child and an owl very much in the vein of Rawlings' boy with a fawn. With this book Hiaasen scored the kind of success which the Miami crime novelist aims at: it was made into a movie, and a very successful one at that. With this accomplishment under his belt, and in the bank, Hiaasen had it made and now, living very comfortably outside Miami, he continues to write the way he always has, pointing out the grandiosely fraudulent side of Miami and of so many of its boosters.

Another who was prolific and, because she had been a prosecutor in the Florida State Attorney's office, very accurate in her crime and investigation scenes, was Barbara Parker. Her first novel, *Suspicion of Innocence* (1994), was made into a for-TV movie entitled *Sisters and other Strangers*. This first success was followed by seven other novels with "suspicion" in the title. They all revolve around two Miami lawyers dealing with the changing ethnic composition of the city and all the bizarre new realities it has brought. This is, of course, Miami seen with Anglo eyes. Parker's lawyers even get involved in an escapade in Cuba in her *Suspicion of Rage* (2005). One gets the flavor of how she perceives Miami's realities in the first three pages of her 2008 bestseller *The Dark of Day*. In these opening pages describing a soirée in a fashionable mansion, the protagonist's friend disappears, the protagonist is invited to participate in tooting cocaine, a transvestite is passed out on a couch, and she is nearly raped by two men. It all seems to be summed up in the protagonist's despairing query as to whether on South Beach, "you ever know who your friends are?"

Parker wrote very much in the style of Miami crime fiction and was on her thirteenth novel when she passed away in 2009. From the obituaries it is evident that she will be sorely missed by writers and legions of fans. And yet several others are there to keep the fires of this Miami-based genre burning, including another Florida trial lawyer turned novelist, James Grippando. In his first novel, *The Pardon*, he established the character who would appear in every one of his fifteen novels, Jack Swyteck, a criminal attorney. Grippando's plots are so outlandish that they are only saved by his racy style and intimate knowledge of the growing presence of the Russian Mafia in South Florida. Perhaps most representative of his concern with organized crime is his 2008 novel, *Born to Run*. Swyteck appears again as a criminal attorney, framed by the Mafia and on the run. His father, Harry Swyteck, twice Governor of Florida, is a close friend of the Vice President of the US. Incredible, but true to the script, in a trip to the Everglades the VP has an encounter with an alligator and the creature does not simply bite off a leg or arm as normally occurs in alligator attacks, but eats the whole man. The president then offers Harry the vice presidency, at which point, says the novelist, "the prestige that comes with the job turns lethal." He describes one character named Mika as having "the look of Miami's first generation Mafiya." The truly alarming mobster, however, is "Tarzan" who represents physically and attitudinally everything the Miami *noir* bad guy is supposed to stand for:

> ... Most feared was a guy called Tarzan, famous for his drug and sex orgies on his yacht off South Beach, until he landed in jail for trying to buy a nuclear submarine from a former Soviet naval officer. His plan was to smuggle Colombian cocaine to Miami under water.

Anyone even remotely acquainted with the drug business will wonder why Tarzan wants an easily detectable Soviet submarine for his dastardly deeds when Colombians are already using fibreglass semi-submersibles to successfully move tons of cocaine to Central America and from there to the insatiable market in the north. Nothing, it seems, is too outlandish for the

Miami *noir* writer.

One of the more promising newcomers to the genre is James W. Hall. In his 2007 mystery novel *Magic City,* his protagonist Thor has been in town for just a few hours before he finds himself and his lovely girlfriend Alexandra investigating Miami's "seamy underbelly to its glittering halls of power." Predictably, plenty of dirt is uncovered. Surely we can expect many more such to come from Hall's pen since the specter of the drug trade and the corruption it spawns is not about to disappear from the Miami scene. Proof certain of this are the novels of Les Standiford. His "John Deal" series is composed of nine novels, all written between 1993 and 2003. In 2006 he published an anthology, *Miami Noir*, which included some established novelists and many new names. The reader will have surely noticed that such novels are a Miami growth industry with many other young writers, Anglo and Cuban-American, waiting in the wings.

Among the established writers in Standiford's anthology is Cuban-American novelist Carolina García-Aguilera. Her six novels featuring private investigator Lupe Serrano deal with the conventional themes of sex, drugs, and murder, but García-Aguilera has promised to change course and develop different plots. If in the 1980s it was drugs and nothing but drugs, she told Neal Conan of National Public Radio (NPR) in July 2006, now it is Miami's financial crimes such as money laundering and fraud which grab her attention. This, she said, is what she will write about in the future: "something totally out of the mainstream of what had been done before." Easier said than done, perhaps, for her last novel—with a typical Miami *noir* plot—appeared in 2003 and up to 2012 she had not written another, certainly not one on financial crimes. It is arguably not as easy to unravel financial crimes as it is to follow the Miami *noir* script, as her main character Lupe Serrano suggests in *Havana Heat* (2000): "From my experience as an investigator, I knew that the overwhelming majority of cases boiled down to three factors: money, sex, and pride." On that score, James W. Hall comes closer to linking the constant mayhem with money laundering schemes gone wrong in his eleventh novel, *Rough Draft* (2000). But the prize for superficiality camouflaged by vulgarity has to be given to the celebrated Tom Wolfe in his *Back to Blood* (2012). "I knew so little [about Miami] but had a lot of fun," he tells an audience in Miami (*Miami Herald*, 12 November 2012), a proper confession from one whose central theme is, in his own words: "In Miami, everybody hates everybody." Thankfully, not everybody loves this potboiler; it was shortlisted for *Literary Review*'s "bad sex award" for its "crude, badly written, often perfunctory" passages of sexual description, while the *Guardian* remarked on its "quality of unusually pure bile—an enraged loathing and envy for just about everything." Beyond sex and ethnic stereotyping, there is little of redeeming value, as literature or sociology, in Wolfe's book on Miami.

BLOWBACK

Since drugs tend to engender and enhance virtually all the themes of the Miami Vice novels, both in Miami and further afield, one can well understand how tempting it must be for any novelist to keep on mining this popular terrain. And yet all of the writers discussed admit that without money—and those who facilitate the moving and laundering of that money—there would be little to write about. This makes it imperative, if the Miami *noir* genre is to expand, to explore other issues such as financial crime. To begin, and to further probe some of the historical origins of Miami as a latter-day Casablanca, two distinct but highly interrelated strands have to be pursued: the role of "blowback" from US Central Intelligence Agency (CIA) involvement, and the role of corrupt banks at home and overseas. It is there that the armies of crime writers will find new rich veins of material.

Chalmers Johnson in his book *Blowback: The Costs and Consequences of American Imperialism* (2000) notes that the term "blowback" was invented by the CIA for internal use, but is now generally used in referring to the unintended consequences of secret policies and operations. In layman's terms it means that there is often a risk that a nation will eventually reap what it sows in terms of covert activity. When a Federal Grand Jury, sitting in Jacksonville, Florida on March 22, 1989, indicted thirty people on charges of smuggling 44,000 pounds of cocaine worth $1 billion between 1974 and 1989, it was in part a case of blowback on several fronts. Hinckle and Turner explain the operation of a classical blowback: "Long ago the CIA cast its bread upon the waters of the Gulf Stream. Now it is coming back in the form of death and destruction. Every time the United States even looks benignly toward Cuba, every time an exile steps out of line, more will come back."

We have already seen how the US government turned a blind eye to the fact that, as Guy Gugliotta and Jeff Leen point out, the Bahamas had become a "nation for sale." Cold War considerations, i.e. keeping a secret missile testing base in the Bahamas and having an ally nation next to communist Cuba, allowed Prime Minister Lynden Pindling to make his own arrangements with the Medellín Cartel. At one point the Bahamian archipelago contained one sovereign nation controlled by Pindling and two quasi-sovereign criminal island enclaves: one controlled by Carlos Lehder of the Medellín Cartel and the other by Robert Vesco, a fugitive Ponzi-schemer wanted by the US government. Another blowback was represented by General Antonio Noriega of Panama; once on the CIA payroll, he soon became greedy and sought the Medellín Cartel's money through drug smuggling and money laundering. Both cases involved Miami since it became the main port of entry for the drugs now measured not in pounds but in tons, and consequently the point at which much of the dirty money was collected and then laundered. Yet the blowback which turned Miami into a killing field was the US government's (through the CIA) recruitment of Cuban-Americans to fight a secret war against Fidel Castro.

After the fiasco of the Bay of Pigs in 1961, the CIA created a very large fleet of speedboats, used to infiltrate commandos into Cuba. Located in multiple bays and canals in the Miami area, this fleet of boats was "controlled" out of a CIA station in Homestead, Florida. All such Cold War strategies and the tactics of direct attacks on Cuba came to a halt with the signing of the Kennedy-Khrushchev Treaty, which also brought to an end the missile crisis of 1962. With no war to fight, many of these Cuban commandos turned to crime, smuggling drugs and selling guns, especially to the Colombians who were only then discovering just how profitable the American market was. Well trained by the CIA, the Cubans were the first to utilize sophisticated electronic equipment to outsmart US controls, as Tom Tripodí, a CIA security officer in Homestead at the time, writes in his memoirs, *Crusade: Undercover Against the Mafia and the KGB* (1993). As Tripodí describes it, one of the more pressing problems facing the CIA was "just how to keep the not-so-secret army of Cuban exiles under control." "Now that we had also instructed them in the fine arts of smuggling," he writes, "some of them applied their newly learned expertise to drug trafficking." In addition to drugs, these commandos supplied CIA-provided guns to Miami criminals.

The trade was first in marijuana; cocaine came later. The transportation of marijuana also took advantage of another historical conjuncture involving Cuban exiles. Some 600 Cuban lobster fishermen had left Cuba, seeking exile in Miami with their boats. They made the Miami river their base and the Bahamas Banks their fishing grounds. When the Bahamas became independent in 1966, it banned these Cubans from lobster fishing in its territorial waters. Here was an additional fleet of boats, with experienced sailors now out of honest work.

It is necessary to reiterate just how rapidly the crime scene in Miami changed. Records submitted by the Metropolitan Dade County Comprehensive Drug Program for 1960–71 indicate a growing rate of drug-induced deaths in Miami-Dade County but none was related to cocaine overdoses. Heroin and a legal sedative, Seconal, accounted for most overdoses. Cocaine was a late addition to the Miami drug scene and when it appeared, it unleashed what became known as Miami's "Cocaine Cowboys' War." In the words of Gugliotta and Leen, "Miami was outgunned and overrun." Cocaine was the drug of choice among better off Miamians, while its cheaper and more lethal derivative, crack, caused devastation in

Captured marijuana bales, popularly known as "square groupers"

low-income areas. In addition, Miami was in no position to provide much assistance in the anti-drug trade effort of the federal government. According to hard-hitting pieces of investigation by the *Miami Herald*, the Miami Police Department was riddled with corruption and intrigue. The massive presence of Cuban criminals who arrived with the Mariel boatlift in 1980 put local authorities under additional strain. In the so-called "cocaine wars" Miami was the American battleground.

Soon drug trafficking led to internecine strife, some, but not all, connected to terrorist activities. Since the exiles could not kill Castro (640 abortive attempts, according to the *Guinness Book of Records*), those who were involved in crime began bombing and killing each other. "In Miami," say Warren Hinckle and William Turner in their substantive book *Deadly Secrets* (1992), "the murders continued with an almost occultist fascination for holidays." Hinckle and Turner speak of a "three year bombing and murder binge" in Miami of more than a hundred attacks, with eighty percent of the cases unsolved. The situation was the following: initially the Colombians supplied the drugs to the Cuban-Americans who supplied them, at enormous profits, to the street vendors. Wishing to take advantage of the value-added process, the Colombians sent their hit squads to Miami to remove the Cuban-Americans from the business.

Even in the midst of general criminal mayhem, one of the cases which remained unsolved for years was the murder of speedboat (the "cigarette boat," specifically) builder Don Aronow in 1987. Aronow built these go-fast boats, successors to the rum-runners, for friends as diverse as members of Meyer Lansky's mobster circle, US Vice President George H. W. Bush, the Drug Enforcement Agency (DEA), and US Customs, as well, of course, as for Cuban cocaine smugglers. It was not until mid-1990 that a career criminal with drug trade involvements was formally charged with the hit on Aronow. His defense lawyer, the indefatigable José Quiñones (already introduced), made sure that neither the motive nor the intellectual authors have ever been clarified. Despite this loss, there was some benefit derived since this was a rare case where the authorities gained some assets which leveled the playing field with the bad guys. Aronow's speed boats, including the "Blue Thunder" type, are now part of the US Customs fleet and are still playing their part for the law in the Straits of Florida.

By far the most complex area of research for any fictional plot, however, is corruption in the world of banking. Actions often fall within that grey area between legal and illegal, making judgments very difficult. And yet the importance of fraud cannot be ignored. On February 11, 1990 two *Miami Herald* writers argued that "If you want to ruin the economy of Dade County, just dry up the supply of drug money for one week." It was only a slight exaggeration. With the drug traffic of the early 1980s amounting to some $50 billion per year, $7 billion of which remained in Florida, it is clear that this trade represented by far the largest single financial connection between Miami and the Caribbean. Within this situation, the Miami banking system was the crucial link between the financier, the seller, the market, and the offshore centers and tax havens where the laundered funds were often "parked." From there they were invested in legitimate real estate and other businesses in Miami and the islands. As official after official testified over the years, banks have been an indispensable factor in this traffic. Here again there was blowback. On April 18, 1980 the *Wall Street Journal* headlined a story called "Big Tax Investigation was Quietly Scuttled by Intelligence Agency." The subject of the investigation was the Castle Bank and Trust, Ltd., based in Nassau, Bahamas, and which the *Journal* revealed was the conduit for millions of dollars provided to fund the secret operations of Cuban exiles. In no time at all CIA training, recruiting, and funding had led to the forging of powerful links between drug running, terrorism, and money laundering.

Anyone seriously interested in entering further the labyrinthine world created by the early CIA involvement might want to review the history of Cuban-born Guillermo Hernández Cartaya and his World Finance Corporation (WFC). The *Miami Herald* (22 February 1978) wondered whether, aside from having been a CIA agent, he might have been the banking agent for various Colombian drug lords. With affiliates worldwide and businesses that included the Banco Ambrosiano of the Vatican, Hernández Cartaya's story is best told by Jonathan Kwitney in his 1984 book, *Endless Enemies: The Making of an Unfriendly World*. Kwitney cites this statement in a House Select Committee on Narcotics and Drug Abuse report on WFC's criminal conduct and its contacts with the CIA: "There is no question that the parameters of the WFC can encompass a large body of criminal activity, including aspects of political corruption, gun running, as well as narcotics trafficking on an international level…"

In 1985 a special investigation by the US Senate calculated that "as many as two dozen" banks in the Miami area "are known to be or suspected of handling or seeking out narcotics money." A thorough study by an Argentine scholar of money laundering, Rodolfo Goncebate, attempted to unravel the maze of international routes and operations of the drug trade's finances and concluded that while this "complex and flexible process" showed no single *modus operandi,* it invariably did show "the instrumental mediation of financial institutions" in Miami and offshore.

Financial institutions are especially irritating to US officials because once the funds leave the United States their trail is almost impossible to follow. Indeed, it is only when a major financial collapse takes place or other dramatic event occurs that the general public gets a glimpse of the hidden but wealthy world of the drug trade's finances. The seamy side of Miami as a Caribbean city often reveals itself on those occasions. A few cases will illustrate. In 1981 a Colombian named Félix Correa Maya—who in five years had risen from running a gas station in Antioquia, Colombia, to owning 56 enterprises, including the Banco Nacional de Bogotá—bought the Bank of Perrine in Miami. He renamed it Florida International Bank and immediately offered it as security against his Colombian bank which was showing $150 million "unaccounted for." Investigations by Colombia's new government revealed that an estimated $500 million a year in drug money was laundered through his bank in Bogotá. Correa, said the US Drug Enforcement Administration, had a "trafficking association" with major cocaine dealers. The reaction of the now-jailed Correa's bank manager in Miami reflected the problem: "Officers at the Florida bank say they made no loans to Mr. Correa's group and have therefore been unaffected by his problems [in Colombia]."

No sooner was this banking crisis confronted than Colombia's most important newspaper, *El Tiempo,* exposed another laundering operation at the prestigious Banco del Estado. The president of the bank and the main shareholder, the governor of the state of Cauca, were jailed and the bank nationalized. Aside from the long list of illegalities on the Colombian side, the Miami and "international" dimensions were so complex and multifaceted that the DEA investigation findings are best cited textually.

The DEA investigation disclosed that a Mr. Mosquera had been the head of Unión de Bancos de Panamá, which had been used by the above-mentioned and now-defunct World Finance Corporation to fund its network of Latin American subsidiaries. World Finance suffered a collapse in 1973 in which investors lost $55 million. A Mr. Hernández was con-

Skyline of the Brickell financial district

victed of tax evasion in Florida and was under a Federal Grand Jury indictment in Texas for embezzlement of the Jefferson Savings and Loan Association.

For those further driven by curiosity about what had been unleashed on Miami, a look at the cases of others such as CIA recruit Miguel Recarey, businessman Ernesto Montaner, or State Senator Alberto Gutman will pay dividends. All three were involved in massive Medicare fraud which, next to drug trafficking, was a major source of illicit monies. Some "cold" cases also occasionally resurfaced to remind the city of its dark past. Such was the case of James ("Whitey") Bulger, accused of murdering James Callahan, the president of World Jai-Alai in Miami in 1982. A member of Boston's vicious Winter Hill Gang, Bulger was believed responsible for at least nineteen other murders. Bulger was on the run for sixteen years, shielded by an FBI agent, John Connoly, but was captured in Los Angeles in June 2011. In a typical Miami twist, Bulger and Connoly served as loose inspiration for the 2006 Oscar-winning film *The Departed*.

DIRTY MONEY

Shopping in Miami, meanwhile, seems to exert an irresistible attraction to people with fortunes illegally gained. Of course, it would be grossly untrue to argue that all such shopping is done with ill-gotten gains. The fact is that big and not-so-big spenders from Latin America and the Caribbean find shopping in Miami glamorous and often more reasonably priced than back home. A visit to Saw Grass Mills in Broward any day of the week will reveal throngs of Latin shoppers. Until recently they included the fabulous Venezuelans who upon hearing the price of an object would exclaim, *¡Carájo, que barato. Déme dos!* (Wow, how cheap, give me two!). Venezuelans thus became known as *Déme dos*—to the delight of merchants. Then there was Michelle Bennett, former wife of dictator Jean-Claude ("Baby Doc") Duvalier of dirt poor Haiti. Retailers in the exclusive shops of Miracle Mile in Coral Gables openly lamented the fall of Baby Doc and, by extension, the loss of Michelle's patronage. They need not have worried; there were others eager to shop and, as they say in the Caribbean, "make style."

Few stories could provide a more sensational case of illicit money making-it-big in Miami than that of Gambian (West Africa) con-man, Foutanga Dit Babani Sissoko, eventually known affectionately as "Baba." His was a case of making style on a grandiose scale. When he flew into Miami as if on a magic carpet worth millions, he became the toast of the town, its most generous and most solicited philanthropist. Not only did he donate $1.2 million to Camillus House for the homeless, he actually roamed across the city in his chauffeur-driven limousine handing out cash to the destitute. When news that the inner city school, Miami Central High, was short of funds to send its marching band to the Macy's Parade in New York City, Baba gave the school a cheque for $300,000; it made headlines and put his smiling face on the front pages. He spent untold millions in shopping sprees with any or all of his four wives in the upscale shops of Bal Harbor. His rented condominium on Brickell Key cost $80,000 a month. Hundreds of thousands of dollars were spent on fancy cars, gifts to his lawyers, and certain politicians. In short, Baba was the sensation of the moment. Subsequent investigations revealed that he had embezzled and then transferred millions from the Dubai Islamic Bank to the following banks: in Geneva, $68 million; New York, $37.2 million; and to five banks in Miami, $41.4 million. And, just to make sure he had sufficient pocket money while in Miami, Baba brought $80 million in cash with him. Eventually Baba became the subject of a Miami Grand Jury investigation. He fell foul of the law when he attempted to bribe a US Customs official to sign off on two military helicopters he wished to ship to Gambia. His defense: the $30,000 offered was not a bribe, but a simple "gratuity." After two months of detention he was extradited to France where he received a two-year sentence for embezzlement and money-laundering.

As sensational as the escapades of con-man Baba were, they paled in comparison to those of Allen Stanford, the nefarious Texan financier, and his Stanford International Bank (SIB). This complex story of international financial shenanigans involved an offshore bank in Antigua, then governed by the same Bird family which made the "guns for Antigua" scandal possible, and a prestigious Miami law firm. As this is being written, Stanford is serving a 110-year sentence for defrauding thousands of investors (15,000 in Venezuela alone) in a $9 billion Ponzi scheme. The affair was well covered in all the important newspapers and journals, but even the in-depth investigations published in the *New York Times*, the *Financial Times,* and *Business Week* in February 2009 left out the vital part played by key actors in Miami in making the chicanery possible. This was remedied by two *Miami Herald* reporters, Michael Sallah and Rob Barry, in two sensational pieces of investigation published on 4 October 2009 and 6 December 2009. The key quote was from the vice president of Stanford's Miami office who turned state witness: "Miami," he said, "was the locomotive that pulled the train"; the Miami office was the "generator," Antigua was the "recipient."

With the flair to which Miamians have become accustomed, Stanford had swept into town and bought the garish Alpine-style castle in Gables Estates from George Wackenhut for $10.5 million. He opened fancy offices on Brickell Avenue, rented his own hanger at Miami International Airport for his private jet, and began donating millions to politicians. His major lobbying office was in Washington, DC and his main political consultant was the former Lieutenant Governor of Texas. But it was in Miami that the legal—and not so legal—scaffolding of the Stanford operation both inside and outside Antigua was erected. To be sure, other major agencies were also involved. The *Financial Times* (21–22 February 2009) did an excellent investigation tracing the actions of an English auditing firm which signed off on SIB's books but apparently never did much auditing. The real story, however, was in Miami.

It was the Sallah and Barry investigation which revealed how a large Miami law firm saved SIB, already suspected of laundering money, from being cut off from the global banking community. The key player for the firm became Stanford's top banking lawyer. In 1998 he negotiated with Florida regulators to allow Stanford to set up an unregulated trust office which then moved millions from Miami to Stanford's Antiguan bank "without any fraud checks or money laundering requirements." It was calculated that between 1999 and 2008, $800 million was transferred from Miami to Antigua in pouches and on courier jets.

Another major lawyer was key in helping Stanford dominate the Antigua regulatory agency from where he "swatted away" most of the other 56 offshore banks on the island. There was nothing gentle in the way this was done. When an Antiguan official refused to hand over records of the other offshore banks on the island, the lawyer and an investigator entered the official's office and snatched the files, removing the records to another building. Hardball Miami style played out on a small island pitch.

As often occurs with offshore activities, the initial pressure did not come from any country's regulators but from a paternity case in 2007 when Stanford's mistress and mother of two of his children, feeling abandoned, demanded to know his real worth. Thus began the battle to keep his finances secret and the investigation by the Securities and Exchange Commission.

As things began to unravel, first in Caracas where private analysts were questioning the whole operation, Stanford grew desperate, often responding in outbursts akin to tantrums. After a trip to Libya where he failed to convince General Gaddafi to add more millions to the $140 million he had already invested, Stanford flew to Miami in October 2009. He assembled his employees and other brokers and presumed investors and, according to Sallah and Barry, went into a near-hysterical rant, boasting of "a sweeping plan to invest in Miami":

> We've got a lot of cash… You can go downtown on Brickell, and you can
> see 10,000 condo units coming, coming on stream in the next few
> months… I've seen it, I've been there. I've done it… this is going to be
> a long-term play. We're going to make a huge amount of money off it.

Good Guys

Reviewing cases such as those of Baba and Stanford, one might ask: why does Miami always seem like an easy touch to those bent on scams, big or small? Addressing this query might well be the next well from which Miami *noir* novelists can draw. If and when they do, it would be only fair and factual if they remember the journalists who are invariably the first in the trenches, ahead of the novelist and the academic. They should also remember the state and federal officials who always seem to respond late but who often do their part in scrubbing the scum off "Casablanca." In other words, "Miami vice" is only half the story and it would be incomplete without telling the other seldom told side, "Miami nice," the actions of individuals and agencies which have prevented the city from sliding irretrievably into criminality. Without acknowledging the altogether legitimate and admirable side to Miami's explosive growth as a financial, commercial, and banking center, one would not understand what the city has become. Because parts of this growth were due to illicit monies but most of it was not, it was urgent that, in order to protect the majority who were honest, agencies with the capacity and the political will to clean up the system were called in to help. This required, first and foremost, that the community itself decide to do something about the rot which had corroded virtually every aspect of Miami's political, police, and economic systems. Then, aware that given this rot it could not do the house cleaning on its own, the community needed to invite the involvement of federal agencies. This is how it had always been in Miami, and so it was again: federal agencies, with the support of key members of the community, began to unleash a series of anti-organized crime "operations." These are some of the better known ones.

1988: "Operation Greenback." The US Customs Service discovered millions of dollars regularly smuggled from Miami to the cartels in Medellín.

1989: "Operation Polar Cap." The Drug Enforcement Agency froze hundreds of accounts in 77 Miami financial institutions. It was during the course of that year that it was discovered that Miami-based speed boats were making regular trips to communist Cuba to pick up drugs, cigars, and illegal aliens. The Cuban government arrested one of its highest ranking generals (Arnaldo Ochoa) as well as high-ranking officials of its Ministry of the Interior. During their trial it was revealed that an estimated $5 billion in drugs had been transported to Miami in speed boats based in Miami and that Cuba held over 100 Americans and 65 Cuban-Americans in jail for trafficking. In Cuba, the accused high officials were found guilty of drug trafficking and were all summarily executed.

1995: "Operation Greenpalm." This operation brought down long-time City Commissioner Miller Dawkins, City Manager Howard Gary, Commissioner James Burke, City Manager Cesar Odio, and Finance Director Manohar Surana. The name Greenpalm was apposite: they were all on the take and one of the banks some of them used, Sunshine State Bank, was later found to be another of those Miami money laundering banks. The FBI arrested the Finance Manager of the City of Miami who then spilled the beans on the mayor and dozens of other city officials. A system of *botellas* (sinecures) was handled from the mayor's office. It was what the new interim City Manager, Merritt Stierheim, called a system of "friends of friends" that cost the taxpayers millions. Stierheim, a truly grand Miamian, would be called in every time a department of the City administration needed a housecleaning.

1995: "Operation Court Broom" brought down Judge Philip Davis (also charged with smoking crack cocaine in his law chamber).

1998: "Operation Casablanca" was not meant as a tongue-in-cheek story. The US Customs Service seized 38 major bank accounts belonging to Colombian and Mexican drug cartels. The results of this last operation revealed something which would eventually help Miami but do enormous harm to Mexico: given the determination of major parts of the Miami elite to "take back" their city, the heightened surveillance by federal agencies, and the increased Coast Guard patrols in the Caribbean, the drug trade began to shift towards Central America and especially Mexico. Within a decade 80 percent of the drugs were no longer coming through Miami but across the US-Mexican border.

Reflecting the determination of the citizens of Miami-Dade County to see real reform, in 1997 the city set up a Commission on Ethics and Public Trust. The attempt at "sweeping clean" continued. Miami had made great strides in reducing the more violent effects of the trade though it certainly was not out of the woods in terms of money laundering, Medicare fraud, and other financial misdeeds also known as "white collar" crimes. There is still much muck for the Miami *noir* novelists to draw on.

A bird's eye view from the MetroRail

Chapter Seven

HIGH AND LOW CULTURE
ARCHITECTURE, EDUCATION, AND "TURF"

You can imagine the shock of the small but active elite of Miami when they read in the *Miami Herald* what the famous architect Frank Lloyd Wright thought of their city. Invited with much fanfare in 1955 by a group called, of all things, the Fashion Group of Miami, Wright issued judgments that were highly negative, even insulting. Miami, he told the Fashion Group, had "no feelings," "no richness," "no inspiration," "no quality," "no sense of region," and quite a few other "no's." He ended with a devastating verdict: these "little boxes" Miamians called houses were something "a pig would be ashamed to live in…" Yet there was hope—if Miami and Miamians specifically made some drastic changes. According to Wright, to turn the city around, the first thing to change would be the people. "You folks are Miami and that's the tragedy of it. We can't do anything with Miami until you change…" His preferred vehicle for accomplishing this urban revival? His own *métier,* the carrying out of an architectural renaissance. "We are going to have an architecture of our own. That is the basis of culture." Wright argued that he knew the history of urban revivals and recommended that Miamians learn that history as they searched for a culture and architecture of their own. That, of course, was easier said than done, as Beth Dunlop, Miami's foremost architectural critic, explains in the introduction to the splendidly edited *Miami: Trends and Traditions* (1996).

Even as Miami is, according to Dunlop, a city of "unexpected pleasures" to truly understand it, to find "the real Miami… it is necessary to slow down, step inside, and once in, look back out again." It is not clear that Dunlop had the quick in-and-out sojourner Wright in mind but he certainly could have benefitted from her knowledge of the city. Since Wright arrived by plane, what he saw from the air in 1955 was most probably those neighborhoods which sprang up after World War II to house the large, white working class which decided to settle in Dade County. The visitor with a sharp eye might still be able to discover the occasional bungalow-like structure in places such as Virginia Gardens,

West Flagler and Allapattah. Yet few of those "little boxes" are left for the simple reason that the demographics of the whole area began to change just a few years after Wright's visit. Architectural pluralism, not homogeneity, characterized those changes. This is precisely why Dunlop recommended a careful observation of the area's many architectural traditions. Miami-Dade, then as now, is still characterized by the urban "turf"—that neighborhood or suburb with which people identify—and in Miami-Dade it continues to be an ethnic enclave. Given this urban decentralization, there still is no one central plaza in Miami-Dade; no Argentine-style Plaza de Mayo, Mexican-style Zócalo, Costa Rican Plaza Central, and certainly nothing comparable to Havana's magnificent *malecón*.

It is not difficult to understand why this has been the case. Dunlop, who always kept in mind just how young the city was, did not believe that its short history should be reason to excuse its civil and political leaders from their responsibilities. On this score, she was severe in her judgments, claiming that these elites have never been much interested in city planning and even less in preservation; both, she says, have been treated "with cavalier disdain." Miami she suggests, "is a city where too much is done too fast and without much thought to the ultimate implications." She calls it Miami's "erratic impulse," composed in equal parts of invention and appropriation. The result is that "the metropolis sprawls so endlessly and so inelegantly across miles of former scrub and swampland, it may seem impossible to believe that Miami was ever conceived as a city of gardens." Harsh words, but delivered with the sympathetic understanding she had for a city she loved.

A Tour of Miami, Modern and Less Modern

Because of the variety of its "turfs" it is not surprising that Dunlop believes that as distinct from other older cities, which "virtually jump into your imagination," Miami has to be "discovered." Yes, but how… if one is not an architect or art critic? One way to get to know the city Frank Lloyd Wright never saw, and to see it at minimal cost, is to take the elevated MetroRail which travels from Dadeland in South Miami north to Hialeah and Palmetto. (Along the way at the Earlington Heights station one can transfer to the MIA MetroMover which takes you straight to the airport.) This reasonably-priced sky ride offers a bird's eye view of the

Miami skyline, and should you decide to hop off at any of the 21 different stations, you will sample what is new in the city of Miami.

The first stop is South Miami station. This fast growing municipality does not offer much of interest. The University stop gives access to the sprawling campus of the University of Miami, which actually lies in Coral Gables. This highly rated private institution does not contain much architecture of note but is beautifully landscaped representing a model of what good choices and spacing of subtropical plants can do to enhance otherwise nondescript buildings. Should the visitor decide to explore the restaurants and shops of Coral Gables, there is a free Coral Gables Trolley which does the rounds every fifteen minutes.

The next stop, Coconut Grove, introduces you to two quite different communities and involves a degree of walking. You will have to walk through the black-settled Grove—Miami's oldest modern continuously-inhabited neighborhood—where you will still find a few wooden bungalows built by the original Bahamian settlers. You will then enter the fashionable area of restaurants and boutiques and see the Coconut Grove Playhouse, which opened as a cinema in 1927 and is now lamentably abandoned. The Miami City Hall sits on the platform built to accommodate the Pan American Airways biplanes and has a distinct Art Deco design as well as an informal collection of Pan Am memorabilia.

Continuing north, you should stop at the Vizcaya Station to access the Miami Museum of Science. That nondescript building will soon be replaced by a new structure in Museum Park to be discussed later. However, from there crossing South Miami Avenue leads to what is surely one of the most splendid examples of an early Miami architectural tradition, Mediterranean Revival. This style is most remarkably evident in the Venetian Villa Vizcaya, a must-see residence and grounds. Built between 1914 and 1917 by James Deering of the International Harvester agricultural machinery firm, it now sits on ten acres by Biscayne Bay and is open to the public. Dunlop believes that Vizcaya provides the essential lesson of an architecture which is informed by a waterfront setting and a lush subtropical landscape. Deering's "house in the jungle" led other northern industrialists to build mansions on the Bay, each according to their own taste, or better, fantasies. Except for Coral Gables, Mediterranean Revival is represented by individual residences and buildings, not whole neighborhoods.

Gardens of Villa Vizcaya

There are three stops on Brickell, formerly a cluster of high-rise finance and banking buildings but since 2011 alive with restaurants and pubs catering to the multinational condo-living folk in the area. Its many amenities can be accessed at www.brickellarea.com. Since this will soon be incorporated into the area linking Brickell with Downtown, Brickell will be discussed later.

At the MetroRail-Government Station Downtown, you can transfer to the free MetroMover. Again, after a good walk, you will reach the Bayside Market Place. This was once a wharf for both sports and commercial fishing boats. Today mighty little of this remains, replaced by an international shopping and dining complex. In that same general area one finds the American Airlines Arena where the professional basketball team, the Miami Heat, play and many a Latin American crooner or troupe performs. Also in that area are the Miami Convention Center, the Knight Center, the Bayfront Park, and the Adrienne Arsht Center for the Performing Arts.

The stop at the Omni Station on the MetroMover "loop" provides a bus service to Miami Beach, specifically South Beach. The bus will travel over the MacArthur Causeway built in 1920. Venetian Causeway also brings you to South Beach but that you will have to do on your own. This is where most of Miami's beaches are to be found and they are several and varied, to wit:

Miami Beach at South Pointe Park: Ocean Drive and 5th Street;
Miami Beach Central: 21st to 46th Streets, Collins Avenue;
Miami Beach at South Beach: 5th Street to 21st Street, Ocean Drive (this
    is Miami's gay and lesbian beach);
Haulover Beach Park: 10800 Collins Avenue. This is the northern end
    of Miami Beach and is the only clothing-optional section.

Of course, Miami Beach is much more than just beaches. It is in South Beach that you will find an architectural tradition belonging to another era of Miami's history, the Art Deco tradition. To Dunlop, these seaside resorts, which often look like "so many ships at berth," represent the true spirit of Miami. Built at the height of the Depression, "they are an ode to optimism, their spires reaching skyward, their architectural attitude uncompromisingly buoyant." While Art Deco is found nearly exclusively in Miami Beach with only traces of it in Miami proper, it surely has to be considered the iconic style of the Miami-Dade area. It certainly is what makes the revived South Beach scene, with its many small hotels, the most popular entertainment spot in the county. As far as architecture is concerned, however, a little discrimination is recommended. Art Deco comes from the French *arts décoratifs* and emerged in Paris in the 1920s not just in buildings but also in furniture, lamps, even sculpture. The style is found all over the world and very much so in much of Latin America. It is especially prevalent in Havana. The question of what exactly qualifies as Art Deco can be seen in South Beach by comparing two buildings designated as such. The 632-room Eden Roc Renaissance, designed by Morris Lapidus in 1955, is certainly elegant, but what, except for a naval type structure on its roof, defines it as Art Deco? Even the much smaller James Royal Palm hotel with its porthole windows and its rectangular balcony shapes does not appear to qualify. To fully appreciate classical Art Deco structures you should go to what is justly called the Art Deco Historic District. This is composed of thirty blocks of hotels and apartment buildings dating from the late 1920s to the 1940s. The real jewels are to be found on Ocean Drive and between 10th and 15th Streets on Collins

Small hotel in Art Deco Historic District, Miami Beach

Avenue. Among the cluster of invariably small hotels look for the zigzag lines, the bold pastel colors, the entrances decorated with exotic tropical or Egyptian scenes and motifs. Especially representative are the hotels Carlyle, Cardozo, Colony, and Delano and the restaurants, 11th Street Diner, and Jerry's Famous Diner (now closed).

The wisdom of making the Art Deco District a historic preservation area cannot be disputed. Miami Beach hotel occupancy is booming—from 4.9 million annual overnight stays in 2008 to 5.5 million in 2011—and much of this is in the small, so-called boutique hotels. The *New York Times* (7 November 2012) reported that between 12,000 and 15,000 of the 19,000 rooms in Miami Beach are in small hotels and they are fetching astronomical prices. The Art Deco Delano (194 rooms) was for sale for $900,000 per room.

Before leaving South Beach, however, one should visit the condominium building called "One Ocean" and witness what the future of architecture in South Beach will probably look like. There is nothing Art Deco about this, but pure modernism *à la* Oscar Niemeyer, a structure which would blend perfectly into the rest of Brasilia. Its curving lines, meant to imitate the waves of the sea, make it seem very much at home in its waterfront location. Priced at between $2 and $10 million a condominium, it was already completely sold out—on a cash basis—soon after becoming available. The same trend towards modernism is evident in the sketches of the yet-to-be-built garage designed by the Iraqi-British architect Zaha Hadid for the Collins Park neighborhood. At the time writing, several city boards had yet to approve the avant-garde design whose swooping and curving bare concrete levels are supposed to imitate Miami Beach's undulating sand dunes but have nothing to do with Art Deco. The same can be said of the other parking garages design by leading architects discussed below.

Because night life is not all that Miami Beach offers, stay a while longer there. A stroll down the dynamic and diverse Lincoln Road in Miami Beach is a must for tourist and local alike. There you will notice that Enrique Norten's avant-garde garage at Drexel and 16th Street stands out, looking nothing like a parking garage. On that same road the Swiss team of Jacques Herzog and Pierre de Meuron designed a masterpiece of visual kitsch, 1111 Lincoln Road, which uniquely combines parking garage, retail shops, office space, and condominiums. Indeed, such are the garage's stunning views that one of its levels is used for lavish weddings and parties. The *New York Times* calls it a "carchitecture… an ode to Miami's flashing automobile culture." Also in Miami Beach, where garages are elevated to the status of art forms, Frank Gehry paired his New World Symphony Center with a parking facility, covering the exterior in metallic mesh. It competes in appeal with Argentine architect César Pelli's Adrienne Arsht Center for the Performing Arts in Downtown Miami—which has no garage.

DOWNTOWN

Finally, by 2015 there will be a MetroMover Station on Museum Park, which is supposed to house the planned New Miami Science Museum and the Jorge Pérez Miami Art Museum. You will never be far from Biscayne Bay and the largest cruise port in the world, connected by an extraordinary tunnel which frees the above-ground traffic from the heavy trucks going to the Dodge Island container port. Having left the MetroMover, you begin to explore specific sites and structures. Since one of the sites you will necessarily get to know is Downtown, it makes sense to repeat the truism that the development of urbanity does not occur by happenstance but rather, as Jacobs argued, it has to be planned and nourished by people who are themselves part of a movement to make even a downtown area a *beau monde* which sets the standards of high culture, leisure, and learning. These people require more than just a good commercial setting; they require elegance and aesthetic discrimination in their physical environment. On that basis, how was downtown Miami doing by 2012?

Pictures available in the Archives of Miami History reveal an early urban setting with a broad boulevard along the Bay and much green space. Anchoring the whole complex was Henry Flagler's Royal Palm Hotel with its wide and airy verandas providing views of the Bay and the Miami river. The downtown seemed to be bustling with activity. The city then suffered a series of blows which laid it low: a terrifying hurricane in 1926, the Depression and the bursting of the building bubble, World War II and the drying up of the tourist trade, all followed by the bloody cocaine wars and the spectacle of the boat people. The result was an exodus of Anglo residents to the suburbs, and downtown Miami turned into a ghost town after nightfall. There were two "towers" which survived: the Freedom Tower—built in 1925 in Mediterranean Revival style to house the *Miami News*—and the 1925–28 Miami-Dade County Courthouse. Also surviving is the first Art Deco building in South Florida, the Scottish Rites Temple on 471 NW 3rd Avenue, and two of Miami's original churches: the Central Baptist Church at NE First Avenue and 5th Street, and the Roman Catholic Church at 118 NE 2nd Street. The latter exemplifies much of what has been occurring in the area. Built of wood by the Jesuits at that same location in 1896, it was rebuilt in 1925 as an attractive Spanish colonial revival-style stone structure. The church, like so much else in downtown Miami, is now surrounded by modern condominiums which tower over it but which have contributed to its revival in unexpected ways, as the Father Superior who administers the church explained in the *Miami Herald* in December 2012: "We have always wanted to revive our presence in the heart of downtown because the area itself has been developed and the Catholic Church was not going to fall behind… We need to modernize and attract new Catholics who have moved into the area." The church is packed on Sundays with Latin American parishioners who now inhabit these condominiums and can walk to church. The Anglo parishioners of the Baptist Church are not so lucky since they largely moved out of the city.

Miami's Freedom Tower, formerly the Miami News Tower, surrounded by new construction

Aside from these few noteworthy original buildings and the many new condominiums, downtown is dominated by some very large and nondescript structures. In the very center lies the massive, fortress-like cultural center which James S. Russell in *Art in America International Review* (5 December 2011) dismisses as the "small, isolated downtown pomposity by Philip Johnson." If Johnson's creation was supposed to be a new center for downtown Miami, it failed, and this explains the plan to create a much more accessible set of museums in Museum Park. It is anybody's guess as to what will happen to this terribly expensive plaza occupying prime downtown space. Nearby is the ever-expanding Downtown Campus of Miami Dade College built on the site of the demolished First Methodist Episcopal Church whose splendid design once earned it the affectionate nickname the "white temple." The saving grace of this urban campus is that its students have brought a youthful presence to the area, at least during the day. The various federal, state, and county offices make up the other new buildings. Fatal for any sense of green urban spaces are the massive parking garages which accommodate the majority of commuters who do not use the public transportation system.

It should be understood therefore that when the *New York Times* (19 May 2006) carried a story on the "building explosion" taking place in downtown Miami, it was referring to developments outside of what is inner-city Miami. Miami is now featured in all the architecture and design magazines, which have taken to calling those designing the new Miami-Dade the "starchitects." This is only one of the neologisms born from the need to describe the new.

One such "starchitect" is César Pelli who performed one of the few acts of preservation when he integrated the old Art Deco tower of the Sears building downtown into the new Arsht building. It remains to be seen whether Pelli's decision to split that building in two with a major thoroughfare, Biscayne Boulevard (US 1), running through its center will eventually do what he hoped: integrate the Arsht Center into downtown Miami's ongoing life. Nearby is Richard Meier's twelve-story, glass-enclosed oceanfront condominium building which provides panoramic vistas of the sea. This structure reverses that atrocious tendency of early Miami architects to design buildings with their backs to Biscayne Bay. Indeed, integrating the splendor of Biscayne Bay has become one of the hallmarks of the new Miami architecture.

Having explored Miami's changing downtown, it is time to get to know the various ethnic enclaves, old and new. Miami's Cuban-American world is by far the most extensive but there are several others worth knowing. To start with, one should note that less than half the residents of Miami-Dade County are native born, and these new arrivals populate the ethnic turfs. Half the Cuban-Americans were born in Cuba and they continue to arrive from Cuba at a rate of 40,000 a year. Whether arriving from Cuba, Spain, or New York, most Cubans tend to gravitate towards the specific ethnic enclaves of Miami-Dade. This trend has made Miami-Dade a cluster of cities which both renew themselves and entrench themselves. New arrivals mean new enclaves springing up with surprising speed, demonstrating the explosive energies of the immigrant entrepreneurs. Such is the case, for instance, with one of the newest municipalities, Doral. Made a city as recently as 2004, it is today 80 percent Hispanic, 21 percent Venezuelan, 15 percent Colombian, and only 20 percent non-Hispanic white. Much of the atmosphere, however, is Venezuelan, all the way down to the restaurants offering Venezuelan fare such as *arepas*, *cachitos*, and *hallacas*. There is already a street named after the Venezuelan crooner Jose

Luís ("El Puma") Rodríguez. Not surprisingly, the area has already been baptized "Doralezuela." Similarly, Miami Beach has seen an Argentine enclave develop on Collins Avenue. Now called "Little Buenos Aires," the district has developed with great rapidity and to great accolades for its restaurants. The best way to know the area is of course by walking. Even in "Little Buenos Aires" you cannot miss the number of Brazilian establishments along the way.

CUBAN CULTURE

As much talk as there is about multi-ethnic Miami, the one culture which has dominated the scene, culturally and linguistically, is the Cuban. Cuban culture is the anchor of Hispanic Miami, historically and presently, and its beating heart is most definitely the older Cuban community in Little Havana with Calle Ocho its main artery. There is not much high art or *beau monde* here, but instead a vibrant scene of restaurants, art galleries, theaters, and small shops with residences just a few blocks away. Jacobs would have approved. It is on this street that one finds the iconic Versailles Restaurant, the meeting place for Cuban-American politicians and most American presidential candidates. No espresso coffee tastes better than that served at its indispensable coffee window… if you can get past the locals who act as if in church, with a minimum forty-minute attendance.

What is lacking in Little Havana is what the Cuban critic Ricardo Pau-Llosa chastises the Miami community for—not ever establishing a Cuban museum of art. What exists in Miami, says Pau-Llosa, are many galleries. This has been so since the boatlift of Mariel in 1980 brought dozens of artists to Miami. But of galleries, he says, "while they sell much art, they understand (know) little about it." Pau-Llosa is wrong only when he says that there was never a Cuban museum of art. There was in fact a very valiant attempt in the late 1980s to establish such a museum. But alas, it was very short-lived. The Museo Cubano de Arte y Cultura in Little Havana made the mistake of exhibiting paintings by artists still in Cuba and—at least in the minds of Calle Ocho's fervent purists—the organizers were branded *fidelistas*. The museum closed its doors in 1988. The ideological ardor of so many exiles pining for "their" Cuba is still too hot-and-heavy for such cosmopolitan experiments. In a neighborhood where one notes many a "For Sale" sign, yellowed by age but testament to

Mural along Miami Avenue in Wynwood

the undiminished determination to be ready to sell and return to the beloved land, one should not expect receptivity to "cosmopolitanism."

Be that as it may, Miami does have its cosmopolitans. It was the raw tenacity of Cuban-American Ramón Cernuda which broke the embargo on Cuban art. He began exhibiting and selling Cuban-American, Cuban, and Latin American art at his gallery on Ponce de Leon Boulevard in Coral Gables. Cernuda resisted the harsh criticism of part of the exiled community which would have made a lesser man wither and move out. Instead, he began the happily-established tradition of wine and cheese events on the first Friday of each month—now a fixture of so many galleries on Ponce de Leon Boulevard. There is also a Wynwood Art Walk on the second Saturday of each month in the up-and-coming Wynwood area. Driven by a rapid influx of artists of various nationalities, the Wynwood area has become one of Miami's most dynamic turfs. Its wall paintings are especially appealing. As is so often the case in Miami, visiting the galleries in Coral Gables and Wynwood has become a festive party-like occasion as well as being a must-stop for those interested in Miami and Latin American art. As distinct from the two weeks of Art Basel (of which more below) this is a year-round affair.

Another area of art which has bucked the parochialism of the area and experienced dramatic growth is the local showing of documentary films about Cuba, filmed mostly by Cubans on the island. Many have been added to the annual Miami International Film Festival, which only lately began showing Cuban-made films. Especially noteworthy are the recent films *La vida es silbar* and *Suite Habana*, the latter a dramatic portrayal of the daily hardships endured by the inhabitants of that erstwhile seigniorial city, Havana. At the end of a particular showing not one dry eye could be observed in the audience. It is testimony to the cross-generational nostalgia of Cubans in Miami but also to the slow-but-sure relaxation of tensions across the Straits of Florida that more and more films and documentaries of Cuba's *Cine Sumergido* (submerged cinema) and *Cine Alternativo* (alternative cinema) are appearing on Miami screens. The reverse, the showing of American films in Cuba, has not been so promising despite the fact—or perhaps because—they are extremely popular. An exception was Wim Wenders' *Buena Vista Social Club*, which was launched in Miami before going across to the island. Word is that the bureaucrats of Cuba's Instituto de Arte e Industria Cinematográficos were little pleased by these events. Whether this is true or not, the young cinematographers in Cuba and Miami give every indication that they will continue to take all necessary steps to reach across the divide.

A similar trend is evident in publishing. In Little Havana's Calle Ocho stands the oldest and most successful Spanish-language Miami bookstore and publishing house, Salvat Ediciones. Juan Manuel Salvat carries on the business which his father started in Cuba and brought to Miami in the early exile. It is hard to believe that this tall hefty man was for years a commando attacking targets in communist Cuba. All that ended in the early 1960s and since then this grand Miamian has published hundreds of titles and become a beacon for Cuban-American authors. Things have changed enough in Miami to reveal one of Salvat's secrets: for years he stored Cuban-authored books in a back room, providing US university libraries and sundry exiled intellectuals with the hard-to-get items. Today these books are on Salvat's shelves.

Another cultural survival is the tradition of *viernes culturales* (literally "cultural Fridays") of Latin *macho* society, celebrated on the last Friday of each month. Do not expect to see only single *macho* men on the hunt, however. That tradition has been transformed and brought up-to-date so

185

both men and women, single and married, go to enjoy the galleries and the restaurants, and to dance to the ever-present music of this Cuban enclave. Also on Calle Ocho and 15ᵗʰ Avenue sits the Tower Theater, another cultural icon of Miami. Very much in the Spanish tradition, it is the venue for a variety of Spanish-language films, musicals (especially *zarzuelas*), farces, and the always popular Cuban comedies.

The Cuban experience also informs one of the United States' enduring TV comedies, *¿Que pasa USA?*, the first bilingual sitcom in the country. It deals with a three-generation Cuban household in Miami and has been on the small screen for the past forty years. Its first episode was aired in 1977 and its last in 1980, but it has played continuously on public television ever since. Its hilarious but believable sociological contents were largely the product of one of Miami's earliest recorders of the evolving bicultural scene, the late Manuel (Manny) Mendoza of Miami-Dade College. Manny produced and wrote much of the dialogue which explores the myriad issues of differential acculturation and assimilation in the Peña family: the grandparents speak no English, the parents work in the English-speaking world but switch to Spanish when at home, and the grandchildren who are at home and at ease in both worlds and languages speak in "Spanglish" with their peers. Steven Bauer, who played one of the Peña teenagers, went on to Hollywood stardom.

MIAMI CUISINE

With the end of the age of the sturdy Miami pioneers, so ended any type of "typical" Miami cuisine and began the domination of undistinguished, traditional American foods. There is, however, one very notable survivor from the original fare: the stone crabs and spiny lobsters which come from Biscayne Bay or further out towards the Bahamas. The place to enjoy these in some fashion (and at an appropriate price) is Joe's Stone Crabs in Miami Beach. It is no exaggeration to claim that since it is virtually impossible to find more delicious sea food than at Joe's, the place is always crowded and accepts no reservations.

Reflecting the diversification of Miami's restaurant scene and its fine international cuisine in relatively sedate surroundings—whether it be French, Italian, Argentine, or Brazilian—it is best to go to Miracle Mile in Coral Gables, South Beach and increasingly the new strip of restaurants and clubs on Brickell Avenue. Otherwise expect festive, even noisy atmospheres in most other eating places. Spanish cooking is abundant in Miami and Spanish-inspired locations are popular for both food and entertainment. Casa Juancho on Calle Ocho often features Spanish university musical groups (*tunas*), while Taberna Giralda in Coral Gables offers flamenco performances to go with its excellent selection of wines and *tapas*. Music and dancing is *de rigueur* at virtually all Colombian, Peruvian, and Cuban restaurants. Good examples are the usually packed Yuca restaurant on Lincoln Road, Miami Beach, and the suggestively named Hoy Como Ayer (Today Like Yesterday) on Calle Ocho, where patrons can brush up on their salsa moves before, during, or after dinner.

It should be borne in mind that Cubans never had their own *haute cuisine*. The hard-working immigrants from Galicia, Asturias, and Catalonia brought their preference for flavor and substance with them to Cuba, and basic food meant combining Spanish spices with tropical ingredients. Cuba's classical cookbook, Nitza Villapol's *Cocina al minuto*, or as it is now called *Cocina criolla*, was originally published in 1954 and is now available everywhere in numerous unrevised (and unauthorized by her) editions. Villapol, born in New York, became Cuba's main TV cooking star in the 1950s and she remained in Cuba after the Revolution. Given the shortages of virtually all ingredients and staples in socialist Cuba, her program *Cocina al minuto* taught Cubans how to get by or *resolver*— the common verb to define survival skills through innovation in all phases of life—in revolutionary Cuba. In cooking it means devising substitutes and stretching what is available. Given the dire food shortages in Cuba, the Cuban tradition, as food critic Ivette Leyba Martínez says, moved to Miami which has become, in her words, the "sanctuary of traditional Cuban cooking." Although the iconic Cuban restaurant is Versailles on Calle Ocho, there are over one hundred recognized Cuban restaurants that preserve and popularize traditional Cuban fare: *ropa vieja, picadillo, bistec de palomilla*, etc., any of which is usually accompanied by white rice and black beans (*moros y cristianos*), cassava (*yuca*), or plantains fried ripe (*maduros*) or green (*tostones*). Dessert is a must and every one of them is super-sugared: *flan de coco, pudin diplomático*, or *cáscaras de guayaba con queso blanco, dulce de leche* (the latter is an Argentine import, while the new favorite, *tres leches*, was originally Nicaraguan). In all Cuban restaurants, and Latin establishments in general, portions are generous, and service is friendly bordering on the familiar. For the late post-theater snack

Cubans and non-Cubans ask for a *medianoche* or a *sandwich cubano*. "Cuban" coffee is more like espresso, invariably dark roasted. A *cortadito* is an espresso coffee cut with warm milk, while a *café con leche* is a full cup of coffee topped with milk, usually breakfast or very late-night fare.

In Miami many of the Cuban staples are in fact imported from the Dominican Republic and Central America, which share many of the same tastes in food. But South Florida is also home to a strong contingent of small Cuban farmers (*guajiros*) who grow traditional fruits and also raise large numbers of pigs, indispensable for the *lechón asado* (roast pork) served at any celebration. Virtually all the soft drinks once popular in Cuba are now produced in Miami: the Cawy, Materva, and Jupiña sodas loaded with sugar and fruit flavors. Beyond the retention of time-honored tastes nostalgia plays an important part in preferences for traditional foods. A front-page story in the Spanish-language *El Nuevo Herald* announced a new brand of fruit-based ice creams and carried the headline, "Delicious Ice Creams with the Flavor of Cuba." "When I ate one," said a Cuban-American client, "I was transported to a happy place of my childhood." Similar taste-based nostalgia explains the success of traditional Cuban coffee brands—Bustelo, Pilón, and La Llave—locally ground from imported coffee but roasted as it used to be in Cuba.

In explaining this dimension of cultural persistence one should not leave out the ubiquitous *comidas por libra* establishments which allow mostly working-housewives to purchase a complete meal and then set a table just as *la abuela* (grandmother) used to do. Also providing this service is the group which in Cuba used to cook for the working class, the Chinese-Cubans, who now cater to Miamians of all classes. Similarly, Cuban and Hispanic family dining traditions are sustained by quick service outlets such as Pollo Tropical restaurants, which feature the typical McDonald's-style drive-through windows.

Sadly, the otherwise vibrant Haitian culture, with its *art primitif* in painting and sculpture and its sensual dancing rhythms (*kompa, meringue,* and *zouk*), has not made a significant mark on Miami generally. Because ethnic cuisine is invariably an initial draw to the outsider, there is lamentably no outstanding restaurant in Little Haiti proper. There is the popular Bakery Café, which very much in the Haitian style doubles as a fast food outlet and occasionally offers *kompa* music. The best-known restaurant serving Haitian food (owned by Americans) is the Tap Tap (the name of

Haitian Market in Little Haiti, Lemon City

the ubiquitous small buses in Haiti) but it is located in Miami Beach. There one will find traditional Haitian fare of pumpkin soup *(soup joumou)*, conch salad *(lambi salad)*, grilled goat *(taso kabrit)*, fried pork *(griyo)*, okra soup *(kalalou)*, and other tasty dishes usually accompanied by a glass of Prestige, that superb Haitian beer. The food and the service is acceptable but for the real flavor of all these Haitian foods one has to go all the way to the middle-class area of South West 88 Street in Kendall to Le Lambi. This establishment is itself testament to the social mobility of the Haitian community, moving out of Little Haiti as soon as their finances allow. Surveys indicate that the move is as much motivated by employment opportunities as it is by the search for better education for their children.

This trend means that the valiant efforts to create a truly Haitian cultural enclave in Little Haiti has had only modest success. Visits to two important cultural centers, the Haitian Cultural Arts Alliance and the Haitian Heritage Museum, reveal very little foot traffic during the day and virtually none after sunset. The Libreri Mapo is a specialist Haitian bookshop and a meeting-place for cultural activities. There is real life and color on

Sundays at the creole mass at the Catholic Cathedral and when Haitian politicians come looking for funds. What the residents want to hear most of all is that the Haitian constitution will be changed to allow dual citizenship. Jamaicans, Trinidadians, even Mexicans, they note, have it, but why not the Haitians?

CITY OF MUSIC

As far as music and entertainment is concerned, it is good to recall that Miami had a musical tradition before the present Latin age. One might begin such a tradition with the likes of Hank Meyer, publicist of Miami Beach and a great promoter of everything South Floridian. It was Meyer who persuaded Jackie Gleason to bring his show to Miami Beach and, not coincidentally, play golf 365 days a year. He had previously worked with Arthur Godfrey and his Talent Scouts. Both Gleason and Godfrey participated in the early days of television and put Miami Beach on the map of musical talent show business. Larry King began his broadcasting career in 1957 from a houseboat anchored off the Fontainebleau Hotel in Miami Beach. This was the age of dance music. Rhythms such as the Boogie-woogie, Doo-wop, Swing, and Rock 'n' Roll were all spin-offs from Rhythm 'n' Blues, originally African-American music. Radio stations such as WQAM-Tiger Radio in Miami kept up a steady diet of music from Little Richard, Chuck Berry, Bill Haley, Elvis Presley, Fats Domino, the Platters, and a host of other popular performers who often made it onto TV shows. Today, those nostalgic for this age and its music can download it from multiple internet sites though they will not find it on the plethora of TV and radio programs covering the air waves of South Florida, except possibly on WPBS public television. Music in Miami now means Latin music.

Beyond nostalgia for ethnic foods, there is also nostalgia for ethnic rhythms and in that regard Miami is the undisputed center of popular Latin music. Listen to the Colombian singing a *ballenato* of his hopes of reaching Miami so that the great musical entrepreneur of that city, Emilio Estefan, can help him become a star. Go to a concert of Dominican Juan Luis Guerra at the American Airlines Arena and watch thousands dance in the aisles to *merengues* and *bachatas,* or the Colombians Shakira and Carlos Vives singing *ballenatos* and *cumbias.* As far as music is concerned, it is in-dividuals with outstanding aesthetic qualities as well as entrepreneurial energy who contribute to what is truly grand in any city's cultural life, and Miami has attracted many of the best.

The era of Latin rhythms arrived some three decades ago and among those who pioneered the city's new sound were Cuban-Americans Emilio and Gloria Estefan. The launching of Gloria's album *Miss Little Havana* was announced on half the front page of *El Nuevo Herald* on September 24, 2011, but her career goes back to the 1970s. In 1974 Gloria's future husband, Emilio Estefan, began playing the accordion with the Miami Latin Boys. It is when he met Gloria that they founded the Miami Sound Machine. Soft rock and ballads sung in Spanish were their repertoire until 1986 when they shifted to Latin *salsa* music. "Bad Boy" and "Conga" were their major hits as they appeared eight times in *Billboard's* Top Ten. Their real break, however, came in 1987 when Fidel Castro objected to their selection by the Pan American Games authorities in Indianapolis, Indiana to play at the games' closing ceremonies. With the assembled athletes dancing joyfully to the conga beat, the Estefans were given publicity of incalculable value. By 1989 they were selling five million records a year, and in 1990 Gloria received a Grammy for her recording of traditional Cuban music, *Mi Tierra*. In 1995 two great successes followed: the CD *Abriendo puertas*—a mix of Latin American rhythms—and the opening of their own recording studio, Crescent Moon Recordings. The Estefans were awarded the US Congressional Medal for their contributions as they helped launch some of Latin America's most popular artists: Miamian Jon Secada, the Colombians Shakira and Carlos Vives, and the Puerto Rican Ricky Martin. Nearly all these artists decided to make Miami their home, just as Spaniard Julio Iglesias and American Madonna already had.

The arts in Miami also include a full-bodied populist strain evident in the number of ethnic festivals that bring people into the streets to dance, to gawk at the flamboyant costumes, and to listen to music. This is definitely the case with the mid-October Miami-Broward One Carnival, a replica of the spectacular Trinidad Carnival held in pre-Lent February. Calypso, soca, and "road march" music dominate, just as many costumes previously used in the Trinidad Carnival are on parade. The festival draws on the increasing number of West Indians in both counties.

However, for raw musical exuberance and partying by *los de a pie* (people in the street) nothing matches the Carnaval de la Calle Ocho held in mid-March. In 2010 one million "regular people" danced to bands set up on Eighth Street, Little Havana from SW 2nd Avenue to SW 28th Avenue. Major Miami-based and Latin American and Caribbean bands participate. Much smaller in scale and certainly much more sedate is the Miracle Mile Carnival of Coral Gables held in early March. The city calls it a "fusion of jazz and art" and the setting is one of upscale restaurants and boutiques—a far cry from a Puerto Rican reggaeton or Jamaican reggae bash. As already mentioned, every second Saturday of the month the Wynwood and the Design Districts of Miami (Biscayne Boulevard from NE 20th Street to 36th Street) come alive with the late evening wine-and-cheese offerings of the clutch of art galleries which have suddenly appeared in the newly revitalized Miami downtown.

A different kind of musical affair is the Urban Beach Week, since 2001 celebrated in early August in Miami Beach. The nearly exclusively black celebrants are mostly affluent young people from outside South Florida and arrive in very large numbers to listen to hip hop and also parade the latest in beach wear and evening styles. Lizette Alvarez of the *New York Times* (January 2012) noted that locals, residents, and businesses alike "take a collective deep breath and do not exhale until it is over." When you have 200,000 to 300,000 young people concentrated in an area of a few city blocks, as occurred in 2010, it is not difficult to fear considerable confusion. This is especially the risk with this affair which has no central or official sponsor but is rather a purely spontaneous gathering of the young attracted like everyone else by the charm of Miami Beach and its inviting warm waters.

More or less at the same time, Miami celebrates the Salsa Congress which brings many of the Caribbean's most popular salsa bands to perform in several hotels in Miami Beach. In 2012 the iconic Dominican *salcero* Johnny Pacheco received the Celia Cruz Humanitarian Award. It is interesting that Miami Beach is the site for such Latin recognition, and what characterized the some 5,000 people who attended the various presentations in 2012 was that they came to listen and to dance. The dancing went on until 6 a.m. and, extraordinarily, many were ready to take salsa dancing lessons from 2 to 6 p.m. Salsa is probably the Puerto Rican version of the Cuban *guaracha* and the *guanguanco* but in Miami where music hardly exists without dancing, no one stops to ponder such details. *Alegría* is what counts and this is what gives the area the legendary "Miami flavor."

"HIGH CULTURE"

There can be no doubt that all such *alegría* is a major part of Miami's attraction, to Americans and foreigners alike. That said and despite the city's ethnic vibrancy, it is by no means certain that these ethnic enclaves will engender the kind of pan-urban synergies which make for great cities. This is because small urban concentrations are not in themselves capable of creating two of any city's fundamental "anchoring" institutions: universities and institutions of "high" culture such as museums, classical dance, theater, and symphonic orchestras. Miami has only in the past four decades turned its attention to establishing these institutions. But none of this is enough to turn the place into a more complete cosmopolitan city. As recently as four decades ago, one institution vital for creating urbanity and cosmopolitanism in a multi-ethnic city such as Miami was conspicuous by its absence—a major public university. There is no doubt that higher education had been casually dismissed by city elites who continually spoke of creating a global city despite the fact that a strong public university presence is indispensable for the global functions the city is already performing. The story of the struggle to achieve such a presence is *prima facie* evidence of how parochial the area's history has been.

It was Alvah Chapman, chairman of the Knight Ridder Corporation which owned the *Miami Herald*, who repeatedly spoke of "the shameful reality" that Miami-Dade was the only metropolitan center in the country without a state university. This was so notwithstanding the efforts since 1943 of one of the area's most influential men, dairy owner Ernest R. Graham. Graham had proposed the creation of a public university in Miami-Dade in the face of resistance by several forces, including the existing universities located further north. First, reflecting the origins of the state, Florida's state universities were all in the northern part of the state, but drew their students from the populated south. They naturally feared competition. A similar fear of competition came from the private University of Miami (UM), established in 1926—a less understandable case since, given its high costs, it recruited very few local students. Added to these forces was the lack of support from the local elite. The CEOs and upper echelons of the major banks and corporations were mostly recruited from outside Miami and cared little about the city, as Jack Gordon, himself a banker and one of Miami's grand promoters, explained: "For three decades, while other cities demanded public universities, Miami's power structure resisted having one, and, in fact, did not want a state university."

Mitchell Wolfson, a major business force and long-term chair of the two-year Miami-Dade Community College Board of Trustees, was adamant that "We do not need a state university in Dade County." At the time, the small community college was beginning to grow. It later blossomed into the largest community college in the US and has gathered increased influence under the very able leadership of Cuba-American Eduardo Padrón.

While other Florida cities with much more active civic leadership—Tampa, Orlando, Boca Raton, and Jacksonville—were securing funding for state universities, Miami finally received permission to begin planning in 1965, and opened its doors in 1972 as Florida International University (FIU). Reflecting the pent-up demand, the new public state university boasted the largest first-year enrolment of any university in American history: 5,700 students, 90 percent of whom came from Miami-Dade County—precisely the student population the university was intended to serve.

Despite its pretentious name—all knowledge, after all, is "international"—the place kept growing. By 1986 a search for its fourth president began and with that the schisms in the community reappeared. The black community, including the black-owned *Miami Times*, lobbied for the black finalist noting that the university exhibited a "chronic inability" to attract and retain black students and faculty. The *Miami Herald* editorialized that FIU should not be turned into "a university for minorities, run by minorities." Further, the paper commented, clearly reflecting icy relations between the Anglo and the Cuban communities, it should certainly not be "the Miami campus of the University of Havana." The victorious candidate was of Cuban origin, but hardly an ethnic parochial. Modesto "Mitch" Maidique was cosmopolitan, focused and determined to set standards well beyond those of a "frontier town." He was also, as the *Miami Herald* described him, "brash to the point of cockiness." Given the turf, one wonders whether anyone with less panache and verve could have achieved what he did in the 23 years he was president. When he retired in 2010, FIU had 45,000 students from all 50 states and 120 countries enrolled in all the faculties of the traditional university, including architecture, law, and medicine. Maidique left a truly beautiful campus complex in southwest Miami. Reflecting the youth of the institution and the speed with which things move, Maidique's successor, the political scientist Mark Rosenberg, was originally recruited as an assistant professor but soon gained a national reputation as Provost and Vice President at FIU. He was appointed chairman of the body which supervises all eleven of the state's public universities, the Florida Board of Regents, before being selected president of FIU.

The university gives every indication of having successfully entered into a pattern of sustained growth, linked to the nature of its ethnic environment. In terms of ethnicity, the university's student body reflected the Miami-Dade community: Hispanic, 59 percent; black, 12 percent; white (non-Hispanic), 17 percent; Asian, 4 percent; and the rest ("international"), 8 percent. It complements the University of Miami, which has 15,000 students. In terms of ranking, however, the UM at 36th in the US in the accepted *US News and World Report* league of universities, outshines FIU and indeed all other universities in the state. The energetic administration of UM president Donna Shalala, former Cabinet member in the Bill Clinton Administration, has much to do with the university's success.

Tram similar to those which ran in Miami in early decades of the twentieth century: exhibit in the History Miami Museum

A review of the two institutions' budgets tells much: FIU, $650 million; UM, $2 billion, a reflection of the latter's enormous medical school and teaching hospital. The University of Miami's medical school includes three highly regarded specialized hospitals as well as an affiliation with other major medical facilities. Both universities have established deep roots in the community, with FIU in particular having a contingent of 170,000 alumni who now include many state and federal representatives as well as several who have served as mayor of the City of Miami.

The outreach of these two universities has enriched the local community enormously. FIU owns and administers the Wolfsonian-FIU Museum in Miami Beach, donated by Mitchell Wolfson, Jr., the son of the Wolfson who once pronounced that Miami did not need a public university. The Wolfson Museum holds a unique collection on Western architecture, design, and art history. The University of Miami's Lowe Art Museum, in the middle of its campus, is the oldest in Miami-Dade and is best defined as a boutique museum rotating some of the finest pieces of its mammoth 18,000-piece permanent collection. The university also contributes through its highly regarded symphony orchestra.

And then there are the smaller museums with respectable collections. Among them is the History Miami Museum containing excellent collections of early local history and a splendid collection of maps of the Caribbean. It also houses a vast historical photograph collection and one of the few remaining complete sets of James Audubon's Everglades bird prints in existence. Yet as valuable as the many small museums with special collections are, there can be no doubt that Miami needs a larger, more accessible, and aesthetically appealing museum complex. Such a project is in the works and if it in fact materializes as planned, it will be the jewel of Miami's architectural and cultural renaissance. The plan is to build two museums surrounded by a vast public park on what is now Bicentennial Park in downtown right off Biscayne Bay. One of these, the Jorge M. Pérez Art Museum, designed by Jacques Herzog and Pierre de Meuron is described by Nicolai Ouroussoff of the *New York Times* as "mesmerizing architecture." Local commentators note that the design seems inspired by the architecture of Stiltsville, a group of private houses which stand high out in the waters of Biscayne Bay off the southern end of Key Biscayne, while others hope that because the Herzog and de Meuron-designed Tate Modern Museum "instantly became the emblem of London's rise as an art world capital," the same might occur in Miami. Certainly the Art Museum, pairing with the new Miami Science Museum designed by the London-based Grimshaw Architects, will be a necessary stop for both locals and cultural tourists.

This, however, is merely the proposed architectural part of the equation. Even before the Art Museum took physical shape, events proved once again that making anything truly aesthetic is never easy in Miami. The first director quit soon after arrival; again because of budgetary problems. But as always occurs in Miami, someone new appeared promising a fresh start. The new director, Terence Riley, who left his job as curator of architecture at the Modern Art Museum in New York, remained optimistic through it all, making the simple but persuasive argument that "We're the only major city in the United States that doesn't have a major art museum… This city deserves one. It *needs* one." He went further in his observations about the architectural future, predicting that "Miami has burst through the line between being design-conscious in general and having more detailed awareness of the top architects worldwide."

This is what is being said about the team behind the building of the magnificent performing arts center designed by Bernardo Fort-Brescia of Miami's Arquitectónica teams in the new city of Cutler Ridge, twenty miles south of Miami. Architecture critic Beth Dunlop calls it "grand without being grandiose" and notes that the setting is currently suburban but that the expectation is that "some day there will be a 'there' there in Cutler Bay." The ambition is that such architectural jewels will serve as anchors of urbanity for the new city at the center of a series of smaller cities which spread out from the urban hub like the spokes of a wheel. Despite the general enthusiasm for such plans, many ask whether at this relatively early stage of Miami's development as an urbane city, one should place such high hopes on the drawing power of megaprojects. To start off with, there is the issue of priorities.

Local builder and art collector Martin Margulies (in a letter to the *Miami Herald*, 22 August 2009) argues that all this new building caters to "an elite group of private individuals" at the expense of social services and grassroots arts. "A great city," he says, "is taking care of the needs of citizens… not building monuments." There are those who raise the eternal Miami question of initial investment and later running costs. Some of the historically dependable sponsors of the arts are already making worrying noises. Very much related to this question of costs is the issue raised by Daniel Shoer Roth of *El Nuevo Herald* (27 February 2008) who points to a consistently harmful feature of Miami planners: starting one expensive project before others are completed and paid for. The Spanish saying, *bienvenido y hasta luego* ("welcome and goodbye") applies. He cites the example of the delays and cost overruns of several major projects, most conspicuous of which is the North Terminal of Miami International Airport, originally budgeted at $500 million and finally costing $2.9 billion.

This comes on top of the approval of Miami-Dade County funding for the new Marlins Park baseball stadium, a cool $525 million of public funds even as the deep-pocketed owners of the team committed only $155 million of their own money. As the *Miami Herald* remarked about the funding of the stadium, once the county pays off the bonds, it will have cost "a staggering $2.4 billion." Aside from the fact that a poll of Miamians showed 57 percent opposed to using public monies on the stadium, the idea that a great city needs sports cathedrals won the day.

The city demolished the erstwhile iconic Orange Bowl and now has major sports arenas for each of its professional teams: in football, the Miami Dolphins use the Sun Light Stadium; in basketball, the Miami Heat use the American Airlines Arena as does the Panther ice hockey team; and in baseball, the Marlins use their own new Marlins Park. The city elites did consider and do promote an interesting angle to the question of attendance at sports events, taking advantage of Miami's ethnic and immigrant populations' enthusiasm for all sorts of sports and for attending the games as part of a festive outing. Given that Latins especially are sports crazy, the Marlins Park owners have contracted with the World Football Challenge organization to bring professional soccer (football to the rest of the world) matches in the off season. Five international matches played in the spectacular stadium brought in over 250,000 ticket holders to see teams such as Boca Juniors from Argentina, Santos from Brazil, Manchester United and Arsenal from England, Celtic from Scotland, and AC Milan from Italy. It might be that the calculation that Miamians love soccer as much as they love baseball is correct, which means the stadium will have year-round usage. Indeed, reflecting the mix of fans, there is already developing—very slowly to be sure—a plethora of small ethnic restaurants and watering holes around the new stadium. The biggest complaint is, not surprisingly, the lack of adequate parking. Could it be otherwise for a stadium in the middle of Hialeah, a densely populated neighborhood which has little public transportation and where virtually everyone uses a car. Calls to extend the MetroMover to the Stadium have gone unanswered.

PROJECT FEVER

In 1965 the Miami Downtown Development Authority was established. Although a very belated response to unplanned development, it at least indicated that City leaders understood the need for central regulation and planning. The claim that that agency had much to do with the phenomenal burst of building which has taken place in the past two decades—94 new condominiums worth $13 billion—is debatable. The 95 percent occupancy rate (representing 80,000 new residents) stems from the arrival of Latin Americans paying in cash. Everyone now awaits what might be the jewel in the crown of all such development: the Zaha Hadid-designed condominium which will be within walking distance of the Carnival Auditorium.

Given that this development has been private sector-driven, it is acknowledged that no private business began promoting Miami more than the Related Group, by far the largest builder of condominiums in Miami-Dade and Broward counties. Its newest building, My Brickell, right in the middle of Miami's financial center, is a 192-unit condominium designed by Egyptian architect Karin Rashid. The Related Group now has offices in Brazil, Uruguay, Panama, Colombia, and Mexico, but not in Argentina, however, where paradoxically it was first established. The explanation for its purchases in Miami was given by the president of the Related Group, Carlo Rosso, in *Fortune* magazine, Buenos Aires, in November 2011. "Miami presents a great opportunity. In 2006, the square meter in Buenos Aires cost US$2,500, now it costs US$5,000. In Miami it is just the reverse." He explained that 30 percent of the units in the My Brickell building were sold to Latin Americans within ten days of being put up for sale. He further explained the fundamental difference in real estate financing between these Latins and Americans:

> We are bringing Latin American models of financing to the United States. The world has turned around [*El mundo se dió vuelta*]. The

Argentine, the Colombian or the Mexican pay for the projects from their savings [*desde el pozo*] because they are accustomed to saving and much of those savings are invested in bricks. The American is a consumer, not a saver.

These savings are part of the enormous capital flight which enters Miami. Quite evidently, and from the historical record predictably, all attempts by the Argentine government at currency and foreign exchange controls are for naught. It is calculated that Argentine capital flight in 2011 was US$26.1 billion, double what it was in 2010, and three times that of 2007 before stringent currency controls in several Latin American countries were in place. The Buenos Aires press reported in November 2011 that the preferred vacation spots for Argentines were Brazil, Miami, and Spain.

The story of the Related Group is the story of its founder, Jorge M. Pérez, whom the *Miami Herald* calls "Miami's *über* developer" and *Time* magazine tags as the "Donald Trump of the Tropics"—who at first seemed to represent the new cosmopolitan citizen the city needs. But was he really? To read Pérez's 2008 book, immodestly titled *Powerhouse Principles: The Ultimate Blueprint for Real Estate Success in an Everchanging Market* (foreword by Donald Trump) is to know that Pérez has the kind of chutzpah necessary for personal success in Miami. Born in Argentina of Cuban parents, he was educated in the US and then came to Miami-Dade in 1968 where he became Director of Economic Development for the City of Miami. By 2004 his investments in low-income, multi-family apartments and later in condominiums led to revenues of $2.1 billion. He was soon said to own fifty condo towers in various stages of completion in South Florida, Fort Myers, and Las Vegas. He is building new hotels in Miami Beach and paid $100 million for the all-but-abandoned Omni Center in downtown Miami. He then sold it to the Malaysian Genting Group which is planning a downtown casino. As we shall see later, Genting expects to make this a multi-use complex which, it is hoped, will join with many other condominiums in revitalizing downtown. It is a daring move given that the state has yet to approve casino gambling outside the Indian-areas.

The question still stands unanswered: is this nearly feverish determination to build enough to elevate Miami from global city to global and cosmopolitan status? It is not at all evident that much thought is being given to answering that query in a city which goes from one grand celebration to the other. Two of these have received world-wide recognition: Art Basel and the South Beach Wine and Food Festival.

CULTURAL RENAISSANCE: ART BASEL

Brett Egan of the Kennedy Center claims quite adamantly that "without any hesitation, I can say that Miami is one of the—if not *the*—most exciting arts communities in development today." Similarly, Hannah Sampson, art critic of the *Miami Herald* (3 October 2011) observes, "The arts have never been hotter in South Florida." Beyond any doubt, a major part of this effervescence is due to Art Basel Miami Beach (ABMB). This multi-location show and its international appeal have incubated the vital *élan* which promises continued success. It is centered on Art Basel studio in Miami Beach, but spread through 25 "satellite fairs" taking place during that same period. It has grown so large that fairs are held in Miami Beach hotels and have spilled over to the galleries in Miami's Design District and Wynwood. The *Miami Herald's* art critic calls it with predictable Miami-style bombast "the most prestigious art show of the Americas." (Note the plural "Americas" reflecting the increasingly popular claim that Miami is in all things the center of the hemisphere.) At least the *New York Times* was geographically more modest, calling it "the hottest contemporary art fair in America," while the *Wall Street Journal* (1 December 2002) described it as "The Art World's Biggest Party" and "the Nation's largest art fair." The *Journal* then immediately admitted that many of the thousands who visit come for what it calls "the glitzy social scene and beach bacchanalia" rather than the art. "Net Jets," a private jet company, announced it flew in more planes for the Art Basel week than it used for the football Super Bowl held in Miami in 2006. At least it can be said that for once that this is partying for a cultural cause and a multinational one at that. In 2011, 260 galleries (26 from Latin America) exhibiting over 2,000 artists were part of Art Basel. The main art show is held in the Miami Beach Convention Center, but in 2011 it also inaugurated an Art Public sector for emerging artists.

Utilizing the green spaces around the Bass Museum of Art on Collins Avenue, Miami Beach, this provided an even more festive atmosphere to the art show. There was also for the first time an Art Video sector with outdoor projections on the wall of the New World Center. Even Martin Margulies, a pioneer of art in public places, has to applaud such openness.

The comments of art critics collected by *Ocean Drive's* art editor, Eric Newell, are illustrative of the impact of ABMB:

> Normally it takes decades to create urban places of culture, but Art Basel and Miami have reinformed and readapted and reinterpreted each other. (303 Gallery owner, Lisa Spellman).

> Where else can you see galleries represented from China, Russia, India, France and New York, all within one square mile? (Jane Nathanson, Los Angeles Museum of Art trustee).

> It's a different kind of collector base, with the South American community, the Cuban-American and Miami communities, and the New Yorkers who come in for the parties but end up loving the fair. (Jeanne Greenberg Rohatyan, Salon 94 owner).

Perhaps most telling is the comment by Miami grandee Norman Braman: "Back in the '90s, Miami was experiencing image difficulties… Now international visitors say to me, 'I never knew Miami was like this.' They are buying homes and condos… Why not do that very American thing—combine art and business."

Most of Art Basel, of course, is a Miami Beach festival. It began across the Bay, with the restored Art Deco architectural backdrop framing it. True, it has branched out to the mainland to include the former Puerto Rican enclave Wynwood, now, as already noted, very much in the process of gentrification. Indeed, such is the change in Wynwood that even that new celebrity of the "back to the city movement," the aptly named Richard Florida, has decided to live there half of each year. We will return to Florida's bestselling *The Rise of the Creative Class* (2012) in the next chapter.

Of course, since not everyone in the art world is interested in waterfront cocktail mixers and "blowout reggaeton concerts" some will not attend. In *Back to Blood*, Tom Wolfe's narrator calls the whole affair flaky and attractive only to "maggots." Others are not so insulting but equally turned off. "Why would I go?" asks a top art advisor to Christie's rhetorically, "I'm not interested in partying—I'm interested in buying good art."

Design Miami building in Miami Beach

In which case, this art connoisseur but non-partier should go to the original Art Basel in more sedate and proper Switzerland. Miami, as noted in Chapter Four, has developed that tropical and Cuban style of accompanying virtually every event with music and dance. It is one of its very attractive features of Art Basel in Miami. But, there is more. Three years ago a separate fair called Design Miami moved from the downtown-based Miami Design District to a location smack in front of the Miami Beach Convention Center where Art Basel is based. The result in 2012 was a smashing success. Despite the fact that a few labeled this presentation of furniture "pretentious and opportunistic," the *New York Times* (13 December 2012) called its exhibits "a bracing combination of living legends, vintage masters, and young talents." The 30,000 people who visited Design Miami in five days quite evidently approved.

Hardly at the level of popularity of Art Basel or Design Miami is the South Beach Wine and Food Festival. It began in 2001 as a small function of the Chaplin School of Hospitality and Tourism Management of Florida International University, and has blossomed into a major three-day food and wine event under the sponsorship of the Food Network, the TV program whose ratings have soared, and over one hundred other major sponsors. The program for 2013 listed some of the world's most celebrated chefs and wine connoisseurs. Predictably, the festival ended with an official dance party featuring reggae star Ziggy Marley.

Such is the enthusiasm for Miami Beach, for instance, that even FIU, catering to a majority Miamian and environs clientele, has opened a branch campus housing the School of Architecture and many an arts program. Naturally it is on Lincoln Road, ocean-side, and is booming as an academic center. Miami is attempting to give the lie to the old saw that education does not prosper in beautiful "tropical" environments. It is just possible that educational developments such as this School of Architecture will eventually change Miami Beach's *beau monde* into more than a mix of cocktail parties, fashion shows, and the once-a-year Art Basel fête, though evidently it will never be even remotely a staid and starched town. Its beating tropical heart will always have the counterpoint so well described by the editor-in-chief of the glossy magazine, *Miami*. Miami, he writes, is "really about sunshine *and* substance, brawn *and* brain, fun *and* forward-thinking." This is so, he brags, because as a native Miamian he knows that "our natives are fearless."

It would be mean-spirited indeed to rain on this parade by adding that the natives have also been known to be feckless, down-right parochial, and much given to the "erratic impulses" Beth Dunlop spoke of. We have dealt with examples of that parochialism throughout and will do so again in due course, but as the discussions in this chapter point out, there can be no doubt that the elites of Miami seem to be infused with a new spirit as they try to catch up with the enthusiasm of the multi-ethnic urban populations which now make this city what it is. It remains to be seen whether the project of building grandly, and often grandiosely, will be the formula which will bring urbanity and cosmopolitanism to Miami-Dade.

Chapter Eight

CITY OF THE FUTURE
GLOBAL OR COSMOPOLITAN?

In 1994 the United States seemed to have scored a major victory when every hemispheric country, except Cuba, sang from the same hymnal of free trade and pluralist democracy. Miami, just recovering from the devastating Hurricane Andrew of 1992, then had a success of its own when, despite significant competition from Atlanta and Mexico City and opposition from the US Department of State, it was chosen to host the first Summit of the Americas Conference. Miami hoped to be the headquarters of the proposed hemisphere-wide free trade agreement. That proposal did not prosper but Miami did receive some noteworthy plaudits. In his opening address of 11 March 1994, President Bill Clinton noted the opposition to the selection of Miami but believed that it was a good choice precisely because in a world in which societies were torn by ethnic rifts, the city had managed to confront that problem successfully. He was adamant about his decision:

> I've had the opportunity to go to Miami and to South Florida and see the heroic efforts that people have made to deal not only with the aftermath of the hurricane, but to build a genuine multicultural, multiracial society that would be at the crossroads of the Americas; and, therefore, at the forefront of the future.

Miami, he concluded, was what the rest of the country should be, "a place that can symbolize the future toward which we are all tending." Certainly the president's advisors had listened carefully to the sales pitch of the Miami advocates led by the Chamber of Commerce and the Beacon Council. The theme of these two agencies of promotion had been consistent since the Beacon's creation in 1986, invariably hitting all the major selling points. They noted correctly that Miami-Dade County is a part of the sixth largest Metropolitan Statistical Area (MSA) in the United States, and that "our community serves as a hub of international commerce between the Americas and Europe, Asia, and Africa." Thanks to its strategic geographical location within the heart of the Western Hemisphere, its diverse population and economy, and beautiful year-round weather, Miami-Dade County had developed into "a world-renowned and advantageous international business center."

Proof that the Beacon Council was not merely engaged in public relations was the fact that close to 1,000 multinational corporations were located in Miami-Dade County—and not just major corporations. When the Trinidad-born Lieutenant Governor of Florida led a trade mission to the island in August 2012 she mentioned that there were thirty Trinidadian corporations already operating in Florida and that over 40,000 Trinidadians resided there. She could have said the same thing about virtually any of the nations of the Greater Caribbean. Again, geography and infrastructure mean that Miami-Dade's banks, airport, air service cargo port, and storage facilities all make it easier to operate from Miami than from any individual nation. Thence its consistent claim to be the "business center of the Americas" rings true… to an extent. Several other cities with deep water ports such as Baltimore, Maryland and Charlestown, South Carolina also make that claim. It is most notably Houston, Texas, however, which is Miami's main competitor as a hub for trade with the Americas. Just as Miami is doing, all these cities are spending enormous sums preparing their ports and rail service to receive the supersize ships which will transit the expanded Panama Canal, scheduled to go into operation in 2015.

That said, how true it is that Miami is fulfilling its often-proclaimed role as a "city of the future?" T. D. Allman had said literally that in his readable but ultimately implausible 1987 book, *Miami: City of the Future*. To Allman, it was not that Miami was becoming like the rest of the country but that the rest of the country was becoming like Miami. Such a claim cannot be sustained without specific comparisons, which he does not make. Yet his lively style and unconventional views make you want to believe him and others who argue like him. Caution, however, is called for. When analyzing Miami, one must be careful not to confuse what is salient and attractive with what is probable in an objective sense. It is a sociological fact that when elites have difficulty dealing with intractable existing realities they tend to talk about glowing futures. The constant claims that Miami is "the city of the future" falls within that tendency. That said, it is also a sociological fact that there tends to be a silver lining to such a belief in a promising future: the operation of a self-fulfilling prophecy. The idea that Miami is a city of the future is very much a self-fulfilling prophecy which has worked in its favor. In a self-fulfilling situation, the prediction, the hoped-for future, becomes a driver in the achievement of that wished-for future. As the sociologist William I. Thomas stated, "When people define situations as real, they are real in their consequences." It is in that sense that T. D. Allman's idea that Miami is a state of mind rings true.

In case after case, the Miami *noir* novel has chosen to frame the city and its inhabitants in terms of vice. But, as we have seen throughout this book, the novelists and film producers have had to share their stage with many grand Miamians and informed outsiders whose words and actions have consistently promoted the alternative image of "Miami nice." Certainly many outsiders tend to look beyond what is superficial about the place. One has but to consult the various issues of the respected architectural magazine *Next American City* to be made aware that to many observers Miami is making real strides on the path to becoming more than a global city, a metropolis. Tony Goldman, whom *Next American City* calls an "urban visionary," asserts without hesitation that "Miami is going to be the city of great new architecture… the next great international city of this country, without a question." Goldman spoke with considerable authority. Arguably more than any other single individual he was responsible for the renaissance of South Beach and Wynwood. His passing in September 2012 was a real loss to Miami-Dade's small cosmopolitan elite.

Despite the contributions of people like Tony Goldman, however, it is also true that Miami was more often than not promoted through hyperbole which often had a graceless edge to it. In 1994 the Board of County Commissioners of Metropolitan Dade County published a very comprehensive study, "Destination 2001," which concluded not only that Miami was a global city but indeed that by 2001 it would be the "City of the Future." Two decades later, the very active and very elite-centric Beacon Council commissioned another set of comprehensive studies of Miami-Dade and its future entitled "One Community One Goal" (7 December 2011). Predictably, the study concluded that Miami-Dade County was "unique," that "major changes are on the horizon," and although the city is already an international community with global brand recognition as the "gateway to the Americas" it is set to become an even more significant destination within the next five years.

No wonder that such projections are very much part of the self-fulfillment syndrome that drives the elites of this very young city. The fact is that no one doubts any longer that Miami is a global city, but this begs the question as to whether it is in reality what it aspires to be, a cosmopolitan city. Is it the kind of place which attracts what Richard Florida (yes, that is his name) in his enlightening book, *The Rise of the Creative Class,* calls precisely a "creative class?" Tony Goldman was representative of that class but how many are there like him in Miami? "Creative centers," says Florida, "provide the integrated ecosystem or habitat where all forms of creativity—artistic and cultural, technological and economic—can take root and flourish." One of the attitudes essential in achieving such creativity is tolerance. In other words, beyond its global commercial functions, is Miami sophisticated and free from small village-like prejudices and intolerance?

The term "cosmopolitan" has a Greek root meaning a center of and for all people of the *kosmos* (world), their art, and ideas. As Florida points out, this ideal cannot be achieved purely through the exuberant promotion of certain objective facts about the number of settled multinational offices, multiculturalism, and the volume of trade. Nor is it, as T. D. Allman believes, equivalent to exuding "urban excitement." Some prominent urbanologists doubt that Miami has reached cosmopolitan status even as they agree that on many accepted objective criteria Miami is a "global city." A global city is one which contains the capabilities for servicing, managing, and financing the regional and global operations of firms and markets. Saskia Sassen calls this the capacity to build and maintain many "cross-border circuits," and in her definitive book *The Global City* (2001) she argues that in a world of transnational processes a global city becomes the hub, and thus meets the needs, of an ever-expanding network of operations. Miami certainly does that for much of Latin America and the Caribbean. But in her study of global cities Sassen mentions Miami only twice and then only in passing and without much comment.

To Sassen, Miami does not appear to rise to the level of exceptionality. Similarly, Edward Ludwig Glaeser, in his *Triumph of the City: How Our Greatest Invention Makes Us Richer, Smarter, Greener, Healthier, and Happier (2011)*—an optimistic view of cities which, he says, are man's "greatest invention"—compares two cities which have experienced unfettered construction, Houston and Miami. Both are competing to be the "gateway" to the Americas in terms of trade. But it is Houston, not Miami, which he believes has succeeded as a city which magnifies humanity's strengths because Houston has successfully combined building and education. "Human capital," Glaeser remarks, "far more than physical infrastructure, explains which cities succeed."

Richard Florida would heartily agree. Richard Dobbs and Joana Remes of the McKinsey Global Institute list what they say will be the "powerhouse" cities of the world. Miami is among the 75, ranking 44th. In the US, New York, Los Angeles, Houston, Dallas, Washington DC, and Chicago outrank Miami, and Atlanta is only three places below it. Should not any of these be considered "the city of the future?" Certainly any one of these cities is older than Miami and had origins as a center of industry very different from Miami's beginnings.

Two urban sociologists, Alejandro Portes and Alex Stepick, argue in their *Miami: City on the Edge* that Miami did not originally rise in the traditional way cities tend to do; in fact, they say, its birth was "accidental": "The origins of the city were… economically underdetermined, more the result of chance and individual wills than of any geographic or commercial imperative." It is this which, in their opinion, "accounted for Miami's sense of suspension above real life and the feebleness of its civic organizations…" As objectively true as all this scholarship may well be, all the academic commentators (even Portes and Stepick) underestimate the role not so much of "chance" but of geographical positioning, historical conjuncture, and human will all unleashing a self-fulfilling prophecy. These elements and processes alone should convince Miami's elites that they should tone down the overhyping of the city but should not stop promoting Miami as *one* of the global cities of the future.

BANANA REPUBLIC?

That said, what about the other claim, that Miami is a cosmopolitan city, a city free from small town prejudices, what the Spanish call *la patria chica*—a conglomerate of people sharing a common set of ideas and preferences? The claim to being cosmopolitan is on much shakier ground. A few examples may explain why.

On 1 August 2012 the Spanish-language newspaper *El Nuevo Herald* published a cartoon by its celebrated cartoonist Garrincha portraying a clown carrying a bag full of dollar bills to a building labeled "Miami" over which flew a flag with a banana in the center. The suggestion that Miami was a banana republic was clear and followed the revelation of a string of corrupt affairs in City Hall which made the allegation believable. There were scandals of every sort: sales of absentee ballots, Medicare fraud so rampant that Miami was identified as the center of such fraud in the US, and much more. The most scandalous case in 2012, however, involved the accusation by the Federal Securities and Exchange Commission (SEC) that Miami's authorities had—once again—been found guilty of "manipulating its books to deceive bond investors." It was an exact repeat of infractions committed in 2001. The reactions of key players who have time-and-time-again been brought in to perform the Herculean task of cleaning up Miami's dirt reflect a certain emotional exhaustion. "Why is anyone surprised?" asked former City Manager Joe Arriola. "I am not surprised at all," joined in former City Manager Merritt Stierheim. And attorney Thomas Tew, who had defended the City in 2001, summed it all up when he asked rhetorically, "You would ask, 'when are they going to get religion here?'"

Is it any surprise that the flag of the Banana Republic was flying over Miami? It was not the first time that this very pejorative label had been applied to the city. After the Elián González case (discussed more fully below) hundreds of specially-designed Banana Republic flags were displayed from houses and cars, especially in the more Anglo neighborhoods. The difference between the "Elián" case and the 2012 "cooking the books" case is that the vitriol which followed the former seems absent in this more recent one. Could it be that even the Cuban-American community has become jaded by so many tales of corruption that ennui has set in? If that were not the case there would be more local investigations and revelations and less dependence on federal action. The *Miami Herald* (19 August 2012) editorialized after reviewing the sordid history of corruption: "Better policing is not the federal government's role alone." It appears that after two decades of grand jury investigations, the community seems emotionally drained by the constant revelations and worried that Miami-Dade's reputation is suffering.

On the other hand, it is quite understandable why Miami-Dade's social and political leaders—no matter what their ethnicity—are not in a self-critical mode. They are well aware of how delicate tourist-based economies are, and stand eternally vigilant and ready to respond to any and all negative comments by finding plausible excuses or explanations. This explains why they did not scream bloody murder when the influential magazine *Forbes* named Miami "America's most miserable city" in 2012. Crime, foreclosures, unemployment, and poor education are all cited as reasons for this misery. It is great, said *Forbes*, for the 1 percent who builds multimillion dollar homes on gated island communities. "But, if you are among the 75 percent of households with an annual income under $75,000, it can be a hard place." Showing the new public relations attitude, the Miami-Dade Mayor's office had a ready response: "Miami is a sexy city to highlight. Of course they'd pick Miami as No.1." "Sexy" it is to be sure, but that does not explain away the ugly facts raised by the magazine. These same elites could hardly be pleased but did not make a federal case of it when the Illinois Institute of Government and Public Affairs ranked Miami as the fifth most corrupt city in the country and Florida the fourth most corrupt state. The ranking was based on the number of convictions of public officials over the past 25 years.

A "homeless" on Miami's South Beach

The fundamental challenge in the pursuit of a cosmopolitan identity, not just as a city with global functions but also as a city with a creative class and sophisticated population, is how to separate the wheat from the chaff when reading reports paid for by City officials. How does one strike a balance between retaining the charm of the *patria chica* while discarding its parochialism? This is the only way to know what the real, systemic challenges are. For instance, delving deeper into the "Destination 2001" study cited above, one discovers that after all the hyped claims to being the city of the future, there is the following sobering statement: "Today, 40 percent of the Greater Miami Community either lives in poverty, is under-employed, is less educated than the national average, or classifies as medically indigent. We are the third poorest large metropolitan area in the country." This was 2001. But on 18 February 2012 the *New York Times* published a "Poverty Top 40" ranking, and Miami was still third as the city with the highest percentages of poor. The worrying thing is that while the first and second poorest, Detroit and Cleveland, are old rust-belt cities, Miami is quite new and has had nothing to do with the deindustrialization process which affected the first two.

The real-life implications for Miami of this situation were pointed out by Willy Staley in a piece in the magazine *Next American City* in 2010. Older, poor cities compare their inequality with other cities, but in richer cities "the inequality is put side-by-side, in an uncomfortable, loathsome way." Such comparisons engender inter-ethnic resentments and urban conflict of the type we have often witnessed in Miami. It is true that Miami-Dade has made significant strides in the past decade. But, again, note how the above-mentioned 2011 "One Community One Goal" report, which was keen to celebrate these strides, concludes with a less congratulatory caveat on what is achieved locally and what is due to national inputs:

> In summary, the unfortunate truth of Miami-Dade's industry perform-
> ance during the past decade is that when industries experienced positive
> growth, *it was primarily due to national trends—not improvement in local
> competitiveness.*

Emphasis has been added to the quote because of the critical reality it spells out. Even as the national recession which began in 2007 had a very negative impact on construction, mining, manufacturing, transportation, financial activities, professional services, and a slew of other sectors, Miami's lack of autonomous initiatives meant that it performed worse than the national norm. The only services which performed better than the national trend were private education, health services, leisure, and hospitality services, with a slight positive shift in trade and transport. These sectoral successes are not enough to push Miami-Dade into the top rank of global and metropolitan cities.

The facts are that by July 2011 Miami-Dade had an unemployment rate of 13.1 percent, 3.9 percent higher than the national average. Translated into human terms this meant 170,000 residents without work. Granted that unemployment was a problem Miami shared with much of the country, what was very much unique to Miami-Dade County was the sharply defined dual or bimodal nature of this unemployment and of its economy and society in general. The stark divergences between the three fundamental ethnic groups which compose Miami-Dade's society indicate that two groups made progress but one remained stagnant. Miami-Dade's black community did not show—and has not shown since it was ghettoized from the very origins of the city—any capacity to develop its own internal growth, or indeed to piggy-back on the growth of the others. It has been bypassed in many fundamental ways by the other two sectors in the much-desired voyage to a cosmopolitan future.

If, as the quite evidently wishful thinking "One Community, One Goal" report says, Miami-Dade lacks its own internal dynamic of growth, then the black community is an extremely negative expression of that problem. By whatever institutional measure one approaches the question, whether it is structural issues such as low educational levels; inadequate capital investments in jobs, housing, and health; or problems ultimately within their own domain such as high levels of crime and the desperate poverty of single-parent female-led households, the black community has not benefitted so far from Miami-Dade's nationally and internationally impelled development.

A comparison with the other two groups, the Hispanics and the Anglos, attests to this as well as providing a sobering window into the real "guts" of this city. In so doing we anticipate our conclusion: cosmopolitan urbanity cannot be achieved without bringing into the mainstream all parts of the society, including this depressed and deprived black sector.

This will require moving away from the parochialism which characterizes important segments of the city's elite.

The first thing to notice in the 2000–2010 interval between the two reports prepared by the Miami Chamber of Commerce noted above is that while the Hispanic population of Miami-Dade grew 25.7 percent (from 1,291,737 to 1,623,859), the non-Hispanic whites lost 17.7 percent (from 465,772 to 383,551). Among those whites under the age of 18 the decline was 28 percent, and we have yet to study why this is so. Young and not-so-young whites were being educated in Miami but leaving to work elsewhere. In contrast, the majority of the non-Hispanic black population was stuck, having—it would appear—nowhere to go, seen in the fact that they lost only 0.3 percent of their numbers (from 427,140 to 425,650). The result was that in 2010 Miami-Dade County was 65 percent Hispanic, 17.1 percent black, and 15.4 percent non-Hispanic white. Important in terms of race relations, however, is that since the majority of Hispanics listed themselves as white, Miami-Dade was, in 2011, approximately 80 percent white.

It should be clear that, as was noted in Chapter Four, Cubans and Hispanics in general take the matter of being white very seriously, an attitude which is probably enhanced as they compete with white Anglos in a society where whites dominate. But beyond race and ethnicity there is economic performance, and in that the Hispanics excel. Again, there is nothing unusual here. We have seen this pattern of immigrant entrepreneurial behavior in other cities. The history of the success of black Caribbean immigrants to New York is often cited as a case where culture trumps race. Similarly, the great success of the Dominican *bodegero* (small shopkeeper) in New York is always held up as an example of immigrant optimal efforts. As far as Cubans are concerned, their entrepreneurial skills are legendary not just in Miami but in virtually every other part of the world where they have settled. They are famous for putting out maximal efforts in their work and for using their high rate of savings for opportune investments. The Cuban participation in the Hispanic successes in Miami is evident in the following data from the 2010 US Census, best presented in the form of a table:

	Hispanic		Black American	
	1987	2007	1987	2007
Number of				
Firms Owned:	47,725	244,148	9,747	46,072
Total Sales:	$ 4.5bn	$ 45bn	$ 260m	$ 2.6bn
Employment:	+/- 80,000	169,525	16,783	11,607

In 2007 Cubans represented 48.2 percent of all Hispanic firms and 54.8 percent of total sales. Of the black-owned firms that year 43,643 were sole proprietor and had no paid employees. Black paid employees averaged $23,126 per year, only 57.1 percent of the county average of $40,469. Black participation in the Miami-Dade County business community declined from 2 percent in 2002 to 1.2 percent in 2007. With over 17 percent of the population, the black share of Miami-Dade's annual payroll was 1.4 percent, mostly in the public sector. It is a community which is not just stagnating, but falling behind. The assessment of the Miami-Dade County Office of Planning Research (June 2011) is hardly reassuring: "Overall, Black-owned businesses in Miami-Dade did improve their participation in terms of firms in 2007, but for most of the other measures, such as receipts, employment, and payroll, the rate of their entrepreneurship remained the same or declined."

How different their description of the situation of Hispanic economic power. Noting the fast pace of growth of Hispanic firms and employment but specifying that by 2007 they had not "reached their potential," the Planning Department believed that given their present situation and rate of growth, hitting that theoretical but plausible potential would mean 327,000 new jobs and $76.3 billion in receipts.

As Miami-Dade's population increases, the growth of Hispanic-owned businesses in size and capacity becomes critical for job creation and this should be encouraged by the area's public and private leaders.

It is worth observing for its future relevance that should the 1.6 million Hispanics in Miami-Dade reach their potential earnings of $76.3 billion, this would be $26 billion more than the whole Gross National Income of Cuba in 2010, a country of eleven million people.

The Cuban Paradox

Shifting the analysis from economic to broader social concerns, one has to enquire whether the economic advantages of the Cuban-American community and its successful assimilation have made a significant contribution to Miami-Dade as a whole, not just as an economic global city but as a cosmopolitan one. Former Mayor Maurice Ferré worried in 2001 that Miami was rapidly becoming a global city but "not yet a cosmopolitan city." In Chapter Four we described the responses of certain Cuban-American leaders regarding their sentiments about Cuba vis-à-vis the US. What is revealed is a community still living on memories, feeding a quite understandable nostalgia for the beautiful island, and essentially geographically and culturally compartmentalized by its ethnic concerns and indifferent to the concerns of other members of the community. Four incidents reveal how the parochial *patria chica* depth of these in-group feelings can lead to bad, self-harming decisions.

It is the essential characteristic of parochialism that there is limited interest in the views and existential realities of those who do not belong to the *patria chica*. It is especially true of a community which sees itself not as immigrants like all the others around them, but as refugees. Refugees, as previously noted, are motivated by deep psychological injuries not easily healed. In this lies a paradox: the intensity and passion of the Cuban-American community contributes enormously to the making of this global, even metropolitan, city, those same sentiments stand in the way of its becoming a cosmopolitan one.

The first was the snub in June 1990 of the visit by Nelson Mandela to the city of Miami. Mandela's refusal to denounce Fidel Castro and Yasser Arafat was deeply resented, and the Cuban elite showed no hesitation in demonstrating their feelings. The Cuban mayors of the cities of Miami, Hialeah, West Miami, Sweetwater, and Hialeah Gardens, and the then-Governor of Florida, Bob Martinez (not Cuban but of an old Tampa Hispanic family), all boycotted Mandela's visit. Newspaper advertisements and small airplanes trailing banners protesting against Mandela's friendship with Castro were everywhere during his stay in the city. Not even four thousand black Americans gathered in Miami for a convention caused much concern to the Cuban-American leadership. When offended black officials threatened to boycott Miami it did not make the least difference to the adamant Cuban-Americans. Because there was no national interest

Cuban-Americans celebrate

involved (at the time Mandela was not a head of state, nor was he in Miami on an official visit but at the invitation of the American Federation of State, County and Municipal Employees) there was no Washington interference. To the national and international communities, the Cuban-Americans seemed awfully intolerant.

An incident which did involve the US government directly was the so-called Elián González case in 1999. Stubbornness made any resolution far from easy. No one disputed the fact that the young child, Elián, was found by the US Coast Guard floating in the Straits of Florida. An ill-fated attempt by his mother and others to reach Miami by boat had left him orphaned of one parent. The Coast Guard put him in the custody of an uncle in Miami. The father, who had not authorized the trip, was in Cuba and demanded that the boy's relatives in Miami return the child to him. United States law was clear: the father had parental rights and thus legitimate claim to the boy. The US Departments of State and Justice requested that Elián be turned over to the authorities for return to his father's custody in Cuba. But ethnic politics and ideology intervened in a boisterous way. The Cuban community stood firm: 79 percent of them believed Elián should stay with his relatives in Miami. When US Attorney General Janet Reno (a Miami native and former elected state attorney in Miami-Dade) ordered the Miami family to give up the child, they barricaded themselves in their Little Havana home and called on the community to rise to their defense. After considerable and ultimately futile negotiations between the US government officials and the family, federal agents and local marshals with their faces covered stormed the house and took the crying child away. All this was captured on camera and televised nationally, causing total revulsion in the Miami Cuban community. The fact that other communities in Miami approved of the operation was irrelevant to them. A poll taken by Schroft and Associates indicated that 91 percent of Cubans disapproved of the federal operation, but 82 percent of Miami's non-Cuban whites, 85 percent of black Miamians, and 40 percent of non-Cuban Hispanics approved of the efforts to restore Elián to his father in Cuba.

This long, drawn-out process had further polarized the community and the big loser was the national image of Miami. Polls taken by Schroft and Associates and one done by Florida International University revealed that 81 percent of non-Cuban whites, 64 percent of black Americans, and even 82 percent of Cubans themselves believed that the Elián González case had a very negative impact on the image of the Cuban community and of Miami. Where they differed was in attributing blame. Cuban-Americans generally associated the operation with President Bill Clinton and with the "history" of Democratic Party "betrayals" of Cuban exiles, not unlike what they believe John F. Kennedy had done to them during the Bay of Pigs invasion many decades previously. Little different from other communities of exiles, Miami Cubans have long but also selective memories. One can readily understand that the one thousand five hundred Cubans, who landed in Cuba in the 1961 Bay of Pigs invasion (and let it be said, fought bravely to their last bullet) felt betrayed by President Kennedy's decision to remove air support. However, there is seldom any analysis of whether such air support would have guaranteed the success of a mission badly conceived by the CIA. Beyond this sad Bay of Pigs incident, fairness would have Cuban-Americans recognize that it was Democratic President L. B. Johnson who provided them with millions of dollars in assistance through the Cuban Refugee Act, and Democratic President Jimmy Carter who facilitated the settlement of over one hundred thousand arrivals from Mariel through the Refugee Act of 1980.

The anti-Democratic Party atmosphere in Miami-Dade was still boiling when the campaign for the 2000 presidential elections began twelve months later. The Cuban-American radio and press were determined to exact revenge on Al Gore, the Democratic candidate. They had, said columnist Soren Triff, been "sharpening their teeth" for the political kill. The expectation was that with George W. Bush's brother Jeb Bush Governor of Florida, with both houses of the State's Congress in Republican hands, and with Katherine Harris, the Secretary of State in charge of the state's electoral system serving as Bush's campaign manager in the state, he would win handily. He eventually won, but hardly "handily." When Bush's total in Florida reached 537 votes more than Al Gore's, Secretary Harris ordered the counting stopped even though there were still 111,000 ballots left to count which by law had to be counted by hand. The whole nation came to a standstill and was on tenterhooks for over 35 days while the "Battle of the Chads" unfolded in heavily Democratic Miami-Dade, Broward, and Palm Beach counties. People were transfixed by the differences between acceptable hand-punched paper ballots showing "descended chads" and questionable "dimpled" and "hanging" chads. The Florida Supreme Court, after a two-week legal argument, ordered that the count be continued, only to have the US Supreme Court order it stopped. The vote in the US Supreme Court was five to four on an evident ideological divide. Before this decision and with Cuban radio stations calling on their partisans to stop any further counting, suddenly, a well-organized mob of some 500 young Republicans recruited in Miami, Texas, and Missouri stormed the offices where the votes were being counted, successfully stopping the count of the ballots in Miami. An influential Cuban-American radio commentator on the most listened-to Spanish-language station, Radio Mambi, when asked whether his broadcast accusations that Democrats were anti-Cuban and that they were trying to "steal" the election were fair play, answered: "We Cubans are politicized, we cannot be impartial. Radio Mambi is not an impartial station."

Bush eventually won the election by 537 Florida votes which gave him the entire 25 Electoral College votes of the state, even as Gore had bested him by 539,947 popular votes nationwide. Again, the divide in

Miami-Dade was evident in the vote: for Gore non-Cuban whites 42 percent, Cuban-Americans 21 percent, black-Americans 90 percent, Jewish 79 percent, Central Americans 74 percent, South Americans 69 percent, Mexican-Americans 69 percent, and Puerto Ricans 71 percent. Gore received 21 percent of the Cuban-American vote but 79 percent voted in favor of Bush.

Cuban ethnic solidarity was on display when the highest-ranking Democratic official in Miami-Dade, Cuban-American Mayor Alex Penelas, purposely went on vacation in Spain absenting himself from the fray and refusing to return calls from the Democratic candidate. He did, however (according to the *New York Times*), stay in touch with Cuban-American leaders of the Republican Party. Predictably, such collective hysteria in Florida—and in Miami in particular—was made the butt of a thousand jokes and the object of national and international ridicule. The most commonly heard insult was the one which has always hurt the most: that Miami was a "banana republic."

The fourth illustration of counterproductive political sectarianism occurred at the ribbon-cutting of the Metromover's link to Miami International Airport. The construction job, praised by one and all for being within budget and more or less on time, was one of many carried out in Miami by the Brazilian multinational corporation Odebrecht USA. As the Brazilian representative got up to speak, the four Cuban-American members of the US House of Representatives rose in unison and left the room. The reason given for such boorish behavior in a city now full of Brazilian tourists, buyers of real estate, and other investors? A branch of Odebrecht (which has seven distinct business divisions working in twenty countries) is working on the modernization of the port of Mariel in Cuba. The flag of the Banana Republic can justly be flown over Miami on such occasions.

These four incidents reveal a community of exiles—not immigrants—who bear profound psychological scars from having "lost" their country. In a way they are similar in psychological, though not ideological, terms to those Russian "romantic exiles" described by E. H. Carr in his 1933 treatise *The Romantic Exiles:* people who lived their lives "refusing to make compromises with reality." They feed on Rousseau's "apotheosis of the feelings" or, as Carr put it, the belief in "the natural goodness of human emotions and their sufficiency as a guide to human conduct." They are what Alejandro Portes and Alex Stepick call "a moral community" and engage in what Damián Fernández calls "the politics of passion."

This explains the tenacious persistence of partisan attitudes so evident in the attitude of those Cuban-Americans who have been successful in national politics. A case in point is ex-US Representative from Miami, David Rivera. As a young law student in 1987 he told the *Miami Herald*: "We've pulled ourselves up, why should we restrain ourselves? I don't think the Cuban community in Miami owes anything politically or economically to anyone. The Cuban community succeeded because it's been loyal to itself." This is the same David Rivera who as an influential member, first in the Florida House and then in the US Congress, continually initiated legislation punishing anyone who was or is even mildly interested in promoting US-Cuban relations. At the time of writing, this same politician was under investigation by the FBI and the IRS for his financial dealings with the owner of the local Flagler Dog Track, who hired him to promote the legalization of slot machines in Florida. On 22 August 2012, both the *Miami Herald* and *El Nuevo Herald* carried with banner headlines the accusation that Rivera was involved in a classical case of Banana Republic-style political high jinks: funding with "envelopes stuffed with crisp $100 bills" the campaign of a "ringer" to oppose his nemesis, Joe Garcia, in the primaries of the rival Democratic Party. Bernadette Pardo of *El Nuevo Herald* (25 August 2012) called him a magician, surviving on his strident anti-Castroism. The dean of Miami journalists, Michael Putney, agreed but believed that his "magic" is coming to an end. Putney was prescient: Rivera was defeated in his 2012 re-election bid by a Democratic rival, also Cuban-American.

It is this affinity for raw emotions, kept alive and fresh by selected memories, which explains the proliferation of naming streets after Cubans, some heroic and others not-so-heroic and most not even remotely related to Miami's history. Should leaders of the Cuban-American political elite wish to promote cosmopolitanism they will have to recognize the debt they owe to other minorities who blazed a path which they emulated. Miami-Dade's Cubans benefitted quite early on from nationwide minority-group pressure which had generated a social and political climate propitious to ethnic bargaining. In Miami it was the liberal Jewish community which pushed reforms. In the Hispanic population it was the Mexican-

American sector more than any other through their labor mobilizations that had stretched the boundaries of political participation by all Hispanics, whether citizens or not. Blacks at the national level also made their contribution. The Voting Rights Act of 1965 was a direct result of Black civil rights agitation, and the "Hispanic Amendment" of 1975 to that act was due mostly to Mexican-American lobbying. The amendment provided for bilingual voting materials and instructions as well as bilingual poll workers in any precinct with more than ten Latin voters. It is significant that the defeat in 1980 of Miami-Dade County's bilingual statute in no way affected these federal regulations, an indication of the value of ethnic bargaining that targets federal rather than local legislation. That said, much credit must be given to the community of Cuban-Americans for not sitting on their hands.

There is, however, a crucial and admirable indicator of Cuban political culture: the early trend toward acquisition of citizenship, a move strongly encouraged by the influential Jorge Más Canosa and his Cuban American National Foundation. Rejecting violence, he argued that Cuban-Americans should become US citizens and begin lobbying as Americans do. Because what was involved was a deliberate act to acquire citizenship, the figures contain broader implications for the collective outlook of this community. In 1970 it was calculated that only 25 percent of Miami-Dade's Cubans were US citizens. By 1980 43.3 percent of a representative sample of foreign-born Hispanics (mostly Cubans) had become citizens, and 77.2 percent of those with permanent resident status indicated their intention of becoming citizens. Fully 90 percent of those who arrived before 1980 (generally known as *históricos*) are US citizens, in contrast to 60 percent of those who arrived in the 1980s, and only 18 percent of those who came after 1990. Regardless of such differences, it is very impressive that 86.9 percent of Cubans who are citizens are registered voters, and of these an amazing 85.4 percent tend to exercise that vote. (Compare this to the 50 percent of Anglos, 44 percent of American blacks, and 31 percent of other eligible Hispanics who vote.) On that score alone they are exemplary.

The trend toward citizenship clearly provides another indicator of permanence in the United States and in Miami-Dade County. Perhaps the most significant feature of this process, however, is that it symbolized the climax of a successful Cuban-American political journey rather than the beginning of it. An approximation to local power was achieved prior to citizenship, not because of it. Citizenship achieved, it facilitated the retention of that power and for its exercise at state and national levels, not just locally. Unsurprisingly, therefore, the decision to adopt US citizenship caused little erosion in the depth of ethnic attachments and loyalties, which after all were and are the true foundations of political culture and action. Given the intensity of feelings of *cubanidad*, citizenship was a matter of instrumental, strategic choice not primordial attachment. Cuban-Americans had assimilated without fully acculturating.

Direct participation in the political process explains the success of the community as a whole. Date of arrival, however, is crucial in explaining political leadership. This explains the controversy over the claim by Cuban-American Senator Marco Rubio—rising star nationally and darling of the Tea Party—that his parents were "exiles." In fact, his parents migrated to Florida in 1957, two years before Fidel Castro took power. In his 2012 autobiography *An American Son* he fudges other dates and begs many a question as to his family's attempt to return to Cuba in 1961 as well as the seedy background of his brother-in-law. But this has made no difference to his extraordinary popularity in the community, or, indeed, at the national level. He is the *patria chica*'s favorite son, and woe betide anyone who dares raise delicate questions. A case in point is the community's angry reaction when Mexican-owned Univision TV, with the largest Spanish-language audience in the US, revealed that Rubio's brother-in-law, Orlando Cicilia, had been convicted and sentenced to a long prison term for drug trafficking, and that the federal government had confiscated Cicilia's house and many other properties because they could not locate $15 million in drug profits which the jury concluded he had received. Manuel Roig-Franzia in his largely sympathetic book, *The Rise of Marco Rubio* (2012), dedicates ten pages not so much to Cicilia's crime as to the spineless response of the local press to Univision's investigation. National media such as the *New Yorker* and the *Columbia Journalism Review* did full analyses of the affair from the point of view of journalistic courage and the lack of it. The moral of the story is that in the *patria chica*'s favorite sons are not to be scrutinized too thoroughly.

What reigns is not so much forgiveness as indifference towards nefariousness, as we noted in Chapter Three. In that Cubans cannot be singled out. Miamians in general tend to turn a blind eye towards what is often regarded as garden-variety malfeasance.

GAMBLING ON THE FUTURE

How, in a city in the midst of a collapse of the real estate sector (and thus with plummeting revenues from property taxes) could all the grand projects be funded? Once more, chance or, more accurately, historical conjuncture intervened. Just as Miami-Dade was in recession, with thousands of condominiums sitting empty, many countries to Florida's south were starting to expand economically and the traditional trickle of capital flight became a torrent. Brazilians, Argentinians, Colombians, and Venezuelans began buying up what to them was relatively cheap vacant property in Miami. They also began setting up businesses under a US immigration visa geared towards foreign investors who create at least ten new jobs.

In 2012 Brazil's largest state-run bank, Banco do Brasil, bought a small Florida bank, EuroBank, for $6 million. It was clear evidence that Brazil—as of 2010 the world's sixth major economic power—was interested in Miami and that there was already a serious Brazilian presence in Miami-Dade. As Eike Batista, Brazil's richest man and most active entrepreneur, told the *New York Times* (21 January 2012), "Brazil today has the wealth that America had at the turn of the century." Every week American Airlines makes 52 flights to Miami from five Brazilian cities. These flights transport 1.1 million Brazilian tourists who on average spend $2,053 each (compared to $1,432 spent by Canadians). This brings the total spent by Brazilians in Miami-Dade County in 2011 to $1.6 billion, and in the US to $5.9 billion. These "tourists" were also buying property. The reason, aside from the fact that they liked the security and the ambiance which Miami had to offer, was economic. In São Paolo and Rio de Janeiro real estate prices had been rising by 25 percent per year while in Miami-Dade they were decreasing by 10 to 25 percent. Mexicans, who have traditionally invested in towns on the American side of the border, were also buying in Miami. It is not known what percentage of the $31 billion Mexicans invested in the US in 2008 came to Miami, but several new real estate offices in the city were catering to Mexican buyers. As was discussed in Chapter Seven, much of this capital flow is contributing to Miami's urbanization. It is potentially a game-changer for the city's political culture. Is it, however, enough to engender a cosmopolitan culture?

Miami's elites seemed to have overlooked the historical fact that moving from being merely urban in buildings and demography to urbanity in culture and behavior requires major, holistic changes in the nature of a city's development—in housing, commerce, and the ethnic composition of new residents. There is evidence that Miami is heading that way. The creation of a true urban mass with the kind of mixed-use of residences, shops, and parks so recommended by Jacobs appears to have started on Brickell Avenue and is moving north to downtown Miami. The key to understanding Brickell is that the rows of condominiums occupied by Argentines, Brazilians, Venezuelans, Central Americans, and Cubans will now have an urban core. It is called Brickell CitiCentre, a $1.05 billion urban shopping complex and mixed-use development built by Swire Properties on three city blocks west of Brickell Avenue. It will front the southern bank of the Miami river and connect to the northern side by bridges and covered walkways. It is expected to open in 2015. The president of Swire Properties might not have overstated the case when he predicted that this project was about "changing the community." Again, it was Miami's Arquitectónica architectural firm with its signature open-air

Architectural mock-up of planned Brickell CitiCentre

concept which designed the entire project. The seven new condominiums built by the Related Group and called "My Brickell" will also access Brickell CitiCentre. The redevelopment of downtown will be further enhanced when the Omni Center and its Hilton Miami Downtown, a property which occupies fourteen acres north of downtown, is developed. It lies just north of the Arsht Center for the Performing Arts and both the MacArthur and Venetian Causeways to Miami Beach.

Fundamental to the creation of this urban cluster is that the residential population in what is already being called the Downtown Miami/Brickell area reached 71,600 in 2011 and, given the building taking place, will probably reach 100,000 within five more years. It is also calculated that over 200,000 work-day persons will come to work, shop and use the restaurants. A Publix Supermarket and a Whole Foods Market will be there, as well as a Metromover station to serve the area. This Brickell complex will be just south of other poles of urban development including the gentrification of Miami's Design District, a proposed upscale shopping and gallery destination led by developer Craig Robbins, who wishes to make it resemble New York's SoHo neighborhood. Additionally, the Genting Group has plans for the forty acres it bought, including the Miami Herald property right on Biscayne Bay and the Omni International Mall right across the street. In December 2012, Miami's Historic Preservation Board decided against designation of the Herald building as a protected landmark, opening up the opportunity for the Genting Group to completely redesign downtown. Even the editors of the *Herald*, having already shifted their operations to Doral, approve of the Preservation Board's decision. Genting's vision for that property includes a $3 billion casino complex, the planning of which is now in the hands of Arquitectónica. The complete realization of these plans, however, depends on securing State of Florida permission to build and run the casino on the property named Resorts World Miami.

It has not been easy going for the Genting Group. Powerful interests oppose the granting of a license for a casino. Perhaps most influential is the Walt Disney Corporation, which argues that a casino will tarnish Florida's reputation as a family-oriented tourist destination. This position is supported by the Florida Chamber of Commerce and existing gambling establishments such as the race tracks (horse and dog racing) and the Seminole and Miccosukee tribes' casinos. These groups fear the competition. A different motivation drives an association of conservative religious groups which have joined the opposition. To understand the principled position of these groups one has to recall the days when Mob-dominated gambling ran amok in South Florida. The reality they face, however, is that Florida is already one of the major gambling states in the US, with various types of lottery, legal and illegal operation of slot machines, gambling at Jai-Alai games, pari-mutuel gambling on racetracks where slot machines are legal, and, of course, the enormous casinos run by the Seminole and Miccosukee Indians. In other words, the Genting Group is not introducing a new form of behavior into South Florida. As if all these gambling opportunities on US soil were not enough, there is also a gambling cruise ship which departs Miami every evening and opens its casino as soon as it is outside US territorial waters and into Bahamian waters.

As if to send Florida a message, the Genting Group has other options regarding a casino within reach of South Florida clients. In August 2012 it signed a deal to open the sole casino on Bimini in the Bahamas, a project called the Bimini Bay Resort and Casino. The complex is owned by Cuban-American developer Gerardo Capo and sports a 250-room Conrad Hotel (Hilton's luxury brand), 500 condominiums and houses, a 550-slip marina, and an eighteen-hole golf course. It covers one-tenth of the 9.5-square-mile island, which has at most 2,000 inhabitants. The advantages of this casino, should Genting's Miami project not be approved, is that it is a mere 48 miles from the coast of Florida—a half hour plane ride or two-and-a-half-hour boat ride. A high-speed ferry will make the trip in ninety minutes. Capo Group executive Sean Grimburg describes the project precisely when he says, "We're building Bimini as Miami's next playground. And it's just a hop, skip, and a jump away." In a way, it is an extension of metropolitan Miami-Dade, but in a sovereign country. There will be no long delays in getting permits for a casino there.

As extensive as all this urban development certainly is, it is not at all certain that it will represent a transformation for Miami-Dade as a whole. There is no guarantee that the new foreign urban dwellers filling the condominiums will be active participants in the area's life. How many will settle and become citizens, and of those who do how many will vote and elect more cosmopolitan leaders? The results of the 2012 national elections in Florida gave a surprising victory to the Democratic candidate Barack Obama. Even more surprising was the fact that for the first time ever 48 percent of the Cuban-American vote went to the Democratic candidate—certainly less than the 63 percent of Hispanics overall who voted Democrat but nevertheless 10 percent higher than the vote for Obama in the 2008 elections and so a significant change. Even if it is entirely possible that Miami-Dade will remain segmented by turfs with the most parochial ones still doing the electing, things are beginning to change. If the new residents populating urban Miami do not adopt the indifference evident in the Anglo and black communities, much more will change.

CONCLUSION: ACROSS THE STRAITS

Should the hypothesized loosening of the grip of the Cuban *históricos* materialize then another fundamental event just might be by far the greatest agent of change: the opening of Cuba and its relations with Miami. At present there is a modest relaxation in Cuba to American and Cuban-American trade. A complete opening of trade, however, would involve every sector of Miami-Dade's community. The activities of the cruise and cargo port, the airport, the export of agricultural and manufacturing goods, exchanges of educational and other technical personnel, and expertize would all expand. Given Cuba's present underdevelopment, a concerted effort by all Miamians can contribute enormously to reversing that condition. The *patria chica* would become the *patria grande*. In the same way that Fidel Castro's active dislike of Havana and its cosmopolitan elite led him to abandon the city to its sad decline and, consequently, fuel Miami's expansion, so the new *apertura* will surely draw Havana into Miami's exploding metropolitan reach and Miami into Havana's fading but still smoldering enchantments. In a short time the number of emotion-laden personal, commercial, cultural, and social interactions which are the fundamental elements of broad metropolitan areas will have multiplied at an ever-increasing pace.

In many ways there is already a Miami-Cuba transnational community in place and it is invariably the people of these communities, much more than any formal, institutional city or country administrations—in the US or Cuba—who shape metropolitan areas. All this transcends formal geographical definitions of "the city" to become a virtual or post-city phenomenon. Even without the lifting of the futile fifty-year-old embargo and its evident revanchist tendencies, Miami and Havana, from whence 70 percent of the Cuban refugees come, have moved, slowly but surely, closer together. All the measures of the Cuban-American politicians attempting to stop this movement have been in vain.

By 2009 Miami had already been supplying Cuba with much of what it needs for its expanding tourist industry: fancy beef from Florida, Bertram yachts for its tourist industry, and even Daiquiri cocktail mix for both its legendary and the newer drinking holes. Given that the chartered flights to Havana were frightfully expensive but the demand continued, shipping by sea began. Crowley Maritime, operating out of Port Everglades in Fort Lauderdale, has a weekly ship carrying humanitarian and other products allowed by law, and in August 2012 a once-a-week ship began ferrying similar goods to Cuba from Miami. Since no trade is allowed under the US embargo legislation (the Helms-Burton law) the ship returns empty. This will eventually change.

The reforms in Cuba are painfully slow to come, but come they will, at least in the economic arena. The failures of the Cuban socialist model are too severe and generalized to delay reforms much longer. By 2011 Cubans were already allowed to hold foreign currency and to buy and sell automobiles and houses. With these changes in place, the flow of remittances from Miami, calculated in 2009 to be between $600 million and $1 billion, will take on greater importance in accelerating them. Understandably, it is the group which emigrated after 1985 which sends the most money to Cuba, but perhaps more revealing of lingering emotional ties and ethnic sentiments is that 58 percent of all Cuban-Americans remit funds to their relatives on the island. The number of businesses announcing *Envíos a Cuba* stands as evidence of this trend. A 2010 survey by the Inter-American Dialogue of 300 Cuban recipients of money from Miami revealed that they planned to use the money to open a small business, to become a *cuentapropista*, a small capitalist. What the millions spent on Radio and TV Martí have not been able to achieve, the Miami community's actions have: unleashed pent-up desires for more private initiatives. This is the theme of a fine book on the relations between Miami and the island, Maria de los Angeles Torres' *In the Land of Mirrors: Cuban Exile Politics in the United States* (2001). Governments, she argues, cannot much longer impede the tremendous human desire to belong as Cubans because, no matter how hard they try, "they cannot legislate identities, they cannot erase our history."

Can there be any doubt that the Miami community is integrating itself into the Cuba which is developing in a slow but inevitable process of economic decentralization and low-level privatization?

It will not be easy to change some of those who reject any form of reconciliation. Local reactions to the efforts of Cuba's Roman Catholic Cardinal Jaime Ortega to establish bridges with the regime reflect that hard line. Note that the head of Radio and TV Martí, an official US government agency, called Cardinal Ortega a "lackey," Guillermo Martínez of the *Sun Sentinel* called him a "bootlicker," and the babalú blog labeled him a "despicable man." As a cardinal, it should be recalled, Ortega takes his orders from the Vatican and two popes have visited Cuba. If one is to understand why on 10 September 2012, for the first time in five decades, Cubans in Miami and in Cuba held processions for their patron saint, the Virgen de la Caridad, it is important to follow Vatican policy enacted through its cardinal in Cuba. Note that the Vatican has refused to name a Cardinal for the Miami Church. Ortega is the Cardinal of all Cubans. Continued intransigence on both sides will not stop these growing contacts.

Of course, intransigence can continue to reach levels of unreality, as when the former director of TV Martí and principal legal counsel to the University of Miami's Institute of Cuban and Cuban-American Studies haughtily deigns to teach Cardinal Ortega what canonical law dictates about "reconciliation" (*El Nuevo Herald*, 12 August 2012). It requires, he says, three stages: the recognition that a crime was committed, the admission of guilt regarding that crime, and the begging of forgiveness. Since the Cuban military are not willing to do these three things, no reconciliation is possible.

No one who understands the history and present status of the Cuban military believes that they would be willing to do any of these three things. There is a good chance, however, that they will not repeat the recalcitrant attitude demonstrated by the president of the rubber-stamp Cuban Assembly, Ricardo Alarcón. In a quasi-debate held with exile leader Jorge Más Canosa and aired on CBS Telenoticias in September 1996, Más adopted a relatively conciliatory tone; Alarcón was supremely intransigent and denied that Más could have a future role in Cuba because he was "no longer Cuban." Both exile and Cuban resistance to reconciliation will have to change. As Henry Kissinger argued, "a stable social structure thrives not on triumphs but on reconciliation." Not surprisingly, Kissinger has long argued for further opening of US–Cuban relations.

It is evident that one of the most difficult accommodations any diaspora immigrant will have to make in Cuba will be between his or her privileged economic status and the political values of the host society, especially its military elites. To the extent that there are conflicts of accommodation, they will probably have little to do with ideology and international alignments and more to do with legal guarantees for any investments the returnee makes, property rights (including copyrights), and the deference demanded by the Cuban authorities. By the latter we mean simply respect for existing authority. As Harold Lasswell noted, "the common trait of the political personality type is emphatic demand for deference." In other words, the conflict will be more about assigning rights and mutual respect and deference to those with the most to contribute, rather than to those with the most to claim or sense of entitlement. Consequently, while there will be relatively little cultural and psychological trauma, it will make an enormous difference whether Cuban officials as hosts will be open to meeting the returnees expectations as to security of investments and the returnees' willingness to grant deference to those in power.

The upshot of all this is that if, as Robert Penn Warren maintains, "history is all explained by geography," then there is no escaping a future when Miami-Dade and Cuba will truly be what since its foundation in 1896 many of Miami's grand thinkers and builders wished it to be. Of all the changes in Miami's future nothing compares in potential impact to the possible creation of one great transnational community. It will signify coming full circle to the days when Miamians and Cubans reached across the Straits of Florida out of friendship and out of a profound sense that this benefitted both sides in myriad ways. The fervent hopes of closer ties felt by Flagler, the pioneers of aviation, Mayor King High, and so many others will finally be fulfilled. If at one time Miamians wanted to emulate the "tropical" style and flair of the Cubans, now Cubans will want to learn and benefit from the enterprising spirit, global business expertize, and capital of their Miami counterparts. Reconciliation, which necessarily means abandoning parochialism and intransigence, will have to be an integral part of the voyage of discovery. Can cosmopolitanism be far behind?

It all brings to mind a couplet in the poem "The Task" by the popular eighteenth-century English poet William Cowper:

Mountains interposed

Make enemies of nations, who had else,

Like kindred drops been mingled into one.

Further Reading

Allman, T. D. *Miami: City of the Future.* New York: Little Brown & Co., 1987.

Allen, Frederick Lewis. *Only Yesterday: Informal Treatment of the 1920s.* New York: Harper & Row, 1931.

Arend, Geoffrey. *Great Airports: Miami International.* Great Airports Books, 1993.

Ayers, R. Wayne. *Florida's Grand Hotels from the Gilded Age* (Images of America Series). Charleston, SC: Arcadia Publishing, 2005.

Barnebey, Faith High *Integrity is the Issue, Campaign Life with Robert King High.* Miami: E. A. Seemann Publishing, 1971.

Bosch, Juan *Cuba: La isla fascinante.* Santiago de Chile: Editorial Universitaria, 1955.

Brewer, Cynthia A. and Trudy A. Suchan. *Mapping Census 2000: The Geography of U.S. Diversity.* Redlands, CA: ESRI Press, 2001.

Buchanan, Edna. Miami, *It's Murder: A Britt Montero Novel* (Britt Montero Mysteries). New York: Avon Books, 1984.

— *Shadows.* New York: Simon & Schuster, 2005.

— *The Corpse Had a Familiar Face: Covering Miami, America's Hottest Beat.* New York: Pocket Books, 1987.

Cabrera Infante, Guillermo. *Tres tristes tigres.* Barcelona: Editorial Seix Barral, 1998.

Camayd-Freixas, Yohel. *Crisis in Miami: community context and institutional response in the adaptation of 1980 Mariel boatlift Cubans and undocumented Haitian entrants in South Florida.* Boston, MA: Boston Urban Research and Development Group, 1988.

Carlebach, Michael and Maggie Steber. *Assignment Miami: News Photographers.* Miami Museum of Southern Florida, nd.

Cope, Carol Soret. *In the Fast Lane: A True Story of Murder in Miami.* New York: Simon & Schuster, 1993.

Croucher, Sheila. L. *Imagining Miami: Ethnic Politics in a Post-Modern World.* Charlottesville: University of Virginia Press, 1997.

Derr, Mark. *Over Florida.* (Photography by Cameron Davidson, Foreword by Marjory Stoneman Douglas). New York: Mallard Press, 1992.

Didion, Joan. *Miami.* New York: Simon & Schuster, 1987.

Dunlop, Beth, Schezen, Roberto (eds.). *Miami Trends and Traditions.* New York: The Monacelli Press, 1996.

Dunn, Marvin, Bruce, Porter. *The Miami Riot of 1980: Crossing the Bounds.* Gainesville: University Press of Florida 1984.

Dunn, Marvin. *Black Miami and the Twentieth Century.* Gainesville: University Press of Florida 1997.

Eddy, Paul, Hugo Sabogal and Sara Walden. *The Cocaine Wars.* New York: W. W. Norton, 1988.

Eisenberg, Dennis, Uri Dan and Eli Landau. *Meyer Lansky: Mogul of the Mob.* New York: Paddington Press, 1979.

Eyster, Irving R. and Darlene Brown. *Indian Key.* Long Key, FL: Jeannie's Magic Printing, 1976.

Fairlie, Margaret-Carrick. *History of Florida.* Kingsport, TN: Kingsport Press, 1935.

Florida, Richard. *The Rise of the Creative Class Revisited.* New York: Basic Books, 2012.

Gaby, Donald C. *The Miami River and its Tributaries.* Miami: The Historical Association of Southern Florida, 1993.

Gannon, Michael (ed.). *The New History of Florida.* Gainesville: University Press of Florida 1996.

— *The Cross in the Sand: The Early Catholic Church in Florida 1513-1870.* Gainesville: University Press of Florida 1983.

— *Operation Drumbeat: The Dramatic True Story of Germany's First U-Boat Attacks.* Gainesville: University Press of Florida 1990.

— *Florida: A Short History.* Gainesville: University Press of Florida 1993.

García-Aguilera, Carolina. *Luck of the Draw: A Novel.* New York: Harper Collins, 2003.

Garreau, Joel. *The Nine Nations of North America.* New York: Avon Books, 1981.

George, Paul S. *A Journey Through Time: A Pictorial History of South Dade.* Virginia Beach, VA: The Donning Co., 1995.

Gjelten, Tom. *Bacardi and the Long Fight for Cuba: The Biography of a Cause.* New York: Viking, 2008.

Glaeser, Edward Ludwig. *Triumph of the City: How Our Greatest Invention Makes Us Richer, Smarter, Greener, Healthier, and Happier.* New York: The Penguin Press, 2011.

Grenier, Guillermo J. and Lisandro Pérez. *The Legacy of Exile: Cubans in the United States.* Boston: Allyn and Bacon, 2003.

Grenier, Guillermo and Alex Stepick (eds.). *Miami Now!: Immigration, Ethnicity and Social Change.* Gainesville: University Press of Florida, 1992.

Grippiando, James. *Hear No Evil.* New York: Harper Collins, 2005.

— *Born To Run.* New York: Harper Collins, 2009.

Grunwald, Michael. *The Swamp: The Everglades, Florida and the Politics of Paradise.* New York: Simon & Schuster, 2006.

Gugliotta, Guy and Jeff Leen. *Kings of Cocaine.* New York: Simon & Schuster, 1989.

Hall, James W. *Under Cover of Daylight.* New York: W. W. Norton, 1987.

— *Rough Draft.* New York: St. Martin's Press, 2000.

Hatch, Tom. *Osceola and the Great Seminole War: A Struggle for Justice and Freedom.* New York: St. Martin's Press, 2012.

Hiaasen, Carl and Bill Montalbano. *Powder Burn.* New York: Knopf Doubleday, 1998.

Hiaasen, Carl. *Tourist Season.* New York: Warner Books, 1986.

— *Strip Tease.* New York: Warner Books, 1993.

— *Stormy Weather.* New York: Warner Books, 1995.

— *Skinny Dip.* New York: Warner Books, 2004.

— *Hoot.* New York: Warner Books, 2004.

— *Star Island.* New York: Alfred A. Knopf, 2010.

Huff, Van E. and Robert Hardin. *From Mountains to Miami.* Miami: The Franklin Press, 1982.

Isaacson, Walter. *Kissinger: A Biography.* New York: Simon & Schuster, 1992.

Johnson, Chalmers. *Blowback: The Costs and Consequences of American Empire.* New York: Henry Holt, 2000.

Kleinberg, Howard (ed.). *Miami, The Way We Were.* Tampa, FL: Surfside Publishing, 1989.

Kobler, John. *Capone: The Life and World of Al Capone.* New York: Putnam, 1971.

Lacey, Robert. *Little Man: Meyer Lansky and the Gangster Life.* New York: Little Brown, 1991.

Lavender, Abraham D. *Miami Beach in 1920: The Making of a Winter Resort.* Charleston, SC: Arcadia, 2002.

Leamer, Laurence. *Madness Under the Royal Palms: Love and Death behind the Gates of Palm Beach.* New York: Hyperion, 1977.

Lightfoot, Claudia. *Havana: A Cultural and Literary Companion.* Oxford: Signal Books, 2002.

Marshall, Dawn J. *The Haitian Problem: Illegal Migration to the Bahamas.* Kingston: ISER, 1979.

McClintick, David. *Sword-Fish: A True Story of Ambition, Savagery and Betrayal.* New York: Pantheon Books, 1993.

Messick, Hank. *Syndicate in the Sun: An Inside Report On Vice And Corruption in the South Florida Gangland.* New York: The Macmillan Co., 1968.

— *Syndicate Abroad.* Toronto: The Macmillan Co., 1969.

— *Lansky.* New York: Putnam, 1971.

Mormino, Gary R. *Land of Sunshine, State of Dreams: A Social History of Modern Florida.* Gainesville: University Press of Florida, 2005.

Muir, Helen. *Miami, USA (Florida History and Culture).* Coconut Grove, FL: Hurricane House Publishers, 1953.

Navarro, Rick and Jeff Sadler. *The Cuban Cop.* Boca Raton, FL: TransMedia, 1998.

Nijman, Jan. *Miami: Mistress of the Americas.* Philadelphia: University of Pennsylvania Press, 2011.

Nixon, Richard. *The Memoirs of Richard Nixon.* New York: Grosset & Dunlap, 1978.

Okrent, Daniel. *Last Call: The Rise and Fall of Prohibition.* New York: Scribners, 2010.

Parker, Barbara. *Blood Relations.* New York: Signet Book, 1996.

— *Suspicion of Betrayal.* New York: Signet Book, 2000.

— *Suspicion of Rage.* New York: Signet Book, 2007.

— *The Perfect Fake.* New York: Onyx, 2007.

— *The Dark of Day.* New York: Vanguard Press, 2008.

Parks, Arva Moore and Steve Brooke. *Miami The Magic City.* Tulsa, OK: Continental Heritage Press, 1981.

— and Gregory W. Bush. *Miami The American Crossroads: A Centennial Journey.* Needham Heights, MA: Simon & Schuster, 1996.

— and Carolyn Klepser. *Miami Then and Now.* San Diego, CA: Thunderbay Press, 2007.

Portes, Alejandro and Alex Stepick. *City on the Edge: The Transformation of Miami.* Berkeley: University of California Press, 1993.

Powis, Robert E. *The Money Launderers: Lessons from the Drug Wars—How Billions of Illegal Dollars Are Washed Through Banks and Businesses.* Chicago: Probus Publishing, 1992.

Rappleye, Charles and Ed Becker. *All American Mafioso: The Johnny Rosselli Story.* New York: Barricade Books, 1991.

Rieff, David. *Going to Miami: Exiles, Tourists and Refugees in New America.* Gainesville: University Press of Florida, 1987.

Cuba in the Heart of Miami. New York: Simon & Schuster, 1993.

Riley, Tom. *Beyond the Tower: The History of Florida International University.* Miami: Solo Printing, 2002.

Roig-Franzia, Manuel. *The Rise of Marco Rubio.* New York: Simon & Schuster, 2012.

Rubio, Marco. *An American Son: A Memoir.* New York: Sentinel, 2012.

Sammons, Sandra Wallus. *Henry Flagler, Builder of Florida.* Orlando: Tailored Tours Publications, 1993.

— *Marjory Stoneman Douglas and the Florida Everglades.* Lake Buena Vista, FL: Tailored Tours Publications, 1998.

Sassen, Saskia. *The Global City: New York, London, Tokyo.* 2d ed. Princeton: Princeton University Press, 2001.

Shell-Weiss, Melanie. *Coming to Miami: A Social History.* Gainesville: University Press of Florida, 2009.

Smiley, Nixon. *Florida Gardening Month by Month.* Coral Gables: University of Miami Press, 1957.

Standiford, Les. *Last Train to Paradise: Henry Flagler and the Spectacular Rise and Fall of the Railroad that Crossed an Ocean.* New York: Ground Publishers, 2002.

— (ed.). *Miami Noir.* Brooklyn, New York: Akashic Press, 2006.

Stepick, Alex and Nancy Foner. *Pride Against Prejudice: Haitians in the United States.* Boston: Allyn and Bacon, 1998

Stoneman Douglas, Marjorie. *Everglades: River of Grass.* New York: Rinehart, 1947.

Stuart, John A. and John F. Stack, Jr. (eds.). *The New Deal in South Florida: Design, policy, and community building, 1933–1940.* Gainesville: University Press of Florida, 2008.

Torres, María de los Ángeles. *In the Land of Mirrors: Cuban Exile Politics in the United States.* Ann Arbor: University of Michigan Press, 2001.

Tripodi, Tom and Joseph P. DeSario. *Crusade: Undercover Against the Mafia and the KGB.* Washington D.C.: Brassey's, 1993.

Waters, Bruce M. *Miami Beach Postcards.* Atglen, PA: Schiffer Publishing, Ltd., 2005.

Wolfe, Tom. *Back to Blood.* New York: Little Brown, 2012.

Willoughby, Malcolm F. *Rum War at Sea.* Washington DC: Government Printing Office, 1964.

Wynne, Lewis N. (ed.). *Florida at War.* San Antonio, FL: Ralard Printers, 1994.

ARTICLES

Aguirre, B. E., Kent P. Schwiran and Anthony J. LaGreca. "The Presidential Patterning of Latin American and Other Ethnic Populations in Miami" *Latin American Research Review*, Vol. XV, No. 2 (1980), pp. 35–68.

Bach, Robert L. "The 'Freedom Flotilla' Cuban Emigrants" (Unpublished, The Brookings Institution, July, 1980).

Linehan, Edward J. "Cuba's Exiles Bring New Life to Miami" *National Geographic*, Vol. 144, No. 1 (July 1973), pp. 68–95.

Maingot, Anthony P. "The State of Florida in the Caribbean" *CISLA Monographs No. 2.* Universidad Inter-Americana, Puerto Rico, 1983.

"Miami: el caso del Niño Elián y la elección de 2000" *Anuario Social y Político de América Latina y del Caribe*, No. 4. (2001), pp. 94–99.

"Laundering the Gains of the Drug Trade: The Role of Miami and the Off-shore Tax Havens in the Caribbean" *Journal of Inter-American Studies and World Affairs* Vol. 30, No. 2, 3 (Summer/Fall, 1985), pp. 167–188.

Pedraza-Bailey, Silvia. "Cuba's Exiles: Portrait of a Refugee Migration," *International Migration Review*, Vol. 19, No. 1 (Spring, 1984), pp. 4–34.

Portes, Alejandro, Juan A. Clark and Robert L. Bach "The New Wave: A Statistical Profile of Recent Cuban Exiles to the U.S." *Caribbean Studies*, Vol. 7, No. 1 (January 1977), pp. 1–32.

and Alex Stepick "Unwelcome Immigrants: The Labor Market Experiences of 1980 (Mariel) Cuban and Haitian Refugees in South Florida" *American Sociological Review*, Vol. 50, (August 1985), pp. 493–514.

"The Social Origins of the Cuban Enclave Economy of Miami" *Sociological Perspectives*, Vol. 30, No. 4 (October 1987), pp. 340–372.

UNPUBLISHED THESES

Tschesclok, Eric G. "Long Road to Rebellion: Miami's Liberty City Riot" (Ph.D. Thesis, Florida Atlantic University, 1995).

Franco, Alexander "The Impact of the Miami Cuban Exile's Political Culture on the 1996 Fiscal Crisis of the City of Miami" (Ph.D. Thesis, School of Public Administration, Florida International University, 2001).

OFFICIAL REPORTS AND DOCUMENTS

Boswell, Thomas D. and Manuel Rivero "Bibliography for the Mariel-Cuban Diaspora" Paper No. 7, *Caribbean Migration Program*, University of Florida, April 1988.

Division of Archives History and Records *A Guide To Florida's Historic Markers*. Tallahassee: 1972.

Guía Cubana Miami en sus manos, comercial, industrial y profesional Miami, 1976.

Historical Association of Southern Florida *Official Directory of the City of Miami 1904*, Reprint 1974. Miami: Greater Miami Bicentennial Project, 1974.

Luytjes, Jan B. and Anne Yuhaz *Black Entrepreneurship in Dade County*. Miami School of Business and Organizational Sciences, FIU, 1979.

Metropolitan Dade County Community Improvement Program *Profile of Metropolitan Dade County Conditions and Needs*. Miami, 1972.

Metro Dade County Community Improvement Program *Profile of Selected Ethnic and Economic Characteristics*. Miami, 1972.

Metro Dade County Community Improvement Program *Profile of Population in Dade County*. Miami, 1972.

Metro Dade County Community Improvement Program *Dade County Crime Report*. Miami, 1973.

Metropolitan Dade County "Social and Economic Problems Among Cuban and Haitian Entrant Groups, Trends and Indications" Miami, August 1981.

Metropolitan Dade County Board of County Commissioners *Metro-Miami Market Place: Destination 2001*. Miami, 1994.

The Beacon Council *Business Center of the Americas – Miami-Dade*, Miami-Dade County Official Development Partnership, 2006.

The Beacon Council, Miami Business Profile and Relocation Guide. 2006.

The Welfare Planning Council of Dade County, *Social Problem Levels in the City of Miami*. Miami, September 1965.

Permanent Subcommittee on Investigations of the Senate Committee on Governmental Affairs "Crime and Secrecy: The Use of Offshore Banks and Companies," *Senate Report No. 130*. 49th Congress, 1st Session, 1985, p. 83.

United States Senate "Gambling and Organized Crime" *Report of the Committee on Government Operations*. Washington D.C.: March 8, 1962.

United States Senate Subcommittee on Terrorism, Narcotics and International Operations *The BCCI Affair: A Report To The Senate Committee on Foreign Relations*. September 30, 1992.

Zucheli, Hunter and Associates *Miami River, Economic Study*. Miami, 1986.

Index of Historical & Literary Names

Index of Places & Landmarks